WHAT THEY

False Prophets Among Us:
mation and why is it dangerous? is written by someone who has had deep personal experience with the NAR movement, which gives his powerful theological insights into this movement even more honesty and compassion. Kent Philpott is not an alarmist, but he carefully and thoughtfully expresses the dangers of the NAR and why it must be opposed. A must read for anyone who has encountered the NAR or who is considering embracing the movement.
– Dr. Frederick Osborn, MDiv, DMin

***

Modern day Gnostics trouble the church today. Increasingly prevalent is the New Apostolic Reformation movement. These NAR teachers claim new revelations from Christ denying the completeness and fully adequacy of the Bible. Kent's book shares the pervasive danger this movement represents to both those outside and inside the body of Christ.
— Brian Bailey, MTh student TCCTC, author of *Joseph: A Life of Providence, Injustice and Forgiveness*

***

Kent Philpott has taken on a very important issue for the contemporary evangelical church in writing about the New Apostolic Reformation . . . The movement the author addresses is controversial, with many feeling that it is more of a sect than a movement. Philpott brings facts and direct quotes from NAR leaders' publications so the reader will be in a better position to make a correct appraisal of this growing so-called reformation.
— Dr. William L. Wagner, ThD, DMiss, MDiv
Director, Olivet Institute for Global Strategic Studies

***

Kent Philpott's book is like a roster of the players and a review of the playbook of a little known yet powerful team called the NAR. After reading it, I feel much better prepared to recognize and deal with this phenomenon that has been working behind the scenes to infiltrate and take over the move of God.
— Lyle Metsker, Itinerant Minister, Redding, California

False Prophets Among Us

What is the New Apostolic Reformation? and Why is it Dangerous?

Kent Philpott, MDiv, DMin

EVP
Earthen Vessel Publishing

False Prophets Among Us

Earthen Vessel Media, LLC
San Rafael, CA 94903
www.evpbooks.com

ISBN: 978-1-946794-03-1

Library of Congress Control Number: 2017913654

Cover and interior design by KLC Philpott

CONTENTS

Section Two: Essays

vi

Section Three: Recovery and Other Issues

*

PREFACE

Forty-five years ago I started pastoring churches in the greater San Francisco Bay Area. I quickly learned that a primary aspect of the work of a pastor is to protect the flock against all threats.

During the thirty-three years that I have led Miller Avenue Baptist Church in Mill Valley, California, I have become increasingly aware of the dangers posed by what is widely known as The New Apostolic Reformation. After years of merely noting it and following its progress and its leaders' activities to some extent, I realized the need to speak out against it directly and wrote a few essays about certain practices associated with it. A number of those essays are contained in section two.

Recently, a member of our congregation asked what I thought about a book written by Bill Johnson, one of the top names in the movement, who is the lead pastor of Bethel Church in Redding, California. Reading it finally woke me up, and to make a long story short, I knew it was now time to tend to the sheep's safety.

The tremendous growth and influence of the New Apostolic Reformation (NAR) is shocking, and I was rather unaware of how extensively the movement has taken hold all over the world, with a very large presence in Asia, Africa, and Latin America, as well as significant advancement in North America. What could and should I do?

A CIVIL WAR?

Some NAR "apostles" and "prophets" are speaking of a civil war currently being fought within Christianity. NAR advocates seem surprised that not all Christians are jumping on board the "final movement," which they are sure will usher in the kingdom of God in these last days. However, many are contesting the NAR; I am only one in a long line of Christians to question them.

Another reason for my opposition to the NAR apostles and prophets and their organizations is their tendency to say and do wild and crazy things that will certainly be an embarrassment to Biblical Christianity. Most non-Christians are not able to discern the differences within Christianity and see even the Bible-based cults like Mormonism and Jehovah's Witnesses as belonging to mainstream Christianity. The offense of the Gospel is obstacle enough, but the absurd nature of proclamations made by the NAR-aligned prophets and apostles is beyond offensive.

Mainstream media has largely ignored the antics of the NAR folk, though a few reports of weird happenings get out, and the bizarre nature of the events and claims are interesting enough to spark more interest. I predict that the public's awareness of NAR activities will increase. Some film crew is bound to do a documentary that the secular community will embrace as representative of what the Christians are up to now. And then Christians and Christianity will look more foolish than is already the case in the minds of many.

We Christians are indeed divided about this, and necessarily so. Soon after this book is published, my next project focuses on what unites Christians, whether they be Catholic, Eastern Orthodox, Protestant, Messianic, or charismatic/Pentecostal: Biblical Christianity is Evangelical, which is the working title for the new book. By "evangelical," I mean that all Christians are given the commission by Jesus Himself to be witnesses of His saving grace to the entire world. The primary objective of evangelical Christianity is not to take over the world, known as dominionism, but to present to the world Jesus and His finished work on the cross.

WHAT IS MY STANDING?

Do I have a right or platform to speak out against the NAR in the first place? It is clear that I have the right and the obligation that comes with being a pastor. But I have additional background, experience, and understanding of what this movement can perpetrate.

When I was twenty-one years old, mid-way through a four-year enlistment in the Air Force, I became a follower of Jesus Christ. This was in 1963. After my discharge from the military (serving as a medic) I moved to the campus of Golden Gate Baptist Theological Seminary in Mill Valley, California. During two and a half years of my student term I pastored the Excelsior Baptist Church in Byron, California. Also, beginning in February of 1967, I engaged in "street ministry" in the Haight-Ashbury District of San Francisco, leading to my involvement in the Jesus People Movement from 1967 to 1972. Around the middle of that time period I was plunged fully into the charismatic/Pentecostal movement. Yes, in 1968, I woke up one morning speaking loudly in tongues and became engaged with the charismania sprouting up everywhere.

Despite my being a faithful Southern Baptist, I became rather "wild-eyed," as we used to say. I was also much engaged with Catholic charismatics, attended and even spoke at Full Gospel Businessmen meetings, and participated in other charismatic events. Lonnie Frisbee was a close friend, and when he requested my opinion, I urged him to unite with Chuck Smith and the beginnings of the Calvary Chapel days in Costa Mesa, California.

My Jesus People ministry focused on the San Francisco Bay Area where we established house churches, bookstores, high school and college ministries, and much more. I completed a MDiv degree in 1969 and went on to do a ThM, both at Golden Gate

Seminary, but was denied the ThM degree due to being a tongues speaker. (My major professor finally told me this was the reason for the continued rejection of my thesis, A Manual of Demonology and the Occult, which Zondervan did publish in 1973.)

While mid-point in a DMin degree program at San Francisco Theological Seminary, my major professor told me that the church I pastored was unhealthy, which shocked me beyond words. The very next week I brought him a copy of our doctrinal statement. His response was that we were theologically orthodox enough, but our methodology, our ecclesiology, was errant.

I had little choice other than to take this acknowledged authority on cults and conversion seriously. It was a "dark night of the soul" experience. Without intending to do so, I isolated myself from nearly all the other pastors and elders in our little community of churches that stretched from Sonoma to San Jose. Slowly, ever so slowly, I began to see that what the professor said was true. I will give only one keen example of what I saw was error about the way we did our ministry.

AT A MEMORIAL SERVICE

In 1980 I resigned my position as pastor of the church in San Rafael, California. I went to law school, figured out a way to make a living, partially lost my family, declared bankruptcy, and nearly walked away from anything involving Christianity. (This reactionary response lasted two weeks.)

At some later date, I attended a memorial service for the son of one of the pastors in our community of churches. During the gathering after the service I was accosted by a woman who had been part of the San Rafael church during the 1970s. In front of hundreds of people, she shouted out how I was to blame for her marrying the man with whom she had two children, both of whom her husband had molested, crimes for which he was presently serving a long prison sentence. She screamed that I had forced her to do so by means of a prophecy that she must marry the young man with whom she had been fornicating. She had little choice than to do what I had "heard from the Lord."

The point here is that I had thought it was entirely suitable to ask God to "give me a word" and then prophesy over people. We directed people to do what came to us by impressions—by whatever came into our minds—which was usually what the elders and pastors had already decided should be done. We thought nothing of it and had no idea that we were manipulating people—thus our faulty, cultic methodology. My professor was correct in his evaluation.

Recovery from the Cultic Mentality

That is how it began for me. For the first time I recognized that I needed recovery every bit as much as any addict. I had suffered loss—my position as pastor, my wife, a family identity, and so much more. Later on, when I was once again a pastor at Miller Avenue Baptist Church, I developed a program designed to help people recover from their involvement in cultic groups. Over the course of six years I facilitated twelve sessions, each one lasting twenty-three weeks. Attendees included ex-Mormons, Jehovah's Witnesses, and others, but most who came were former members of the church I had pastored in the 1970s. Those who showed up accepted their loss, and it was painful, very painful to take a close look at what had happened to them and what they had done to others. It is still uncomfortable for me to think about it.

My point is that many of those who have been and are yet to be involved in the NAR will need recovery, because it will and must come to an end. Evidence points to the fact that it is imploding from the inside out. Those who are effected are precious brothers and sisters in Christ. Some may be tempted to suicide, some perhaps to revenge, and most will be emotionally devastated. Many will simply want to walk away from anything Christian, thinking they had merely been duped and used.

I do not intend to bring grief to the Christian family. In speaking out and opposing the NAR I hope to bring peace and healing. Naming names and pointing out blatant error is not mean-spirited; it is what both Jesus and the New Testament authors did regularly. There are counterfeits, there are demons teaching error, there are false apostles and prophets. To leave it all unchallenged is unbiblical and un-Christian.

REFERENCES TO "CHARISMATIC/PENTECOSTALISM"

Please understand that I am not attacking those who are charismatic and/or Pentecostal. The reality, however, is that much of the NAR emerged out of the charismatic and Pentecostal movement, and today it is apparent that the churches and groups that identify as charismatic/Pentecostal are more open to the ideologies of the NAR.

JUST WHEN I THOUGHT I HAD HEARD OR READ EVERYTHING. . .THE WORST OF THE WORST

Just when I thought I had completed the content for this book, our researcher, Margaret Alvarez, handed me a copy of Fredrick Osborn's book, *The Physics of Heaven: The Theology of the New Apostolic Reformation*. Reading this caused me to realize I had not paid enough attention to what must be the very worst aspect of the NAR movement. I refer to the close connection between the theologies of the NAR and what is called quantum mysticism, which is associated with ancient occult, neo-pagan, Hindu, and Buddhist mystics.

Judy Franklin and Ellyn Davis co-authored a book entitled, *The Physics of Heaven*, wherein a number of leading persons in the NAR contribute chapters sounding more like the ruminations of mystical, occult-oriented gurus than Christian ministers. I was so surprised by what I read that I had to break into this preface in order to make this known.

Let me provide just a little of what I found in Osborn's book, *The Physics of Heaven: The Theology of the New Apostolic Reformation*.

Ellyn Davis speaks of sitting under the teaching of Ern Baxter who was an associate of William Branham. Branham's followers believed he was the angel of the church of Laodicea, who taught that the word of God was revealed in the Zodiac, the Egyptian pyramids, and in the Scriptures (p. 32). It seems that Davis bought into this concept or at least was very much influenced by it.

A main argument is that the church lost much of what is found in occult and mystical practices and that these are now being recovered. Everything from clairvoyance, clairaudience, knowing the future, and the full range of what is typically understood as the occult world is to be mined, dug into, and reclaimed as belonging to Christians in these last days. Here is what Bill Johnson says: "We can begin by recovering secrets, mysteries, mantles, and realms of God that have been abandoned and ignored for decades, some of them for centuries" (p. 48).

The authors pay attention to Jonathan Welton, who teaches that "whenever there is a real, there is sure to be counterfeit. We shouldn't be afraid to examine the counterfeits because God's power to keep us is mightier than the devil's power to steal us away" (p. 54). The result is that in the mystical and occult world are truths to be found. True, the occult is not good and is a counterfeit, but hidden in that which is wrong is something from God for Christians to seek out.

In short, much that is hidden in NAR-oriented literature is revealed in Franklin and Davis' book. It is nothing more than a call to the occult world despite dressing it up in pseudo-scientific trappings. It is a siren call to traffic with demons.

What can be worse than this?

FIND THEIR STORIES

Many are now leaving churches with an NAR alignment or affiliation. You will find stories of those who have left NAR churches at http://bereanresearch.org.

*

INTRODUCTION

This book consists of three sections:

(1) **Critiques** of books written by the major players in the New Apostolic Reformation

(2) **Essays** on certain aspects of the NAR

(3) Elements of a **Recovery Program** for those who have and will come out of the influence of the NAR

My view is that those who identify as leaders in the NAR, especially those who claim the status of apostle and prophet, have climbed out on a limb—a limb that is sagging, bending, and beginning to crack under the weight. The grand prophecies have not come to pass, competition from within is increasing, detractors both from within and without are finding a voice, some of the big names have died or are aging quickly, and the strain of it all is starting to show.

Those who identify with the NAR are largely genuine Christians. Of course, as many have noted, church pews have always been filled with un-converted people. Despite that, the NAR is still theologically located within the broad Christian family. And according to Jesus' words in Matthew 24:24, even the elect may be led astray. It is therefore entirely appropriate to follow the counsel of Paul as found in 2 Corinthians 13:5: "Examine yourselves, to see whether you are in the faith. Test yourselves. Or do you not realize this about yourselves, that Jesus Christ is in you?— unless indeed you fail to meet the test!"

The big issue is not whether we have been duped or led astray. This can happen to anyone, and the powerful healing of the Holy Spirit can deal with it. The real issue is to keep our eyes on Jesus all the rest of the way home.

*

Letter

The following letter was sent to the Miller Avenue Church members and friends list in June, 2017

Dear Church Family,

For years now I have ignored the development of what is most often referred to as the New Apostolic Reformation. Yes, I am very much aware of it, but I did not fully realize the global extent of this rapidly growing movement. We are watching a Christian-oriented cultic group, like the Mormons or Jehovah's Witnesses, grow and prosper. However, I can no longer sit back and pretend it will go away. It is several decades now in the making, and it goes back to Fuller Theological Seminary in Pasadena and a professor there, C. Peter Wagner, with whom I conversed extensively. I was unwittingly helpful to him and the development of his views, none of which I can help now: I did not know what would result from my contributions. At that time I was part of the charismatic/Pentecostal phenomena, from which this movement springs.

I have visited Bethel Church in Redding, CA, where Bill Johnson has been the senior pastor, though he is semi-retired, with his son Eric now taking the lead. On one occasion, I was there when

Randy Clark (another leader in the NAR) spoke. Bethel Church in Redding is one of the most influential churches in the NAR, along with Rick Joyner at Morningstar and Mike Bickle of the IHOP ministry in Kansas City. The core idea of the NAR is that God is establishing apostles and prophets to direct and even rule the Church, in order to prepare the world for the kingdom of God on earth and also for the arrival of Jesus—as we know it, the 2nd coming of Christ. The apostles and prophets are charting the way now, since what is currently transpiring is not in the Bible—rather, it is "off the charts." It is a form of post-millennialism in which the Church takes dominion in preparation for the Lord's return. This kind of movement or theology is also known as dominionism.

The NAR is not a cohesive organization; rather, it is network of apostles and prophets and the congregations they pastor or have authority over. There are several churches in Marin, in San Francisco, and in the larger Bay Area that are part of it. They consider themselves a fifth branch of Christianity—no longer Protestants—and are guided by prophecy and personal, direct encounters with Jesus and the Father. All who oppose them are considered to be in opposition to what God is doing here in the last days.

The NAR reaches into many areas of our culture, from politics to music, film, television (God TV, TBN, Prueflix, Hillsong, for example), and much more. One of the wonderful organizations to come out of the Jesus People Movement, Youth With A Mission or YWAM, has come under the authority of NAR leaders.

This movement is very big on signs and wonders, miracles, and especially healings. One of their chief activities is "soaking prayer" in 24/7 prayer rooms, where people lie seemingly unconscious for hours, even days, and enter into altered states of consciousness where they experience direct contact with angels, Jesus, and so on. It is a combination of shamanism or Wiccan forms of spirituality and other religious traditions that rely on going on a "soul journey" while in a state of trance. And all this in the name of Jesus! It has all the markings of being "gospel lite," but the champions of the NAR would deny my charge here.

Large crowds attend NAR conferences characterized by the latest music, including Electronic Dance Music (EDM), formerly known as Rave and Trance music, perfectly crafted to induce dangerous trance states. And "miraculous" events occur, just like those I witnessed during the 1970s with Jim Jones' church, The People's Temple in San Francisco. I did not speak up at that time as I should have. I hope not to make the same mistake again. My apologies, if I have or will offend anyone, but I ask everyone to think through, pray through, and consider whether this movement is of God or not.

Beginning July 9, I will be teaching on the NAR during the evening service, because many well-meaning people are not aware of the nature of the NAR and the churches affiliated with it. It is my job as a pastor to warn the sheep of the approach of the wolf. I sincerely wish I did not have to engage in this—it is far from pleasant. For too long now I have not spoken up, because I have close friends involved in this movement, and I know they must end up rejecting me or at least my message. That is often the cost of speaking out against error. Sadly, some well-meaning Christians are caught up in it.

July 2017

Section One
Book Critiques

Contained herein are critiques of books written by some of the most well-known names connected with the New Apostolic Reformation.

Within the critiques are quotations of significant passages of each work to give the reader direct acquaintance with the actual ideas, doctrines, and beliefs of the apostles and prophets who are the chief spokespersons for the NAR.

My own responses to these ideas are contained primarily in the shaded paragraphs starting with **Note:**

A Critique of

Birthing the Miraculous

Heidi Baker, Charisma House, 2014

CHAPTER 1: TAKE HOLD OF THE PROMISE

Heidi speaks beautifully of Mary, the mother of Jesus, and how it must have been when the angel appeared to her and told her what was to take place. For a number of chapters, the story is delicately and insightfully drawn out.

Heidi has seen angels and felt the Lord's presence (p. 3).

She became a Christian at age sixteen, and the "Holy Spirit overshadowed" her (p. 4). When she told her family about her experience they thought she had joined a cult. At the same time she lost the man she loved; the Lord told her he was not to be her future husband.

At another point a speaker at a college she attended announced to her that God told her He "is giving me a city!" (p. 5). Though puzzled about this, she saw two angels, one on either side of this man, and right behind him she saw Jesus. "He was bright and shining" (p. 5). She says it was an "open vision" and that she was wide-awake. Then Jesus pointed at her and said, "Listen to him, he is telling the truth." However, Heidi cried out that she wanted a nation (p. 5). And that is how it all started.

Some twenty years later Randy Clark, who we recall had the anointing from Rodney Howard Browne, laid hands on her at the Toronto Airport Christian Fellowship (now Catch the Fire) and said, "God wants to know—do you want the nation of Mozambique?"

When the church she was attending (name not given) heard of this, they asked her to sign a statement saying she would never go back to the Toronto or Pensacola Churches which were experiencing "revival" and if not she would not receive any support money from them. She declined.

At another service with Randy Clark, she went forward during the preaching time, lifted her hands, and started screaming. Randy stopped preaching, stepped down, laid hands on her, and asked the same question she heard twenty years before: "God wants to know—do you want the nation of Mozambique?" She screamed, "Yes!"

CHAPTER 2: JUST SAY YES!

This next sentence, quoted exactly, sums up a major theme of the book: "He looks for a Church, for a people, for worshippers who will not care about the approach, who will not care about being stretched or pulled or inconvenienced, who will let the Lord take all of them" (p. 12).

Recounting her conversion experience at an Indian Reservation in central Mississippi, in a Baptist Church, she notes that the next evening she was baptized in a Pentecostal Holiness Church.

Some five months later, while worshipping, she felt overshadowed by the Holy Spirit again and saw the "brilliant light of God," and "she was taken up in a vision" (p. 14). At this time she heard an audible voice, the voice of God. The vision lasted for "three whole hours."

She then attended a Pentecostal Church in Laguna Beach, California, and "bore the reproach" for doing so. The people in that church taught her how to do this and rejoice at the same time. She does say that she lost every single friend she had and her family as well. This made her go deeper into God, into his fullness, the secret place of abiding in the very heart of God.

CHAPTER 3: THE SECRET PLACE

She wants the reader to be clear that there are no "shortcuts to the anointing" (p. 20). It is absolutely necessary to cultivate intimacy with God. Surely, the "secret place is the secret" (p. 21).

In the secret place is where God reveals all actions or movements one is to make. God reveals His strategy to us. For Heidi, God reveals in His Word and in His presence—His secret place—what His will is for us.

CHAPTER 4: DEEPER STILL

One sentence captures the whole of the chapter: "God is looking for a people He can so immerse in His love that for the rest of their lives they will have to survive inside His heart" (p. 40).

CHAPTER 5: REMAIN IN HIM

Again one sentence captures the essence of the chapter: "You see, when you spend time with Him in the secret place, a union takes place that causes you to start thinking like God. You begin to have His thoughts, You take on the mind of Christ" (p. 60).

Note: While studying in a doctoral program I took a course on contemplative Christianity and looked at the lives and words of famous Christian mystics like Therese of Avila and St. John of the Cross. For a period of four months I made an attempt to follow what Richard Foster wrote of in his book, *Celebration of Discipline*. For a period it was kind of "cool" but then I realized how self-focused I was, sitting, listening, for something special, something other-worldly, and it took some time after the conclusion of the course to get back to normal. What I mean to say is that I understand some of what Heidi Baker experiences and I can more clearly see how off the biblical track it is.

CHAPTER 6: PAYING THE PRICE

Heidi writes of a conference at which she appeared in Red Deer, Canada. As she was about to speak, she was lying prostrate on the floor (sometimes referred to as being drunk in the Spirit), and she was crying out to God. She felt as though she was being pulled inside the "Lord's heart." She could not walk or talk after that and had to be carried to her car after the conference concluded that night.

CHAPTER 7: LAVISHLY LOVED

She contrasts here how different her gifts are compared with those ministers and preachers who use quotes and notes. She can't do it, but trying once she went to a bookstore to get some books so she could make notes and quotes. Right between shelves she collapsed and had a vision. Basically she learned from God that not everyone uses notes and quotes.

CHAPTER 8: THE NEED FOR HUMILITY

In a conference in Canada where she was to speak, she spent a whole week lying on the floor absolutely unable to "walk or talk" (p. 103). She says she had no control over her body. She would think about how much she needed a drink of water and then someone would come over and give her a drink of water.

At another conference in Toronto, after her husband Rolland was diagnosed with cerebral malaria, when enemies wanted her dead, their home in Africa was lost, with more than 300 of their kids there now homeless, she tried to listen to the conference speakers, but the Holy Spirit came, and "I ended up standing on my head in the middle of the church! I was literally flipped upside down" (p. 105). This strange behavior was not of her doing, and for an hour, in front of thousands, there she was. "Afterward my body was covered in bruises from head to toe," she reports.

Then some prophet type came up, while she was still standing on her head, and said God had told him to pour water on her head. She said, "why not?" So upside down, with wet clothes, she asked God what is going on, and He replied, "I'm turning your ministry upside down. The apostolic is upside down. It's the lowest place you can go!" (p. 105).

Note: It is not entirely clear from the book what exactly is meant. I am assuming that the conference may have had to do with NAR folks and the theme was the restoration of the apostolic office, which she did not necessarily agree with. Not sure here, but the event is of the weird nature.

For brevity, I am skipping chapter 9, which is very similar.

CHAPTER 10: BELIEVE FOR THE IMPOSSIBLE

Toward the very end of a wild story of impossible rescues with boats, Heidi tells of her husband Rolland being very ill. Besides the cerebral malaria he had a series of micro strokes, lost some short-term memory, and was unable to function much for two years.

Despite it all, Heidi continued to go forward and believe in what God had promised her.

CHAPTER 11: ENTER INTO HIS REST

Heidi had to learn that she needed to rest, to take a Sabbath day's rest. She also learned that play is rest, too.

She reports that God told her "we were to play and pray. I asked if we could strategize as well. He said no!" (p. 143).

Note: It is not clear how this communication takes place, but it seems that it is more like an actual conversation with the two parties being face to face.

She attended a meeting on a day when she was supposed to rest. Jesus came to the meeting; she said she could feel His presence. Suddenly she had a vision in which she was mounted on a white horse. At one point, she found that Jesus was on the horse and had His arms around her. She was completely "swallowed up inside His heart. We rode as one" (p. 145).

CHAPTER 12: EMBRACE THE JOY SET BEFORE YOU

Embedded in this chapter is a paragraph where Heidi gives a list, a partial list I am thinking, about how the ministry Iris Global, the name of the ministry Rolland and Heidi developed, is united with many other ministries. Here is a list of them:

"Assemblies of God, the International House of Prayer, Bethel Church, the Toronto church, the Baptists, Youth With a Mission, the Nazarenes, Operation Blessing, World Vision, and may other movements across the earth" (p. 160).

CHAPTER 13: SUPERNATURAL BIRTH

Heidi had a vision, shortly after arriving in Mozambique, that God was "releasing" a movement of supernatural love. In the story line of the chapter, Heidi hears Jesus say, "Tell the church, 'Release control'" (p. 188). The idea was that the church should essentially let go and let God do His work without interruption. The church, evidently, was not doing right. But there were many elements in the church that resisted releasing control.

Finding this out, Heidi looked to Jesus, who said to her, "The sword is both mercy and judgment" (p. 189). And for those resisters, Jesus said, "For those who will reject My presence, My purpose, My love, there is great darkness and judgment" (p. 189).

Note: This is the most difficult of all the critiques presented here. I cannot help but believe that Heidi Baker is a sincere Christian woman who has given so very much to accomplish what she feels God has called her to do. At the same time, much of what she presents is hard for me to accept as being a part of the normal Christian life.

None of the other authors' books summarized bear any real resemblance to Birthing the Miraculous. I have seen Heidi Baker in person along with Stacey Campbell at the New Life Church in Novato, California, and she ministered exactly as she describes numerous times in her book.

Baker has much more about presenting the Gospel of Christ and people being saved than any of the others discussed in this book. Evangelism will follow the report of healings, with much love and attention shown to very primitive people who may or may not understand the language or dialect of Heidi and company. However, I do not see an ordinary, time tested, process of conversion that normally consists of a conviction of sin, a sense of hopelessness, and then seeing Jesus as Savior. The conversion stories seem tacked on to the more exciting healing miracles. My experience in the Jesus People Movement from 1967 to 1972, when we saw many signs and wonders, was that these were not at the forefront of the ministry. The message of the cross of Jesus was foremost; that unless we were born anew, we were lost forever. At best, the Gospel story is fleeting and sketchy in *Birthing the Miraculous*. It appears that Heidi's desire is for others to bring forth miracles far more than it is to fulfill the great commission.

The "secret place" Heidi speaks of, and alludes to often, is a key feature in her life. This is the same concept as going into the heart of Jesus, or God, and hearing and knowing what cannot otherwise be heard or known. It is the language of the mystic, the contemplative, even the shaman. And once one has such experiences, she will not be talked out of them easily. I have found this to be true with shamans, priests and priestesses of Santeria, and followers of Wiccan cults. There are keen similarities between pagan encounters with spiritual entities and those of which Heidi speaks. I cannot help but become uneasy and wonder if there has not been very subtle put powerful deception.

Baker does not attempt to establish herself as an apostle or a prophet, but she is desirous of being seen as a genuine follower of Jesus by others despite her rather peculiar and unique style of ministry.

There is no question that she is a fine writer. My sense is that she wrote the entire account herself, unlike the other authors covered in this book. She has a keen mind, is obviously well educated, and is a most loving person who has made great sacrifice in her work. Few would ever undertake to go through what she has.

I do have a "however." Some of her stories, miracle stories would perhaps be descriptive, do not hold together very well. There are some implausible parts. Perhaps it is a case of faded memories, or it could be embellishment. I cannot be certain, but I am suspicious.

After fifty-four years of being a follower of Jesus, pastoring for forty-seven years, obtaining three degrees, and reading hundreds of accounts of the deeds of Christians, I have never read a life story such as Heidi's.

It must be asked: Is there anyone or anything in Scripture that compares? Maybe Moses, Joshua, David, Elijah, or Jeremiah fit—those Old Testament heroes. The dissimilarities are too evident, however. In the New Testament, Jesus' life does not compare with Heidi's, nor does Peter's or Paul's. I do not see anywhere in Scripture where anyone exhorts anyone to live a life like Heidi lives, however devoted and spiritual it may seem. Her life is more extreme than that of even the mystics.

In chapter twelve, Heidi lists churches and groups that the Lord showed her belong to the "vast net" that Iris Global (the name of the ministry Rolland and she developed) was also a part of. In the list are mentioned the Assemblies of God, Nazarenes, and Baptists. While individual congregations of these churches may be aligned with NAR groups and networks, whole denominations definitely are not, at least not yet.

In the very last chapter of the book Heidi references, in a very understated manner, the so- called "Christian Civil War" often found in other books of those committed to the NAR. I fall in with those who resist. Some NAR folks speak of only a spiritual war, but others suggest, at minimum, actual violent warfare. Alarmingly, Heidi must be included in this latter group. Is this from someone who lives in the secret place of God's heart? This is as close as she comes to full identification with the New Apostolic Reformation.

A Critique of

Growing in the Prophetic

Mike Bickle, Charisma House, 1996, 2008

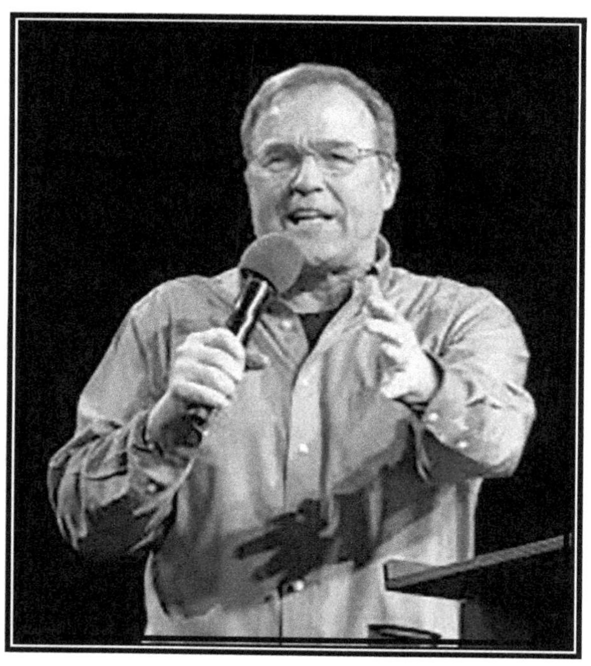

PREFACE

Mike Bickle is writing about prophecy for prophets and would-be prophets and admits there will be clashes among them due to "selfish ambition and lack of wisdom."

Bickle highly values the work of the prophets, and his book is aimed at building them up. He says that many have received "prophetic dreams, visions, and supernatural experiences" (p. x) and that hundreds of prophets have given words from God to thousands of people.

Note: Over the course of my research for this book I see little attention paid to apostles, yet the network is referred to as the New Apostolic Reformation. A more accurate designation might be New Prophetic Reformation, as developing prophets and what they do seems the major focus, by far.

CHAPTER ONE: THERE'S BEEN A TERRIBLE MISTAKE

The "terrible mistake" Bickle mentions has to do with his being invited to charismatic churches when it was supposed he was a charismatic. The mistake was that he was not a charismatic. But that would change, and dramatically so.

This chapter begins with a recounting of a conference held at the Vineyard Church in Anaheim, California, in July of 1989, under the leadership of John Wimber. Bickle spoke on developing and encouraging the prophetic ministry that was then emerging. He reported that many were having dreams and visions, receiving impressions, and hearing God's audible voice. And "some" of the prophecies were confirmed by events in nature such as comets, earthquakes, droughts, and floods.

Many who attended the convention at the Vineyard conference desperately wanted to experience more direct contact with God. In that conference, Bickle reports that many came to him, some hoping he would impart to them the prophetic gift or give them a "word from the Lord," meaning they hoped to hear from

God about what His plan might be for their lives.

Note: I am reminded of Simon the magician in Acts 8 who wanted to receive the power to lay hands on people so they might receive the Holy Spirit, a desire that caused Peter to rebuke him. Passing on the anointing to be a prophet or wanting to hear personal messages from God sounds more like occult divination than biblical Christianity.

In June of 1982, after Mike Bickle had established a church in St. Louis, Missouri, two men came to him, one named simply Augustine, the other a person who would become a well-known prophet, Bob Jones. Both of them told Bickle about hearing audible voices and seeing and being visited by angels, among other spiritual experiences. Bickle at first questioned all of it, but bit-by-bit he began to embrace it, especially when people around him began to accept the two men as real prophets of God.

The prophetic ministry brought Bickle great blessing from 1983 to 1985 while in Kansas City where he planted a new church.

Chapter Two: Confirming Prophecies through The Acts of God in Nature

Bickle supports the thesis that God confirms prophecies by means of events taking place in nature. His illustrations of this include the "unexpected snowfall," the "unexpected comet," and a rainfall coming just at the precise moment.

It is not stated how Bickle knows this is God's method, but he is certain that as the "End Times" approach, more and more prophecies will be confirmed by natural events. After this, and quoting Matthew 24:29-30 to substantiate his prediction, he launches again into the theme that prophets will make mistakes. He even says that "the Lord disciplined us for our pride and errors" (p. 21), citing failures in the lives of some of those in the prophetic ministry at Kansas City.

Bickle struggled with this, questioning whether he should

continue in prophetic ministry. But he eventually became even more committed to it. He writes, "I am resolved to embrace the Holy Spirit's ministry through prophetic people regardless of what it costs" (p. 22).

Note: He has indeed done this; he continues to support the prophetic ministry as of the 2008 publication of this edition. I wonder how the interceding years and all the many wild and crazy things have affected his attitude, but it might be impossible to change direction and thus call into question his whole life's work.

CHAPTER THREE: PROPHETIC ADMINISTRATION: REVELATION, INTERPRETATION, AND APPLICATION

To cope with all that can go wrong in the prophetic ministry, Bickle and company adopt a process designed to minimize errors and failures. They adopt a three-step process of revelation, interpretation, and application, which are three tiers in determining the content, accurate understanding of, and application of a prophecy. He is sure that the Holy Spirit can provide all of this.

Mike Bickle himself has received many of what he calls "flattering prophetic words" that he most often simply "deletes" and forgets. He then wisely says, "A man with an ambitious or insecure heart is more often seduced by an exaggerated or flattering prophet word" (p. 31).

He also notes that prophetic people who seek to be rewarded for their "important words" or be recognized as a real prophet are often corrected rather than credited—talking here again about selfish ambition. Bickle then thinks that it is not the accuracy of the prophetic words but presumptuous interpretations and applications that are problematic. The solution he puts this way: "When we receive a prophetic word from someone, we must hold it at arm's length and not seek to interpret or apply it until God Himself confirms it" (p. 33).

Note: It is my opinion that the foregoing is a disingenuous way of overlooking the prophetic errors, failures, confusion, and harm that is characteristic of so many who suppose they are prophets. And the numbers are growing, considering the schools that teach one how to prophesy with Bethel Church in Redding, California, and the IHOP centers all over the country.

CHAPTER FOUR: OVERVIEW OF THE PROPHETIC MINISTRY

Mike Bickle knows that the words coming from contemporary prophets are not to be treated in the same way we view Scripture. He notes a kind of sliding scale between God's words and man's words, from strong to weak. However, he points out, on the basis of 1 Corinthians 14: 29–30, that Paul warns not to "despise prophecies," and, "For you can all prophesy one by one."

At this point Bickle remarks on the work of Wayne Grudem, a New Testament scholar and a charismatic, who does not believe the Bible teaches there is an office of prophet. Bickle, indeed all those who espouse the NAR, disagrees with Grudem and naturally so, since Bickle considers himself a prophet, is proclaimed as a prophet, and must therefore take issue.

Note: Grudem believes that the designation prophet describes a function and is not a title or an office. With this I agree.

A further distinction, I think, is that the kind of prophecy found in the church at Corinth was when believers spoke of things that they thought or had heard about what Jesus said and did. At that point there was no New Testament, and it is plain from apocryphal material, much of it coming from Gnostics, that there was errant material floating about. We see this, for example, in the Gnostic oriented Gospel of Thomas, to name only one such document. So the early churches had to verify what was being proclaimed as prophecy. Once the Gospels were written, the possibility of falsely attributing words and deeds to Jesus diminished, although historically we have continued to deal with this issue until the present time.

A prophet operating today along biblical lines proclaims the person and work of Jesus Christ. The prophet is a preacher, an evangelist, and one who witnesses to the saving work of Jesus. This is my view of it.

Bickle describes four levels of prophecy:

» The first is "simple prophecy." This is when a person speaks out an impression they think God has brought to mind or a word that comes from a vision or a dream.

» Second is "prophetic gifting." This designates someone who regularly has impressions, visions, and dreams.

» Third is "prophetic ministry." Here the prophet is recognized by others as functioning regularly in prophetic ministry.

» Fourth is "prophetic office." Here the prophet is close to the order of the Old Testament prophets.

Bickle is quick to remind the reader that this does not mean that someone in the prophetic office is 100% accurate. But they do have a regular flow of words, "open visions," and predictions, including those about natural events, weather, and politically oriented occurrences.

Some in the fourth category contend that they have been directly chosen by God for their placement in the prophetic office by such events as a miraculous birth, an angelic visitation, or other means.

Bickle however warns, "I think the church does itself harm when it allows people to quickly identify themselves as "apostles" or "prophets" simply because they consider themselves to be so or because it looks good on a brochure" (p. 43).

Note: The title of "prophet" sells books, garners invitations to speak at large conferences, and attracts exalted designations. It also allows those with this title to go unchallenged when they speak unusual and fantastic words. "Touch not mine anointed" is the rule.

CHAPTER FIVE: THE DIFFERENCE BETWEEN THE GIFT OF PROPHECY AND BEING A PROPHET

Mike Bickle describes people who claimed to have powerful spiritual encounters when he first began the church in Kansas City. They reported hearing audible voices, having angelic visitations, seeing visions in vivid color, seeing literal signs in the heavens, going into trances, and, as Bickle concludes the list, "just to name a few" (p. 49). At first, he did not know what to think about all of it. However, as time went on, his doubts subsided and he began to develop a prophetic ministry himself.

Bickle contrasts Old and New Testament prophecy. In Old Testament prophecy the prophet, to avoid being stoned to death, had to be 100% accurate. He points to John the Baptist as the last of the Old Testament prophets. John proclaimed the arrival of the Messiah and admonished people to be ready for His arrival by means of a baptism of repentance. John was the only prophet at that time, which was often the case during Old Testament history. But now, in the New Testament era, there is what he calls "prophetic distribution" with a multitude of prophets found worldwide. Now the 100% standard no longer applies. He quotes 1 Thessalonians 5:20-21: "Do not despise prophecies. Test all things, hold fast what is good." His conclusion then is that not all the prophecies given in the early churches were expected to be accurate.

Bickle says New Testament prophecy is by faith and that often the impressions of the Holy Spirit are subtle and lack complete clarity.

Note: Here now we find the core of the NAR error. It assumes that the kind of prophecy developed and standardized in the charismatic/Pentecostal movement is just like that in the days of the early church to which Paul was referring in the 1 Thessalonians passage. There is no logical reason to do so, except that it supports their view of prophecy.

Prophecy is proclaiming the Good News of the Kingdom of

God, presenting Jesus, His work on the cross, His deity, and His finished work—and not uttering things like, "God told me you have an illness," or, "You will have a great ministry as an artist, musician, singer, or dancer, etc." Prophecy New Testament style is not predictive; it is preaching.

Mike Bickle once again touches on the mindset or personality of some of the NAR prophets or at least those in his IHOP ministry: "Sometimes we are so desperate to make sure that people know we are special because we receive impressions from the Holy Spirit" (p. 54).

Then, even more startling, he teaches that every believer in the New Testament era has the ability "to hear directly from God through the indwelling Holy Spirit." He quotes Jeremiah 31:31-34 to support his claim. Jeremiah said, "For they all shall know Me."

"Know" not "hear" is what the passage says. The knowing did come with the arrival of the Messiah, and the new covenant became operative. We are no longer law keepers; we have the indwelling of the Holy Spirit. Bickle is employing proof-texting at its worst, because he is trying to support the notion of audible voices that come from angels, Jesus Himself, and even God the Father.

Bickle is keenly aware that not all Christians are in one accord with him. He says that some fundamentalists and conservative evangelicals cling to Old Testament prophecy instead of New Testament prophecy, which of course is what is seen at his IHOP.

CHAPTER SIX: WOMEN OPERATING IN PROPHETIC MINISTRY

At IHOP Mike Bickle says, "we have a growing number of women who are anointed to speak the Word publicly" (p. 65). He describes the ministry he heads this way: "Our prophetic network consists of about two hundred fifty people who regularly receive dreams, visions, and prophetic words from the Lord. The oversight of this network is provided by our Prophetic Council. This council is made up of both men and women" (p. 65).

Note: I find little fault on this point. There are many who disagree with Mike Bickle and me, but women are and must be engaged in ministry. I have heard it said that about half of the world's pastors are women. This is what I refer to as an "intramural debate" as opposed to an "extramural debate." Unhappily, some will say the issue is whether or not one believes in the Word. Many of us see it otherwise.

Of interest is when Bickle quotes Revelation 2:20 toward the end of chapter six: "You allow that woman Jezebel, who calls herself a prophetess, to teach and seduce My servants to commit sexual immorality." (This spoken by Jesus to the Church at Thyatira.) If someone, a woman likely, is prophesying such unbiblical messages, this is clearly a departure from a genuine New Testament proclamation of the Jesus Christ as Lord.

Chapter Seven: Seven Dimensions of the Prophetic Church

The overall prophetic ministry, Bickle understands, has a number of dimensions besides being restricted to those who have dreams and visions. He lists seven of these.

First: The revelation of the testimony of God's heart. Bickle says, "prophetic ministry flows out of experiencing Jesus' heart. It is a ministry that feels and reveals God's heart" (p. 70). He speaks of God having burdens that weigh upon His heart. And these burdens, apparently, God reveals to prophets.

Second: The proclamation of end time prophecy. Bickle refers to Revelation 10:8-10 in which John was told to eat the little scroll, and Bickle says it was the scroll of End Time prophecy in order to "feel God's heart related to the End Times." The point apparently is that John in this manner would be able to grasp the inner feelings God has in His heart.

Third: The preservation and proclamation of the Word of God as His prophetic standard on the earth. He says of this dimension something that all Christians can agree with. "We are most prophetic when we faithfully and regularly proclaim the Word of

God" (p. 71).

Fourth: The reception of prophetic direction. The church must recognize the current move of the prophetic ministry.

Fifth: Prophetic dreams and visions and the power of God. God equips the prophets, Bickle believes, with receiving and proclaiming dreams and visions as well as giving the ability to work miracles.

Sixth: The prophetic outcry against social injustice. This indeed is a time-honored work of the prophets of the Old Testament, and it would be agreed that such is true of Christ's Church today.

Seventh: The prophetic call to holiness. Once again this is standard biblical truth.

Note: Here is a mixture of traditional understandings along with analogies that may well cross the line into that which is not biblically authentic. Specifically there is the mention of "God's heart." And the process of learning what is on God's heart is decidedly on the mystical scale of spiritual experiences. I do not recall Jesus, Paul, John, or any other New Testament writer speaking in such a manner.

In addition is the assumption that the prophetic ministry is the centerpiece of "End Times" revelation. This is far from mainstream understandings.

CHAPTER EIGHT: THE COMING GREAT REVIVAL

Without explanation Bickle declares that in the coming great revival over one billion new souls will be gathered in. This is one of six positive trends we are to see in the End Times.

He tells of an experience he had in September of 1982 while in Cairo, Egypt. During a time of prayer and worship, God spoke to him and gave him a message he will never forget: "I will change the understanding and expression of Christianity in the earth in one generation" (p. 79). Bickle does not directly say that this is or is not happening now. He merely states, "This reformation revival will be by His sovereign initiative" (p. 79).

He makes it clear the revival will not be seen as an evangelistic, healing, prayer, unity, or prophetic movement, but rather it will include all of these at once. And of the prophetic part, this "will include angelic visitations, dreams, visions, and signs and wonders in the sky as well as an increase in prophet revelation" (p. 81).

Note: Bickle refers to "The Acts 2 Model," calling it Wind, Fire, and Wine. Here he refers to Acts 2 and the Day of Pentecost. It is impossible to examine each and every time Bickle slips in something a little fishy, but this is an easy one and exemplary of dozens of other misinterpretations. The passage under consideration is Acts 2:2: "And suddenly there came from heaven a sound like a mighty rushing wind, and it filled the entire house where they were sitting" (ESV). There was no wind, rather there was a sound like the sound of a mighty rushing wind.

Some years back I visited the Bethel Church in Redding with two old friends who had been part of the congregation for years and were fully engaged in the whole movement. Bill Johnson came on stage to introduce Randy Clark, who was the reason I was in Redding in the first place. As soon as Bill took the stage, right in front of me two men rolled out a very large fan, the type you might imagine being used in filming a movie. I was sitting on the aisle about fifteen yards away. The fan was turned on, and Bill began to sway back and forth as though being pushed about by the wind. I nudged my old friend and pointed to the fan. He made no indication that he saw it. On the ride home I asked my dear friends about the fan. They had not seen the fan, but the mighty rushing wind was present from time to time, they said. And I forgot to mention, when the wind blew Bill around, the crowd went wild.

Under the heading, "Cosmic Signs in the End Times," Bickle relies on literalist understandings of passages like that found in Joel 2:30-31 with its "blood and fire and pillars of smoke" and the sun turning to darkness, the moon into blood. Historically, these apocalyptic images referred to the judgment of God and were not to be taken literally. Doing so now, however, fits with the idea that in the Last Days prophets will be foretelling signs in nature. Bickle says, "These cosmic signs are not to be dismissed as symbolic poetry. The biblical approach to these cosmic signs is to take them literally" (p. 88). There is nothing given to back this up—only his word, and he is a prophet.

So many of these nature signs are given out by the prophets with the NAR—by the thousands—that some are bound to be right, or at least close.

CHAPTER NINE: CONTENDING FOR THE FULLNESS OF THE PROPHETIC ANOINTING

"The Holy Spirit will release grace to receive prophetic dreams and visions in the generation in which the Lord returns" (p. 89), and all of "God's people" will receive it.

Note: What about those who do not receive prophetic words? Questions like this could be asked at many points in this book. Bickle will not say straight out that only those aligned with the NAR will receive them, implying that those who are not so aligned will not.

Once again, partially hidden from view is found the ordinary cultic "we-they" division. And it stands to reason for Mike Bickle and others that if prophetic words are not accepted as divinely imparted, then someone is right and someone is wrong. But *they* are hearing directly from God.

Bickle lists five ways of contending for the fullness of the prophetic anointing:

» Have a clear vision for the fullness of the Holy Spirit.

» Cultivate a spirit of gratefulness and faithfulness in smallness.

» Live a life of fasting and prayer.

» Seek to fully obey God without compromise.

» Bear the reproach and stigma of the anointing.

Note: Once again is a list of "musts." Is this particular list at all realistic? Who can measure up? Who will say this is even possible? Consider the first—having a clear vision for the fullness of the Holy Spirit—is this not something only deity could possess?

CHAPTER TEN: FALSE EQUATIONS ABOUT PROPHETIC GIFTINGS

Often Bickle admits that some of the prophets are a bit strange. Some have—gasp—unresolved issues in their lives. He will also admit that there is competition among them, they are difficult to manage, and their lives do not often express holiness. In an attempt to explain or justify the validity of "prophets" he gives three false equations, or three reasons why prophets may be misunderstood:

False Equation # 1: Character Equals Anointing. The point here is that just because one claims an anointing as a prophet does not mean he or she has moved to blameless sainthood.

Bickle recognizes that some prophets "fake it" and will say whatever when the pressure comes so as not to seem to lack giftedness.

False Equation # 2: Anointing Equals Divine Endorsements of Ministry Style. Styles and methodologies are the focus here. By style or methodology, Bickle means what a prophet does in the process of giving prophetic words. Some act quite strange and think they must do so or they will lose the anointing.

False Equation # 3: Anointing Equals 100 Percent Doctrinal Accuracy. Bickle use William Branham as an illustration of this third point. He was acclaimed a great healer, and his prophecies were said to always be correct. However, he did depart from biblically correct doctrines. The error Bickle says is that Branham wanted to be a teacher also, but for this he was not properly equipped.

Note: One thinks of Heidi Baker and Stacey Campbell. I have seen them both in person, and anyone can go to YouTube, type in these ladies' names, and see for oneself.

Heidi usually begins with a darkened stage, and you cannot see her, because she is lying on the floor, but after a while you hear her. It is not easy to understand what she is saying, but it sounds like cries for "more, more, more" of God. She is drunk in the Spirit and cannot stand up. After a while she will get on her knees, and later she will stand.

Stacey at first seems quite normal. But when she gives people a word from the Lord, her head moves back and forth at break neck speed—literally. Her husband Steve holds a microphone up for her as she unreels a word.

In regard to William Branham, this was a healer who said he relied upon an angel named Emma who stood beside him and pointed out an illness someone had in a crowd he was speaking to. And it went from there, but this is a poor defense indeed and lacks credibility when one studies the life and ministry of Branham.

Chapter Eleven: God Offends the Mind to Reveal the Heart

Mike Bickle in this chapter tries to justify the behavior, style, and methodology of prophets. He admits he had a difficult time accepting the eccentricities of Bob Jones, including his appearance, mannerisms, and speech. Bickle was initially offended by this man, but over time Jones at least proved to Mike that he was a real prophet of God. Bob Jones "would talk about feeling the wind of the Spirit or about his hands getting hot during a ministry time." It took time for Bickle to accept this, and he did so by reasoning that yes, prophet Bob Jones offended his mind but it was the heart where the lesson was to be learned.

In this chapter Bickle also talks about "unbalanced people." Some unbalanced people are simply trying to be weird because of their misconceptions of prophet ministry. They are excited about the idea of being some sort of mystical prophet; they therefore intentionally act strange. They suppose their strangeness makes them more anointed. However, some such people are just eccentric, not anointed" (pp. 117–118).

Chapter Twelve: Pastors and Prophets: Getting Along in the Kingdom

Pastors will be needed in the days during the beginning of the new wave of the Holy Spirit coming just before Jesus returns. Pastors who are wise and mature are needed to "lead, nurture, and administrate prophetic people" in their churches (p. 126).

The pastor does not want to be the prophet. Pastors have limited callings and giftings. Bickle says, "Pastors, like everyone else, must be secure in their limited callings and spiritual giftings" (p. 129).

Note: Pastors are fourth in the hierarchy of Ephesians 4:11. Above them, in the general NAR schematic, are the apostles and prophets. Despite the listing, Bickle says little of apostles and pictures the prophets more highly than anyone else. But pastors are rarely mentioned, and when the subject comes up, pastors are not highly esteemed. And why not?

My view is that the pastor is more likely to stand in the way of what the NAR is up to. This is certainly true at Miller Avenue Church. I am the pastor, and anyone who looks approvingly at the NAR knows I will not embrace it. Therefore, I become an impediment to the Holy Spirit in their eyes—and so will many a pastor be.

One does not hear much about the "evangelist" of Ephesians 4. And why not? Also the "teacher" is rarely heard of. And why not? Obviously NAR is all about the two "offices" of apostles and prophets, since they are the power positions. It often seems to be more about having power, prestige, notoriety, and money than anything else.

CHAPTER THIRTEEN: ORIGINS OF THE PROPHETIC CALL

In conferences at which Bickle has spoken, people approach him and ask him to pray that they might receive a prophetic calling. And when this happens, there is an increase in spiritual activity.

Bickle points out three main ways people move into the prophetic world. First are indications while still a youth. Here a young person will perhaps hear an audible voice, and this could even come before conversion has occurred. Then there is a sudden calling in one's adult life. There it is, straight forward. Last is what Bickle calls "stirring up the gift." This is where, due to varying influences, the desire to move in the prophetic comes alive in a person's life.

Note: Again I cannot help but ask again, where is the core evangelical message, the testimony, the witness, the proclamation, the preaching of Jesus? The answer, as I gather it, is that through the fulfillment of prophecy, seeing signs and wonders, witnessing healings and other miracles, people will then be saved from their sin. And there are times, as recorded in the Book of Acts, where this did happen. And such can occur today. But it is not what Jesus directed His disciples to do. They were to bear witness to the core Gospel message.

CHAPTER FOURTEEN: EMBODYING THE PROPHETIC MESSAGE

Prophets must be ethical and above reproach, as all of those who are followers of Jesus need to be. Bickle has honestly spoken of ethical and moral failures among well-known prophets. Thus comes the need for a call to "embody" what a servant of God must be.

Bickle quotes Revelation 19:10, "The testimony of Jesus is the spirit of prophecy," as somehow speaking to the theme of the chapter. His thought is that the testimony of Jesus is what is on Jesus' heart.

Bickle speaks of a period that began in his ministry in 1990, a time when the work in Kansas City was being criticized to the point that the word "cult" was aimed at him. The chapter is essentially the lessons learned as a result, and his appraisal and manner of dealing with the trouble is exemplary and honorable. He ends the chapter with "lessons learned the hard way."

» Seeing our pride

» Need for other ministries

» Understanding the prophetic process or becoming more mature in his or her view of the prophetic ministry

» Becoming accountable

» Having a balanced ministry team

Note: This chapter seems disjointed, and I cannot pick up the primary thread of it. However, what caught my eye is the passage from Revelation 19:10. The "testimony" of Jesus is not what is on the heart of Jesus but is the witness about Jesus, both who He is and what He has done. The testimony is the Gospel, the Good News story. It is not giving a word about what is on the heart of Jesus. It is right here that Bickle's understanding of prophesy is errant. The prophet is the preacher; the prophet declares the Gospel; otherwise he or she is not a prophet.

Chapter Fifteen: Common Abuses and Misuses of Prophecy

Here Mike Bickle discusses "simple" prophecy that he thinks most people are able to do. He is not referring to a ministry or office. Whatever the source of prophecy, whether from a beginner or old hand, he insists the meaning or intent of a prophecy must not go against Scripture.

In 1986 Bickle developed guidelines for those who receive personal prophecy, and he adheres to these yet today. This is a not-to-do list, or areas of people's lives about which not to prophecy. I will simply present these and not attempt to explain them;

some are self-evident, others are not.

Misuse #1: Giving direction in domestic areas
Misuse #2: Redirecting the roles of people in the church
Misuse #3: Giving correction to people
Misuse #4: An overreliance on dreams
Misuse #5: Trivializing prophetic ministry
Misuse #6: Flattery and manipulation
Misuse #7: Prophesying in total privacy
Misuse #8: Assumptions about timing
Misuse #9: "I cannot help/stop myself"
Misuse #10: Drawing attention to ourselves
Misuse #11: Neglecting to give the conditions for prophetic words
Misuse #12: Giving negative words without communicating that they can be averted
Misuse #13: Speaking without clarity
Misuse #14: Not acknowledging the missed prophetic words we give

Chapter Sixteen: Practical Ways to Grow in the Prophetic

The premise of this chapter is that every Christian is able to give "simple" prophecy. In fact, prophecy is intended for every born-again Christian. Bickle quotes 1 Corinthians 14:5 to prove it: "I wish you all spoke with tongues, but even more that you prophesied." And by prophesy he does not mean proclaim the message of Jesus, but to report words God gives through impressions, dreams, visions, direct audible voices, angelic visitations, and so on.

Note: In this section, Bickle also quotes part of 1 Corinthians 14:31. The entire verse is, "For you can all prophesy one by one, so that all may learn and all be encouraged." He quotes only, "For you can all prophesy." However, it is plain that Paul does not say everyone can prophesy but that they should do so one at a time. Bickle's idea is that everyone can learn to prophesy.

Once this is accepted, people are bound to try to do it. And so they are constantly waiting for impressions and words. This becomes obsessive to the point that a dangerously different form of reality is developed. One sees him or herself as being a prophet to whom God is forever speaking, and thus to whom others must listen. A kind of schizophrenic mindset can develop and begin to cause abnormalities that others begin to observe.

Bickle recommends a mechanism in order to do simple prophecy: He suggests asking God, "What are you saying or doing at this time that You want me to participate in?" Then wait for the word or impression and be bold to give it out. Then when present at events involving others this can be on the mind of the fledgling prophet. It is not necessary for the prophet to announce that a "word" has been received. It is enough to speak it out in ordinary conversation without letting on the content was prophetically received.

Bickle states that Jesus asked the Father, "Show Me what You are doing today." In Jesus' heart He was continually asking, "Father, what are You doing?"

Note: It appears that Bickle has special knowledge of how Jesus went about His work. Nothing like what he suggests can be authenticated in Scripture. Apparently also, the Father makes up His mind what He is doing day by day. This is indeed very strange, and I suppose this is an important element in the prophetic movement that necessitates a constant exploring of what is new.

Mike Bickle provides four ways to see what the Father is doing:

» We receive the prophetic whisper or impression from God.

» The Spirit may allow us to feel a physical sensation or pain that may correspond to how He wants to heal someone.

» We may observe the Spirit's presence resting on someone as we see obvious outward manifestations such as their lips quivering, their face flushed, their body trembling, or simply their tears falling.

» The Holy Spirit may show us what He is doing by giving us a prophetic dream or vision.

By "whisper" Bickle means the "still, small voice." By means of whispers or hints the Father can show what He is doing. Bickle refers to this as the "prophetic whisper of God."

Bickle says that prophets require love and strength to prophesy on a regular basis. It can be stressful to always be waiting to receive an impression or a word. But for those who desire to prophesy, he gives the following tips:

» Pray, "Holy Spirit I want to prophesy" or ask, "Holy Spirit, what are You saying or doing?"

» The impressions received must be expressed.

» Cultivate a lifestyle of watching and waiting.

He then counsels: "We must contend to walk in this" (p. 179).

Note: Bickle's counsel seems unhealthy. How could one live a normal life and relate to people properly, as in being present with them? What a burden to bear! Can this be mentally and emotionally, even socially healthy?

Chapter Seventeen: The Prophetic Word in Public Worship

Under the heading, "'Anything Goes' Approach to Prophetic Ministry," he warns that because some are fearful of "quenching the Holy Spirit they will not properly administrate" their words. Therefore, they will utter whatever they are impressed with "just in case" it is from the Lord.

This then sets the stage for how prophets are handled, especially in regard to public worship. He explains how this is managed at his church in Kansas City.

Note: He is right to have a process to manage the prophesying, if one accepts the validity of the kind of prophecy going on there. Upon reading the chapter, I became thankful that I do not have to deal with such deception.

Chapter Eighteen: The Prophetic Song of the Lord

Bickle says that Jesus loves music. He says, "Jesus is an excellent singer, song writer, and musician." He goes on to say, "The Scriptures are clear that God is the author of all the anointed life-giving music that exists in both heaven and on Earth" (p. 191). This announcement sets the stage for validating prophetic singers and songs. Bickle says this happens when "Jesus sings in the midst of the congregation by releasing His Spirit on singers in the church" (p. 192).

Note: Is it appropriate to ask how Mike Bickle knows this? Yes, he uses passages from the O.T. that seem, somehow, to suggest as much, but I think he carries it too far, with the aim of justifying the dynamic taking place in the church of which he is pastor, where apparently there are many God-anointed singers, song writers, dancers, and musicians.

"Angelic Choirs" will be seen and heard as we near Jesus' return, Bickle says, and in 1990 he actually heard one such choir (pp. 195–196). He thinks each piece sung by the angelic choir will carry with it a particular message. He knows of others who have heard angelic choirs, and they report that the music is absolutely wonderful.

And there is more: "The angelic choirs are always functioning in the spirit realm in concert with our earthly prayer meetings" (p. 196).

More still: In the end time conflict—the civil war, I suppose—a battle will be waged between two global worship movements. Satan will head one, that of the evil music.

Chapter Nineteen: Manifestations of the Holy Spirit

"Manifestations" refer to the stranger things that happen among worshippers at Bickle's church and at others associated with the NAR. He says that such manifestations have been known to occur during powerful moves of God down through history. On pages 204 and 205 he lists what he considers manifestations that appear in Scripture.

Bickle believes that "the Bible nowhere teaches that God is bound to do only what He has done before" (p. 206). Essentially, even if some of the current things taking place are not found specifically in the Bible, this is no reason to prevent God from doing new things. He suggests that the issue is hermeneutics, that it is the critic's way of interpreting the Bible that is the problem. He refers to America's first Great Awakening and Jonathan Edwards who wrote of some of the phenomena that took place then.

Bickle has developed a means of testing manifestations:

Does it bring honor to the person of Jesus Christ?
Does it produce a greater hatred of sin and a greater love for righteousness?
Does it produce a greater regard for Scripture?
Does it lead people into truth?
Does it produce a greater love for God and Man?

Note: At first glance many might be satisfied with Bickle's list. But in each of the five, how would this be determined? Who would make the decisions? What if a manifestation failed to meet the test? And would an observer be able to see the manifestation and make a decision on the spot? Would it even be possible to make such judgments at all?

One source of concern is his reliance on Teresa of Avila's life and writings to support strange manifestations. This woman was notorious for engaging in very questionable practices that some thought to be of a demonic nature.

I have personally observed very strange manifestations that were accepted and even applauded at NAR gatherings. I have wondered afterward if what I was seeing was either faked (the wildness and weirdness some see as evidence of the person being very spiritually powerful), a sign of delusion and thus mental illness, or even behavior inspired by demonic spirits.

Mike Bickle gives a list of phenomena or manifestations observed in the sort of worship done at his church in Kansas City:

> Shaking, jerking, loss of bodily strength, heavy breathing, eyes fluttering, lips trembling, oil on the body, changes in skin color, weeping, laughing, "drunkenness," travailing, dancing, falling, visions, hearing audibly into the spirit realm, inspired utterances (i.e., prophecy), tongues, interpretation of tongues, angelic visitations and manifestations, jumping, violent rolling, screaming, wind, heat, electricity, coldness, nausea as discernment of evil, smelling or tasting good or evil presences, tingling, pain in the body as discernment of illnesses, feeling heavy weight or lightness, trances (altered physical state while seeing and hearing into the spirit world), inability to speak normally, and disruption of the natural realm (for example, electrical circuits blown). (p. 210)

Then come six "false equations" about manifestations (p. 213):

» False Equation # 1: If I were more devoted, then I would experience more manifestations of the Spirit.

» False Equation # 2: When many are visibly touched by the Spirit, then revival is here!

» False Equation # 3: The people God uses to impact His manifest presence are usually mature and sensitive to God.

» False Equation # 4: Just be open and sensitive to the Spirit, and you will receive physical manifestations of the Spirit.

» False Equation # 5: If it is truly the Holy Spirit touching these people, then there will be instant and lasting "fruit" in their lives.

» False Equation # 6: If the power of the Holy Spirit touches people, then they should not have control over their responses.

Bickle's answer to each of the six false equations is "No!".

Note: Mike Bickle makes an attempt to right some wrongs he obviously is much aware of and likely has to deal with on a regular basis. Yet, answering "No!" does not mean that what God wants every one of His children to prophesy in the way experienced with the NAR prophets.

Chapter Twenty: God's Strategy of Silence

From vast experience, Mike Bickle talks in this last chapter about some of the "pressures" that come upon those who prophesy. For instance, the notoriety that often comes to those who are acknowledged as prophets can bring pressure from those who want them to prophesy or hatred from others for reasons Bickle does not explain. So the prophet receives either honor or opposition.

Prophets need to be silent when they receive knowledge about others. Maybe the "hatred" spoken above comes from knowing or suspecting that a prophet knows details of a person's life one would not want exposed.

Note: In this last chapter Bickle hints softly at dynamics that would likely take place in a church where there are several hundred people looking to get a word from God or receive a prophecy every Sunday. The very thought could be chilling to many, even if they had no serious secret sins. What a chore it would be to pastor such a church.

A Critique of

THE PHYSICS OF HEAVEN

JUDY FRANKLIN & ELLYN DAVIS,
DESTINY IMAGE PUBLISHERS, 2012

Kris Vallotton, "Senior Associate leader of Bethel Church, Redding, CA" (p. iii), writes a foreword for Franklin and Davis' book. From the beginning we then have an endorsement of the contents of the book from Bill Johnson as well. Indeed, Pastor Johnson is a major contributor to the book. Kris urges the reader, "If you are tired of being a settler, existing on the shores of tradition and riskless living, this book is for you. But beware, because once you get a taste of these authors' insights into light, sound, vibration and quantum physics, and you discover how God has written His personal story into creation, you are destined to see the Almighty all around you" (p. ii).

Note: Destined? Maybe condemned or captured are better terms. Of all the books I have examined in the process of presenting a view of the NAR, this is the most chilling, in that the authors and other contributors constantly encourage Christians to engage in plain, old-fashioned, occult practices.

INTRODUCTION
by Judy Franklin

"My journey into the mysteries of sound, light, vibrations, and quantum physics began with one word—sound" (p. v). This began in 1999, when Franklin heard the single word "sound" and assumed it was from God. She began a search into the meaning of the word and what it was that God wanted her to discover.

First Corinthians 15:46 is a verse she looks to for support: "But it is not the spiritual that is first but the natural, and then the spiritual." By natural she means the creation itself, God putting into the creation information about Himself and thus, quantum physics.

She cites Bill Johnson as support. He said, "We can't just camp around old truth, but should seek newly revealed truth for our generation." And she turns to Jonathan Welton who explains, "Christians need not be afraid of being deceived by counterfeits, but should realize that whenever we see a counterfeit, we should try to discover the 'real' behind it" (p. x).

Note: It is obvious that Christians traditionally look to Scripture and not to science or occult concepts, but the quantum physics she refers to is not science at all. A Wikipedia search will show this to be the case. Johnson and Welton know this as well and thus give a challenge to Christians to go ahead and explore anyway.

Welton uses the idea of the "counterfeit" as he reveals in chapter 5, "Authentic versus Counterfeit." He reasons that, if there is a counterfeit, there must be the genuine article. So then, he says, look into the counterfeit to find the truth. Mine the counterfeit, dig deep, search it out, and there will be truths as well as the counterfeit. He claims that the devil stole from God what we call the occult but that Christians should now reclaim these lost arts. Just like that! And Bill Johnson, Kris Vallotton, and the rest simply swallow it.

CHAPTER ONE: THE POWER OF THE ZERO-POINT FIELD

by Judy Franklin

Franklin states that "no child of God has ever fully realized the power that has been put within us" (p. 2). Power is what it is all about, and now is the time for Christians to grasp and use that power.

She recounts that the Lord "told me that soon He would release a sound from heaven that will literally change the structure of how we think" (p. 2). When this happens we will think like God, in fact, "bringing heaven to Earth is our mandate, and to do that we need to think more like heaven" (p. 2). She also feels the Lord gave her the following: "If we will place our hearts in an upper room posture, He is again releasing a sound that will transform the way we think. I believe that sound is going to empower us to do greater works than He did" (p. 3).

Her research leads her to an astrophysicist named Bernard Haisch who studied and presented his findings on the "zero point field." This is the "background sea of light whose total energy is enormous" (p. 5), and though huge the zero-point field is the lowest possible energy state. All other states of energy have more intensity than this low energy state, she insists.

This energy state is an "underlying sea of quantum light" (p. 6), and it will turn out that we can obtain power from it to do far more than Jesus did during His earthly ministry. She believes that this energy is in us and around us and is the real power of God. Again, the zero-point field was spoken into the creation because He wanted Adam and Eve to be powerful. "The good news is that Jesus reconciled us back to God and to what we should have been in the garden of Eden, but our minds haven't been transformed enough yet to realize it" (p. 7).

Of greatest importance is to know how to access the power. The zero-point field is within us, Franklin states, so we have the power in us to move many mountains. After all, Jesus controlled nature and so should we able to do the same, even more. Doing "greater works" should be just every day events.

Note: The principle behind the occult is the quest for power to control people, events, and the future. What Franklin is speaking of is nothing more than a philosophical rationale for engaging in the occult. She has not one shred of proof behind her pronouncements. Are we to believe God speaks to her?

She would be more believable if she were to cast a few mountains into the sea, but she has shown nothing of this power, so I suppose her mind hasn't been transformed enough. Her state of mind is, however, certainly the gateway into a connection with power—demonic power.

Over and over we hear the charge that we must do something or another, and always it has to do with changing our thinking. The "musts" are unending.

CHAPTER TWO: EXTRACTING THE PRECIOUS FROM THE WORTHLESS

by Ellyn Davis

This chapter is introduced by a quote from Jeremiah 15:19: "God says, 'If you extract the precious from the worthless, you will become My spokesman.'" There is no version given. Then Davis says, "We may have to delve into areas we previously considered off-limits to extract the "precious" from the "worthless" and recover lost truths that belong to the people of God" (p. 11).

Note: Here now is one of the central theses of the book: hidden within much of what is termed New Age, Eastern mysticism, and the occult are teachings and practices previously rejected as demonic by Bible-based peoples, but in reality are truths of God that need to be recovered today.

Probably the translation of Jeremiah 15:19 from which Davis quotes is The Passion Translation, which makes sense, because the passage is a far cry from being accurate. The ESV translation of the passage reads, "If you utter what is precious, and not what is worthless, you shall be as my mouth."

The Passion version, as it does so very often, is used to back up the theology of NAR concepts and worldview. Davis must be desperate for something biblical to back her strange ideas and thus ignores Jeremiah's point completely. The verse is very clear: the people of God are to speak His words not those of the pagan and idolatrous nations.

Davis admits that the Christianity of her childhood in a Baptist setting somewhere in the South of the USA didn't meet the challenges as she grew up. She states she was a "Jesus Freak" and learned a great deal from Ern Baxter, who sat at the feet of William Braham and became one of the "Ft. Lauderdale Five" of the Shepherding movement that caused so much division during the aftermath of the Jesus People Movement.

After pursuing a scientific education, marriage, and having children, she moved to Sedona, Arizona, to accept a job offer.

Sedona is where wonderful spiritual knowledge was captivating many. "I was intrigued by what I found there. I saw healings and mystical experiences and revelation to rival anything I had seen or experienced in the church.... It wasn't that I wanted to become a New Ager, I just wanted to find out if maybe they had uncovered some truths the church hadn't" (p, 14).

She "decided to examine New Age thought and practice for anything precious that might be extracted from the worthless" (p. 15). She wanted to take back any truth that had been rejected or ignored.

The term "quantum mysticism" is the term she uses to identify that which is found to be precious and not worthless in the understanding of most Christians. Her definition of the term is "a set of metaphysical beliefs and associated practices that seek to relate consciousness, intelligence or mystical world-views to the ideas of quantum mechanics and its interpretations" (p. 6).

Wayne Gretzky, the great hockey player, once said that he skated to where the puck was going to be and not where it had been. She employs this idea for what she and others are doing now—skating to the puck—unlike those who are mired in the same old Christian stuff that has been around forever. God is "moving on" into quantum mysticism, which is "unfamiliar territory that seems dangerous and sometimes seems to contradict what He's done in the past" (p. 18).

She believes that the Holy Spirit is "moving again" as do those who contributed to her book, such as Kris Vallotton, Bill Johnson, Jonathan Welton, and others (the predominant NAR notables). "They all agree that the next move of God will cause a shift at the deepest level of who we are—perhaps at the very 'vibrational level' that the New Age movement has been exploring."

The chapter's last sentence is an open invitation: "My hope is that this voyage of discovery we are taking together allows you to be open to deeper understandings of God's reality" (p. 19).

Note: She sounds the invitation to shipwreck. After embracing the occult world, she acts as the missionary, urging others to get on board, and crashing upon the rocks is inevitable. We have the practices of abomination listed in Deuteronomy 18:9–14, and though it is "old" it is still valid. In my view, Ellyn Davis, along with Judy Franklin and the other contributors to the book, have drifted out into a devilish sea. I am trying, in *False Prophets Among Us*, to throw out a lifeline.

Chapter Three: Vibrating in Harmony with God

by Bob Jones

This chapter is based on interviews with Bob Jones. The book's authors introduce the material by saying, "Bob Jones shares that God is beginning to 'breathe' on His people again to prepare for a second Pentecost that 'tunes' us and brings us into harmony with God" (p. 21). This fits in with the concept of quantum mysticism. "God recently showed me that shields were being given to different men and women" (p. 21). Jones does think that many shields—consider them as badges of rank and power—will be given out, and those who receive them will bring in a "divine order" (p. 22).

A point of interest here: Jones references "The Song of Solomon" to say that God's breath smells like apples. So as God "breaths" new things, there will be the smell of apples, and Bob Jones has in fact smelled apples (p. 23).

The word "sound" came up in the interview and also the idea of vibrations, and he thinks the "vibrations take place in us" (p. 23). He also thinks the new move of God will be ten times more powerful than that of Pentecost (p. 24).

Note: Jones' shields may be comparable to Bill Johnson's "mantles," which will be mentioned in another chapter. Again, the idea is that God is doing something new.

The smell of the apples is a convincing event. It strikes me as odd that the apostles and prophets rarely if ever critique one other.

Jones relates that as far back as 1995 prophecies were being given about a "new sound." This sound is different from the ordinary noise or resonance. "This coming new sound isn't just something that you pick up with your ears, but it's greater than anything you can understand. It can change DNA so we are genetically growing up . . . where our genetics come out of the Father in our spirit. We are becoming like an instrument being tuned, where our genetics are getting aligned with the Father's genetics, in harmony with Him" (p. 26).

Then more in line with what Franklin and Davis would like to hear: "We're going to take authority over everything down here back and literally give it back to the Father." Expanding further on the idea he says, "And everything vibrates. But when we get in harmony with God, everything will vibrate to tune with us. Total authority was given to man" (p. 27).

Note: Prophet Jones aligns with what Franklin and Davis and most all NAR-aligned people project: power and authority is coming. This of course is the central draw of the occult. It takes little reflection to realize that such is in complete and absolute contradiction to what God has revealed in Scripture. But never mind, because God is doing a new thing.

In between chapters 3 and 4 is this thought: "From the point of view of quantum physics, as human beings we are not only immersed in energy fields, but our bodies and our minds are energy fields" (p. 28).

CHAPTER FOUR: RECOVERING OUR SPIRITUAL INHERITANCE

by Bill Johnson

Part of the author's introductory statement to this chapter reads, "He [Johnson] emphasizes how crucial it is for us to recover lost 'God truths' as an inheritance to future generations of Christians" (p. 29).

Note: What are these truths? Apparently the Bible is not enough, does not go far enough—more is needed, always more that must be done.

There is a contradiction here, or a departure from some NAR concepts, which promote with certainty that the very last days are upon us. Johnson perhaps has a different view, since he speaks of future generations.

The lost truths—is this a reference to truths found in the occult? Are these truths hidden in the worthless stuff that must be brought back and claimed by the church today?

In the past, Johnson says, those things received from God by previous generations were lost and then died out and were not passed on. He says "There are anointings, mantles, revelations, and mysteries that have lain unclaimed" (p. 30). He believes that it is possible to recover realms of anointing and insight and to do so simply by reclaiming them. But even more, he is convinced that "realms are opening up right now to people because they realize their destiny. They realize that God has ordained and given them access to hidden things" (p. 32).

Note: The usage of terms like "realm," "destiny," and "access" are peculiar in that they are far less Christian than they are occult and mystically oriented. Johnson quotes something Jesus is purported to have said: "The things that are revealed are for you and your children forever." No reference in given however. I searched an analytical concordance and found nothing close, rather that who the Father is was being revealed to little children and to those whom Jesus chose to reveal Him (see Luke 10:22). I am guessing Johnson is quoting from The Passion Translation, thus his citation is highly questionable as to its meaning.

How are realms and destinies accessed? And this is the lead-in to occult practices, which in this book by Franklin and Davis are to be found in the sounds, light, vibrations, and quantum physics arena.

The early Church and subsequent generations essentially failed to pass truth along, but this is a new day, the days of the final move of God, and the ancient truths are being made accessible. Johnson puts it this way: "But we have an opportunity in this generation to grab the concept of spiritual inheritance and see, for the first time in church history, what it looks like" (p. 34). Then on page 35 he restates it: "We have the opportunity to recover lost wealth of prior generations that was, for whatever reason, disregarded."

Next comes the question of how to make a reclaiming. "We can begin by recovering secrets, mysteries, mantles, and realms of God that have been abandoned and ignored for decades, some of them for centuries. They just lie there waiting for someone in this generation to come along and claim them" (p. 37). He even quotes God: "There are things that are lying there, mysteries to be understood, inheritances that are untended, uncared for, unoccupied. But they're there for the taking" (p. 37).

Note: The quote from "God" above must be something revealed to Pastor Johnson. This is the trouble. NAR apostles and prophets continually get messages from God, they contend, and no one can call them to account or they might risk negative accusations or allegations of blasphemous speech.

The question must be asked: How are the discoveries made and/or claimed? According to Franklin and Davis it is by digging into the vibrations, the quantum mysteries, essentially the "precious" parts of the worthless occult world. Johnson leaves us with no other conclusion when he says, "We've been given an inheritance of hundreds of years of mystics, of revivalists, of those who broke into realms of the Spirit to leave something as an inheritance, and it needs to matter to someone" (p. 38).

CHAPTER FIVE: AUTHENTIC VS. COUNTERFEIT
by Jonathan Welton

Note: This chapter is intended by Franklin and Davis to encourage Christians to let down their guard when it comes to things mystical and occult. Jonathan Welton makes a very persuasive case for Christians to embrace what the Church has rejected as counterfeit and demonic.

In the introduction to the chapter, Franklin and Davis say of Welton's piece: "Jonathan Welton teaches that wherever there is a real, there is sure to be a counterfeit. . . . Jonathan tells us that we need to be more concerned about reclaiming all of our stolen goods from the enemy than about being afraid of the deception of counterfeits" (p. 41).

The point is, if there is a counterfeit there must also be the genuine. This is true regarding a counterfeit dollar bill. One does not counterfeit what is not true and valuable. It is our job as Christians to claim the genuine, but the danger, Welton warns, is in throwing out the whole, both counterfeit and genuine together. This means the Christian community has failed to claim power found buried in the counterfeit.

Welton assures Christians that there is no need to fear the supernatural. After all, those who identify and claim Jesus as Lord, are safe and protected from deception. He says, "We need to be much more concerned about reclaiming all of our stolen goods from the enemy than about being afraid of the deception of counterfeits" (p. 45).

"Are psychics and New Agers operating in real power? The answer is yes, but they have climbed in as trespassers. They have not accessed the spirit realm through Jesus" (p. 46).

Welton assures his readers that "I have found throughout Scripture at least 75 examples of things that the New Age has counterfeited, such as having a spirit guide, trances, meditation, auras, power objects, clairvoyance, clairaudience, and more. These actually belong to the church, but they have been stolen and cleverly repackaged" (p 49).

Welton says, "When you see a counterfeit, don't shrink back in fear—let this cry rise in your heart, 'THAT IS MINE, AND I WANT IT BACK!'" (p. 51).

Note: In admonishing Christians to engage with the occult world without fear rather than crying out against it, Welton sets them up for confusion and trouble. He is convinced the follower of Jesus is entirely safe. How wrong and unbiblical he is. We need only examine Matthew 24:24, where Jesus says, "For false christs and false prophets will arise and perform great signs and wonders, so as to lead astray, if possible, even the elect."

"If possible" is a first class grammatical construction that means it is indeed possible to lead astray even the chosen and elect ones of God, those who are truly born again of the Spirit of God. Jesus is clear that there are false christs and prophets who do actually lead true believers astray. Not that salvation is lost; but as to being led astray, absolutely possible. To follow Welton's counsel is to open oneself up to being led astray.

The "realms"—where does Scripture speak of this, or anything close to it? His readers are being set up for accepting an unbiblical construct. "Realms" is an occult designation, and the magician, shaman, and medium claim to move in them, but those realms are ruled over and populated only by the demonic.

Welton is keenly aware of the standard occult practices, listing some of them on page 49. Hearing the voice of an angel, or Jesus, or a dead saint, seeing an angel, or Jesus, or a dead saint— all of these are perpetrated by Satan.

CHAPTER SIX: GOOD VIBRATIONS

by Ellyn Davis

Incredibly, God has opened the eyes of some to the mysteries of sound, color, light, vibrations, and frequencies. Dr. Ellyn Davis, a scientist, is going to show the possibilities latent in the creation. Some have even discovered that they themselves have a "resonance" that helps others move into greater depth with God. For example, "Judy Franklin has found that people who have a hard time 'going to heaven' by themselves can more easily do it if they are around her, so she carries some sort of energy that helps them" (p. 53).

Good Vibrations, the title of a song by the Beach boys, provides an opening for a chapter that is somewhat scientifically oriented. The idea is, if God has placed vibrations in everything He created, why not explore this? (p. 54).

Prophets, maybe like Bob Jones, have been saying for some time that sound, color, and light have healing frequencies in them. Then comes the question, "What if there really are 'good vibrations' that God has imbedded into everything He created and we just need to be open to experiencing it?" (p. 54).

Note: Could it be? Let's find out. What fun! How exciting! We certainly can't look into the Bible for this, since nothing in Scripture even remotely suggests this. We have here some real science in terms of explaining what waves, light, and other physical phenomena are, but it proves nothing in terms of presenting a natural mechanism underlying or overlaying mystical things. This chapter is intended to act as a blinding tool to entice the unwary into the old time occult. The idea is to suggest that we need to discover hidden things God has placed into the natural realm that can be used for various purposes like healing.

In the second to last paragraph in the chapter, Davis speaks of "many scientists" without naming them, providing no references to their work, giving no way of checking to see if what she says is true. She just says it, and I will suppose that NAR-indoctrinated persons will simply accept what she says as true, which is a true characteristic of the cultic mindset.

CHAPTER SEVEN: SOUND OF HEAVEN, SYMPHONY OF EARTH

by Ray Hughes

There is much we don't know yet about sound and its relationship to the unveiling of God's glory" (p. 65). That being true, we yet live in an "information age," when more and more is being revealed, especially in the spirit realm. Now in this chapter, Ray Hughes believes "that the Holy Spirit has given me some of the pieces of the puzzle to heaven's sound, so the information I share with you about sound and light and vibration will be based on scientific fact, confessed speculation, and spiritual revelation (pp. 65–66).

Note: The trouble for the reader is that Ray Hughes does not specify where one ends and the other begins. It is fascinating material but I do not know which is science, speculation, or revelation.

Sound began, Hughes thinks, when God said, "Let there be light" (Genesis 1:3). Sound means vibration, and essentially everything has vibration, which produces the sound of heaven. And Hughes concludes, among other interesting ideas, that "we have been given the creative ability to release the sound of God" (p. 67).

Note: Again we come across the word "release." This is a common expression used by NAR apostles and prophets, and when I see it I become suspicious. The idea of release sounds good, but what does it mean and how does it work? On the face of it Hughes says we have the power, for that is what it is, to release the sound of God. Power indeed!

CHAPTER EIGHT: THE GOD VIBRATION

by Dan McCollam

Sounds, we find in Franklin and Davis' introduction to this chapter, can "open up portals in the heavenly realms" (p. 77).

Note: How may this statement be taken? What are portals? What are the heavenly realms? The writer assumes the reader will understand. It may be that this is insider language, understood by those who have been reading and listening to material from the last movement of God on the planet. I am not making fun of this, I would like to have some definitive explanations of what such important words actually mean. Catchy phrases may wow many, but for those who demand more, there is little information available.

McCollam says that God's voice, the God vibration, is the glue holding all creation together. He states that all creation, everything in the universe, has a vibration at the center of it. Everything vibrates, so there is sound in everything.

On page 85, McCollam states where his chapter is going. "Because God, creation and the angels are constantly interacting, we can expect to hear them at times." So then, how can we hear these sounds? "Open your heart, your eyes, and your ears with an expectancy to encounter the sounds and sights of heaven on a new level" (pp. 85–86). He goes on: "Activate your sensitivity to your aural and spiritual environment. . . . At the slightest impression of the Lord's calling turn aside to meet with Him even if just for a moment" (p. 86).

Note: Here is a prescription for insanity. Anyone who attempts to follow McCollum's counsel will be overwhelmed with all that will come along. Hopefully people will not practice this while driving a car, performing a surgical operation, flying a plane full of passengers, or swinging for the bleachers in the last inning.

In a way McCollum has a point. A person who wants to hear a sound will eventually hear a sound, then more sounds, later a cacophony, and then the ears will pop. If insanity were the worst that could result, well that is one thing. There is more, however, and that is demonic invasion.

CHAPTER NINE: ANGELIC ENCOUNTERS

by Cal Pierce

(This chapter developed by means of an interview with Cal Pierce.)

It all began with Cal Pierce when he had a conversation with an angel, an angel that had been with him for thirty years. Prior to that, Pierce was asking God about the energy crisis. Then he was at a conference where Tim Sheets referred to Psalm 91: "He sends his angels to render service on behalf of those who inherit salvation." And "render service" Pierce discovered actually means "run errands," thus angels run errands "on our behalf" (p. 89).

Note: Pierce does not give the specific verse from Psalm 91. The closest I see is verse 11: "For he will command his angels concerning you to guard you in all your ways" (ESV). This has been variously interpreted. Some say the person in question is the psalmist and others the Messiah. The translation quoted by Pierce is likely (no way to check on this) from the Passion Translation. If so, it fits perfectly with the Brian Simmons worldview.

Later Cal Pierce found that an angel was standing in front of him, and the angel reported that he was sent to answer Pierce's question about the energy crisis, since he is the energy angel (p. 89). The angel accompanied Pierce back to his hotel room and began teaching him about energy. The angel talked about the "water car" and how light and water can produce energy.

Something new was then added—sound. "Sound will literally drive vehicles and produce the power to drive the planet (p. 91). Sound, light, and energy; it is all about producing power with sound.

At some later point, Pierce met a man who had been taken to heaven in some way. This person had been shown how to produce four-dimensional objects with sound (p. 91). Later on, he was at a conference where a Native American talked about "sonoluminescence," where sound creates bursts of light (p. 91).

The angel went on about the connection between sound and the power of the spoken word. The idea is that God's Word produces faith, and faith is "activated by sound" (p. 92). The upshot is, "when you get the will or word of God in you, you have something in you of God that is creative. When the creator releases a word, the word itself becomes creative" (92), and angels are waiting for the sound in order to act. Angels do not know what people think, but they hear the words they speak.

Pierce promotes talking with angels, partnering with them, and speaking out creative words, which is what the angels are waiting for.

Note: One wonders how it could get any weirder. Is there anything like this in the New Testament? What about the ministry of the Holy Spirit? Who or what is this angel who appeared to Pierce? Could it be the angel of light Paul speaks of in 2 Corinthians 11:14? And even worse, how could such a chapter appear in Franklin and Davis' book, one that is supported across the board by leading apostles and prophets aligned with the NAR? The deception is deep and wide.

CHAPTER TEN: SPIRITUAL SYNESTHESIA

by Larry Randolph

(This chapter developed by means of an interview with Larry Randolph.)

Larry Randolph is concerned about preparing people to interact with God in many more ways than ever before imagined. He believes "we are on the verge of experiencing Pentecost on a new level and in a new measure" (p. 95). He explains: "We need to be impacted with the same kind of 'sound' from heaven that penetrated the atmosphere on the day of Pentecost. I'm weary of sermons and teachings that only restate our need for transformation. What I'm hungry for is to experience something fresh from heaven. Now! Not Later!" (p. 96).

Note: Randolph at various points says that the 120 in the upper room at the time of the Holy Spirit's outpouring were drunk in the spirit with an emphasis on drunk. This is typical misunderstanding of the meaning of Acts 2:13, when onlookers assumed the disciples "were filled with new wine." Peter goes on to point out that they were not drunk at all (see Acts 2:15). It was the hearing of the foreign languages that promoted the imagining and accusation on the part of the hearers. The reason why NAR folk like to emphasize "drunk" is that so many of them act drunk, and the chief example of this would be Heidi Baker. It is interesting how deliberate misunderstanding of Scripture is intended to cover serious error and confusion.

Synesthesia comes from the combination of two Greek words, syn which means together, and aisthesis which means perception. Therefore, synesthesia means "joined perception" (p. 107). Randolph cites statistics, without noting sources, that 3–4 percent of the world's population experience synesthesia, which is a mingling of the five senses where they hear colors, smell numbers, taste sound, and so forth (p. 97). And he says this is what happened to the 120 in the upper room on the Day of Pentecost. Randolph's explanation is that "a heavenly 'sound' can create a heightened level of synesthesia that opens our senses to extreme encounters with the supernatural" (p. 98).

He is convinced that the next move of God will radically transform the "realm of our senses" (p. 99).

We must be aware, Randolph warns, that even the slightest things like "inspired thought," "feeling a witness," or "having a gut feeling" are messages from God. So then we must "tune in to the spirit realm with all of our senses and reach out for more of God's Spirit in every way we can" (P. 107).

Note: So many "musts" and this involves those aspects about us that are not at our beck and call. That is one point, but more importantly is how Randolph sets his readers up for accepting the occult world. There is absolutely nothing even close to this in Scripture. Jesus never came close to any of this , but that seems to mean nothing to the NAR apostles and prophets. Are the people under their leadership able to examine what they are hearing and reading?

Randolph believes that to position ourselves for the next move of God we must recover "truths "currently held captive by many unbelievers. "Many New Agers, for example, have already begun to explore the phenomenon of synesthesia and are desperately trying to 'tune in' to multiple realms of spiritual reality. . . . We must take back what is ours." Then he suspects "that many have a fear of being deceived by things they might not understand" (p. 103).

"What if God chooses to speak more frequently in colors and numbers in this next outpouring? What if he uses colors, numbers, smell, feeling, and sound at the same time? Or speaks to us in a combination of modalities that are physical, mental, and emotional, or even vibrational? Are we really open to 'new things' in God?" (p. 106).

Note: I have read very similar statements and theories in books by Wiccans and shamans. Randolph sounds more like an occult spiritualist than he does a Bible-based Christian. Who will rise up and challenge such dangerous nonsense?

CHAPTER ELEVEN: STRANGE THINGS ARE AFOOT

by Ellyn Davis

Note: Dr. Davis presents her version of quantum physics, and strange things are indeed afoot. While I am no scientist , it seems that her explanation of the theory of quantum mechanics is essentially correct. Not that anyone really gets it, but beyond the explanations, she moves on to something else—The Rise of Quantum Mysticism. The reason for this effort is to say that Christians need to take back some of that which is theirs in the first place, which she does in chapter 12.

Quoting Ernest Lucas and his book, *Science and the New Age Challenge*, Davis lists three key concepts of quantum mysticism (p. 113–116):

» First is that "the world we live in is not the 'real' world, but an illusion." Essentially this postulates that all we see and know is illusion.

» Second is "that the universe is a unified, inter-connected whole." Here the idea is, since everything is connected, all is God, we are all God, and our consciousness is God as well.

» Third is that human consciousness "has the power to create material reality."

Davis will detail in the next chapter how she thinks these ideas impact or can impact Christians today.

Chapter Twelve: Quantum Mysticism

by Ellyn Davis

Under the heading "Metaphysical interpretations of Quantum Physics," Davis makes five points (pp. 121–127):

» First, there is the belief in the power of consciousness to influence material reality.

» Second, there is the belief in a single, universal consciousness that permeates all things.

» Third, there is the belief that everything—even the thoughts and emotions—emits energetic vibrations.

» Fourth, there is the belief in parallel universes.

» Fifth, there is the belief that mankind is evolving to higher levels of consciousness.

Note: This is a succinct expression of a worldview that is becoming increasingly popular. It avoids connections with any and all of the world's religions, including Christianity. It is both godless and godly at the same time. It does open the door to the new move God is doing now, however, and in a form that is much more acceptable to those who bristle at the basic Gospel message.

Under the heading "Compatibilities with Christianity?" Dr. Davis says, "It's obvious that the New Age has used quantum physics as part of its belief structure. But are any of the ideas advanced by quantum mysticism compatible with Christianity? Yes, they are" (p. 127).

There are four areas of incompatibility: (1) "where God, Jesus, and the Holy Spirit fit into the picture; (2) what constitutes sin; (3) where the Bible fits into the picture; and (4) what happens after we die."

On the other hand, there is much of quantum mysticism with which Christians can agree, since all truth is God's truth and we must dig out of quantum mysticism that which belongs to the Creator. Dr. Davis gives four areas of potential agreement:

God-Truth: By Faith, We can speak Things into Existence. "It shouldn't be a stretch for us to believe that, as 'observers' to whom Jesus gave all power in heaven and earth, we can, through faith, intent, prayer, and declaration, call things into existence" (p. 128).

God-Truth: Thoughts and Attitudes Are Powerful. "It shouldn't be hard for us to accept that thoughts and emotions might actually give off energetic 'vibrations' that can cause changes in the physical and emotional atmosphere" (p. 129).

God Truth: A Oneness Connection? "Scripture tells us that rocks can cry out, stars can sing, and trees can 'clap their hands' in joy, so we wouldn't be too surprised to discover that they have a form of consciousness too, a 'mind' as it were" (p. 130).

God-Truth: Different Levels of Reality? "So we should have no problem embracing theories about the 'other side' and multiple dimensions of reality" (p. 131).

Note: What power we have then, speaking things into existence. There are the decrees, words to release, expressing faith verbally, focusing on the positive, being loving in our hearts—just a few ways to be powerful. And it is all about power. Though a Bible passage or two are quoted, and these without any real accuracy or relevance, science, occult mysticism, and crazy fantasy all work together for the good and for God, who is, after all, the one and only.

CHAPTER THIRTEEN: KEYS TO TAKING YOUR QUANTUM LEAP

by David Van Koevering.

"Our spoken intent can bring something from the unseen realm into the seen and we can make the non-material appear in material form" (p. 133). According to the author, our faith words spoken out can do wonders. In fact, a large part of our universe is actually non-physical (p. 134).

Van Koevering looks to 1 Corinthians 1:28 for support: "God chose what is low and despised in the world, even things that are not, to bring to nothing things that are." He then states, "This Scripture makes sense only when you understand it at the atomic and subatomic level. Everything is made up of atoms, which are frequencies of energy. These frequencies of energy are the voice of Jesus causing all things to be!" (p. 135).

Note: Apparently Van Koevering believes humans, fallen as we are, limited as we are, can bring something out of nothing. And that he quotes the 1 Corinthians passage to support his theory is completely astonishing. Paul is speaking of Jesus, God becoming flesh, becoming subject to all manner of human punishment, even death, and dying as a criminal. Then, Jesus, taking upon Himself our sin, rises as King of Glory. His victory over sin and death changes everything. This self-serving twisting of the greatest event in history in order to substantiate an unproven and occult theory is remarkable.

Next we are told that the speed of light is slowing down (p. 136). In fact, "When man fell, the speed of light slowed down" (p. 136). This concept, I assume, explains the problems many have with the creationists' view of the age of the universe, or at least of the earth, compared with the billions of years scientists usually state. But here, Van Koevering uses the notion to explain how prophecy works.

The Holy Spirit works faster than the speed of light, is way ahead of 'now time,' especially since time and therefore the speed of light has slowed. The Holy Spirit, whose speed has not diminished, can then reveal what will happen, really what has already happened, to those caught in a time warp. The prophet, by virtue of being informed by the Spirit, can speak of what is to come.

Van Koevering puts it this way: "Here is a quantum leap for someone: If you know something coming from your future, let's say a vision, a revelation, a desire, or even a creative idea, that information has to move faster than the speed of light to reach you. . . . The quantum leap of knowing your purpose and assignment is waiting as a God quaff for you to pop!" (p. 137). He also explains this phenomenon with, "What is a vision? What is a word of knowledge? It is seeing, knowing, getting information before the causation" (p. 141).

Also, Van Koevering understands, based on passages like Habakkuk 2:11 that says, "For the stone shall cry out of the wall, and the beam out of the timber shall answer it," that matter has memory. All matter vibrates and therefore records, as if it were a data-collecting machine.

Franklin and Davis, at the conclusion of the chapter, offer this: "By this point in the book, you've realized that you have a choice to use the energy of your intent and your words to change matter and events" (p. 146).

Note: This book belongs in a bookstore's magic and sorcery section! Please pile a dozen or more exclamations points after that sentence. I suppose there are those who are thrilled to embrace the deception, since it seems to validate all that belongs to the doctrines behind the New Apostolic Reformation. Yes, it is all possible, many will say to themselves; I have not been deceived, I am merely in a flow with real science.

Chapter Fourteen: Whole Lotta Shaking Going On

(Six combined authors)

Here six people relate how the power of God changed them, and dramatically so. The first two are Bill and Beni Johnson, whose chapters are coming up. Then we read about Cal Pierce and Ellyn Davis. Finally, we read about Celeste and John, no last names given.

They all have in common powerful experiences with God. Bill and Beni sound as though they stuck a finger in a wall socket, and for long periods of time. Bill wanted more, more of God—year being 1995—and he got it. Beni, his wife, was not far behind.

Note: I have to be careful here since I do not want to cast disparagement on what happened to these folks, all of whom I count as brothers and sisters in Christ.

Since 1963, I have been closely associated with all manner of Christians. For fifty years now I have either pastored churches or have led para-church ministries, during which I operated a Christian counseling ministry for ten years. Since 1984 I have facilitated a divorce recovery and loss workshop. For six years I led a cult recovery workshop. I simply want to say that I have been intensely involved with people for many years.

Several of the six stories making up chapter 14 sound highly unusual. In fact, I have never heard anything comparable. And this is what I offer: All that is spiritual is not of the Holy Spirit.

CHAPTER FIFTEEN: THE CLARION CALL

by Beni Johnson

The clarion call is to "venture into new realms, including realms of the vibrations of heaven" (p. 163).

Beni Johnson, wife of Bill Johnson, loves to hear the sound of heaven during times of worship. When it comes, it shifts the atmosphere. "When that worship leader and his team of worshippers hit the right note or play the right song, heaven comes a little closer" (p. 163).

Beni has and continues to have dramatic spiritual experiences, which she describes as similar to being in direct contact with live electrical wires.

On one occasion, while she and husband Bill were speaking at a conference in Wales, she heard the sound of what seemed like a large number of birds singing in a tree. This sound puzzled her. She thought it was a message from God. She writes, "I was determined to find out. It was obvious that God was trying to speak." Finally the meaning of the birds singing was revealed. It was God saying, "This isn't your place. Get away! You can't have this" (p. 167). Exactly what she was to get away from is not mentioned.

In the conclusion to the chapter she counsels: "Take time to be alone and listen and wait for His sound to come to your spirit. As you deliberately shift your attention, you can physically feel Him stirring in your innermost being, changing and shifting you. The vibrations of heaven are a powerful life-changing substance. Anything is possible when you plug in" (p. 169).

Note: Beni and Bill Johnson are sincere Christians who live to serve Him. I have no doubt about this. Yet, the expressions I read about are extra-biblical, and they would very likely admit this. Their experiences, however, are so confirming to them as being actual, physical contacts with the spiritual world, and their statements so sure, that most people are prevented from making a critical examination of what exactly is going on. We must not forget that the demonic kingdom is so very "spiritual," perhaps more spiritual than the kingdom of God, at least in the understanding of many.

One last point: The worship experience involved with music is very powerful. It moves the listeners, even the most reluctant. EDM, that is the electrical dance music, will get anyone jumping up and down. And it is all so spiritual.

CHAPTER SIXTEEN: PULLING INTO TODAY

by Bill Johnson

The authors of *The Physics of Heaven* introduce this last chapter with, "Bill Johnson shares how we already own in the present what is not yet. And, because of our inheritance in Christ, we can reach into God for what has been reserved for tomorrow and pull it into our today" (p. 171).

Bill states it himself: "It is interesting to note that we have already inherited tomorrow—things to come" (p. 172).

Note: What is the meaning of this? It is biblically correct that in Christ we have inherited eternal life. I do not think this is what Bill is talking about, however. Rather he is thinking about being able to grasp future events and bring these, somehow, into the present.

After reading one book after another by Bill Johnson, I find his words to seem more like double-speak than direct, clear language. It is as though he is living in another dimension, and I doubt he would refute that.

He attempts to make his views look biblical and quotes Scripture to back them up. In my opinion, these attempts are not convincing.

A Critique of

HEARING GOD'S VOICE TODAY

JAMES GOLL, CHOSEN BOOKS, 2004, 2008

Kris Vallotton writes in the foreword to Goll's book that there is a growing hunger in people to have real spiritual experiences. In the introduction that follows, James Goll lets us know that "God still speaks today" and that the reader will be given practical tips on how to hear God's voice today.

CHAPTER ONE: AS IT WAS IN THE BEGINNING

The chapter begins with John 10:27: "My sheep hear My voice, and I know them, and they follow Me." This well known verse is followed by Revelation 3:20: "Behold, I stand at the door and knock; if anyone hears My voice and opens the door, I will come in to him and will dine with him, and he with Me."

Dr. Goll explains that after his conversion during the Jesus People Movement (1967–1975) everything changed. He was having "impressions, mental snapshots, hunches, knowledge, short thoughts and full phrases" entering or being released into his heart and mind (pp. 22–23).

The author then urges his readers to get into the School of the Spirit and start hearing the voice of God.

Note: Hearing the voice of God is meant to be taken literally by Dr. Goll. Most commentators agree that the intent of Jesus in both of the above verses is that we as Christians can belong to and be followers of our Lord Jesus. It appears that Dr. Goll sets the stage for his readers to attempt to hear the audible voice of God. It is a siren song intended to create a longing for something that is far more cultic, even of the occult, than that of biblical Christianity.

CHAPTER TWO: THE HOLY SPIRIT AT WORK TODAY

This chapter presents the truth that the Holy Spirit is given to us and helps us grow up in Christ. Building on this traditional and acceptable biblical doctrine the believer's next step is to be ready to hear His voice.

Note: Dr. Goll is right; the Christian will not make sense of what it means to be in Christ without the working of the Holy Spirit. The issue comes down to how this works out in a person's life. In my opinion, this book goes beyond what is meant to be the normal Christian life and crosses over into something never mentioned or intended by the Author of the Word.

CHAPTER THREE: THE SOUND OF MANY RUSHING WATERS

On page 47 Dr. Goll gives twenty "tools" God uses to speak to us:

A dream or vision
A voice in a trance
The voice of many angels
The voice of the archangel
The sound of many waters
The sound of the Lord walking in the Garden
The sound of the army of God marching in the tops of the trees
The audible voice of God
God speaking peace to His people
God's written Word
Wonders in the sky and on earth
Visions and parables given to prophets
Words and metaphors given to prophets
The Holy Spirit speaking to a group
Men, moved by the Holy Spirit, declaring God's voice
Heavenly experiences in which one is brought up before the Lord
The Holy Spirit bearing witness to our spirit
A dumb donkey speaking with the voice of a man
One person speaking the revelatory counsel of the Lord to another
God's own Son

Note: I recall hearing about these things from one of our group during the closing years of the Jesus People Movement. He taught us some of what is listed above. He then began receiving directions to do things. He said he was hearing God's voice telling him specific things to do or not do. One day this confused young man called me from a city about one hundred miles away and asked me how to get home. This sort of thing happened to him over and over until his parents had him placed in a mental hospital. It took years before he was able to sort things out and return to a normal life.

Chapter Four: Walking in Our Kingdom Birthright

We begin to hear the voice of God by taking baby steps, learning as we grow up. It is not always pretty, as there will be missteps along the way.

Dr. Goll asks this question of the reader at the conclusion of the chapter: "Are you engaging your spirit to expect to receive revelation from God? Before you know it, you will be hearing His present day voice in your life and you will be passing on this contagious passion to others" (p. 64).

Note: James Goll has set the stage and invited those who want to hear God's voice today to both seek it and accept it. Seekers will be hearing a voice, tangible and believable. It is like those who want to see an angel or talk to Jesus directly—all well within the range and capacity of the demons to counterfeit.

Chapter Six: Ten Practical, Personal Tools

The author makes it seem both right and simple to hear God's voice today. Every one of God's children is invited to listen for His voice. And here is how to do that:

» Don't make it complicated

 a. Submit to His lordship
 b. Resist the enemy
 c. Ask a question and expect God's answer

- » Allow God to speak how He chooses
- » Confess any known sins
- » Obey the last thing God said (Dr. Goll "sanctifies" his heart by three days of fasting.)
- » Tune into God's voice
- » Don't talk about it too soon
- » Know that God will confirm it
- » Beware of counterfeits (Dr. Goll knows that Satan is able to counterfeit that which is actual. He says, "The enemy counterfeits God's voice, and he counterfeits experiences, even rare, supernatural experiences" (p. 87).
- » Practice hearing God's voice
- » Cultivate an intimate relationship

Note: If in 1963, at the beginning of my Christian walk, I had been very impressed with the list above, I probably would have followed each step faithfully. It is no wonder that so many do. It takes considerable knowledge of the Scripture and of what is characteristic of the normal Christian life not to be duped by a slick sell such as the ten "tools" above. Clues here are "allow God," "tune in," and "practice hearing" God's voice. We know now that God speaks to us by His written Word. Yes, there is such a thing as a word of knowledge (I have had at least two), and there may be prophetic words, and likely these two are the same, but to be hearing God's voice regularly, almost on demand, is just neither biblical nor Christian.

CHAPTER SEVEN: WALKING IN COMMUNITY

Dr. Goll talks of an event that occurred in 1992, when he experienced "an unexpected invasion" (p. 94). At one minute to midnight, on the Jewish Day of Atonement, a heavenly visitor entered his house. This being stood in front of the bedroom and at the stroke of midnight began to speak, especially addressing his wife, Michal Ann, who wrote about this encounter in her book, *God Encounters*. For a nine-week period the Golls experienced repeated visitations. They heard God's voice, and the primary lesson Goll learned is summed up in this sentence: "I learned that God can speak to and through whomever He wants whenever He wants" (p. 95).

Note: Either we believe James and Michal Ann Goll or we don't. I do not believe that God spoke to them. The visitor, perhaps a demon in disguise, said nothing much except that spiritual entities could speak to human beings. Who among us would not be deceived?

CHAPTER EIGHT: HEARING WITH DISCERNMENT

Dr. Goll lists three sources of revelation: the Holy Spirit, the human soul, and the realm of evil spirits. He gives nine tests of revelation (p. 108–110):

» Does the revelation edify, exhort, or console?

» Is it in agreement with God's word?

» Does it exalt Jesus Christ?

» Does in have good fruit?

» If it predicts a future event, does it come to pass?

» Does the revelation turn people toward God or away from Him?

» Does it produce liberty or bondage?

» Does it produce life or death?

» Does the Holy Spirit bear witness that it is true?

Note: The Scripture, applied by the Holy Spirit, is the only reliable source of revelation. As for the human soul, there is no biblical support for this at all, but it is a door opener to deception. (My view is that we are soul as opposed to the doctrine that came into the Church during the third and fourth centuries to the effect that there is a separate entity inside us called the soul.)

My view is that the "voice" in question comes from the demonic realm. In my long years of deliverance work (casting out demons), I heard many a demon speak. At times I made the mistake of actually conversing with them, thinking I would learn some secrets about the dark side. That demons can speak, whether out of the mouth of a person or not, there is no question, and we see this in the New Testament. Since they can speak and have access to what I call "the second best computer data base in existence," their words can be accurate, powerful, and deceptive.

Dr. Goll insists that to move in the prophetic, seeing people healed or freed from demonic power, we need to have God's "supernatural anointing" (p. 112).

Note: Applying the tests on Goll's list is virtually impossible. Getting any kind of clear guidance is at minimum questionable. Even test #2, the voice being in agreement with God's Word, would not be easily grasped.

Also, how much time would need to elapse before any clear decision could be made? How would one know if a revelation edifies, consoles, or exalts Jesus? If there were good fruit, what would "good" look like, and as to the event coming to pass, producing liberty or bondage, and bringing life or death, it is nearly impossible to test.

Chapter Nine: He Will Guide You!

Dr. Goll gives ten principles of divine guidance. They will merely be listed here and then be left to the reader to decide their efficacy (pp. 117–124).

» The will of God is made known in the Word of God.

» The will of God is confirmed through circumstances.

- » The Holy Spirit speaks from where He dwells.
- » Divine guidance comes from meeting God's conditions.
- » Peace of God accompanies true guidance.
- » Much guidance from God comes unnoticed.
- » Divine guidance does not mean we know all the details.
- » The process of guidance is not always pleasant.
- » Hearing God speak should prompt us to action.
- » Guidance is a skill to be learned over a lifetime.

Note: Several of the above principles I applaud, especially the first. The rest are so nebulous, subjective, and open-ended, they are rendered unreliable and confusing. "The Holy Spirit speaks from where He dwells"—clear and simple?

The purpose of the guidance given is to be a blessing to others, Dr. Goll declares. However, I have another thought. Might the person receiving guidance by hearing God's voice learn to be dependent upon this guidance? Over time, might such guidance become a heavy burden? Might it rob one of free will? Might it make a person subject to the voice?

CHAPTER TEN: LISTENING, WAITING, AND WATCHING

Dr. Goll speaks of dealing with distractions. Imagine praying, hoping to be still and hear a voice, all of which can easily be disturbed. Only focus on Him until all the distractions subside. Keep on listening, waiting, and watching.

Note: The words and meaning of the title of this chapter may be applied to many spiritual disciplines. It is the mantra of many Eastern forms of meditation as well as forms of contemplative prayer promoted by people like Richard Foster and Dallas Willard. Being quiet and still with a blank mind, hoping to hear something from the spirit world, whether practiced by a Christian, Buddhist, or Hindu, is to open oneself up to the demonic.

Chapter Eleven: Properly Responding to God's Voice

One must be patient to hear God's voice; it may not come quickly. Persevere, lean in, focus—it may not come easily.

Chapter Twelve: At the End of the Day

The revelations of God may seem fantastic and unintelligible to the mind. The revelation must be grasped by the spirit through faith, spirit here being the human spirit.

Note: The title for this final chapter is a fitting conclusion to the book. At the end of the day no one really knows for sure what is going on. It is mystery; it is also often nothing more than confusion, which may result in chaos or even harm.

A Critique of

THE VOICE OF GOD

CINDY JACOBS, CHOSEN BOOKS, 1995, 2016

There are two forewords: one by Jack W. Hayford and the other by Bill Johnson, with endorsements by Che Ahn, Jane Hamon, Bill Hamon, C. Peter Wagner, James Goll, Cheryl Sacks, Jane Hoyt, John Dawson, Dick Eastman, Chuck Pierce, Jim Hennesy, Banning Liebscher, Samuel Rodriquez, Elizabeth Alves, Marilyn Hickey, and John Loren Sanford.

In the following critique, I attempt to avoid repeating similar ideas found among the other books in this section, selecting instead the more interesting or original points.

INTRODUCTION

Jacob's reason for writing the book is to "demystify" the prophetic. Her hope is that prophetic ministry will be increasingly normalized and accepted.

CHAPTER ONE: THE VOICE OF GOD

Jacobs states that at the onset of her prophetic ministry, when people called her about someone with a serious illness or to report a death, she knew what had happened before the phone rang.

She believes that Christians are eager to learn more about personal prophecy so they can be comfortable with it.

When she was twenty years old it was made clear to her that she was being called to the prophetic ministry. This gift of prophecy, she states, was "poured out" on her during a time of what she refers to as deep worship. She calls it "a deep time of seeking the Lord." From that point on, Cindy began to listen to the "voice of God."

Note: In my experience and understanding, so many of these unusual callings come at times described as deep worship, soaking in prayer, being drunk in the Spirit, toking the Spirit, and so on. These altered states resemble or are identical to the trance, the ecstasy, or the passive or meditative state of mind common to shamanism, Santeria, and numbers of neo-pagan groups like Wicca. This is a warning sign, as there is no support for this in

Scripture. The question must then be asked: In such states of mind do demonic entities have access to the individual? Never in Scripture are God's people instructed to empty their minds, bypass their minds, or stop thinking.

Under the heading, "The Effect of Prophecy," Cindy tells an interesting story about Dick Mills, C. Peter Wagner, and John Wimber, the founder of the Vineyard Movement. She speaks of a time when she was with Peter and Doris Wagner in Peter's study at the Lake Avenue Congregational Church in Pasadena, California. John Wimber had called to inform Peter that a man named Dick Mills was going to contact him about a personal prophecy he had for him. Peter did not know who Dick Mills was, since he was just learning about the prophetic movement. (Dick Mills was one of the early prophets emerging out of the charismatic/Pentecostal movement.) Upon hearing this, Cindy assured Peter that he should talk to him. Cindy told Peter, "He's one of the major hitters as far as prophets go." Dick Mills did call and began to tell Peter "how God would use him to bring three strands of the Body of Christ together for an end-time work" (p. 33). Toward the end of that phone call, Peter informed Dick Mills that Cindy was present in the room. Dick replied that he had, back in the 1980s, prophesied that she would have an international ministry.

CHAPTER TWO: BUT I DIDN'T MEAN TO PROPHESY

When Cindy is interceding for people, circumstances, and so on, she begins to hear the voice of God breaking into her praying. She can identify it by a change in her own voice's "tonality" (p. 40), which indicates that she is hearing not her own but, she assumes, the voice of God.

She relates a story about a person with the reputation of being an intercessor who had been requested to pray for a particular need. (I will avoid the names of the persons and other details.) While praying, the intercessor suddenly saw the man who was the subject of the prayer in some sort of vision, and the intercessor began to speak to him. Quickly, the man seen in the prayer-vision actually walked into the room where the praying was taking place. The prayer was answered, and the situation was resolved.

Note: What troubles me, perhaps more than anything else, is that sincere Christians who want to serve their Lord will attempt to pattern themselves after NAR apostles and prophets. The prophetic word Cindy Jacobs received apparently came true, and likely many words given to others have as well. Does this confirm that the prophetic words were from God?

Chapter Three: Camel's Hair and Wild Locusts

Jacobs admits that some "weird" people are attracted to the prophetic ministry. She writes, "Those who have severe emotional and personal problems have caused real damage to the Body of Christ and have created a serious backlash against others who are used to prophesy" (p. 49).

It is at least refreshing to hear this admission.

Cindy now revisits the early days when she began to "know" things. She relates that while in college she began to experiment with mental control, that is, trying to read other people's minds. An acquaintance told her she would make a good medium.

The theme of the chapter is "generational sin." Her father's side of the family had been involved in occult practices. In such cases, these generational influences must be treated, blocked, and eliminated, and this might be why she adamantly attacks mediumistic practices. So then, despite the fact that Jesus took our sin upon Himself on the cross, we must still be concerned with issues like generational sin and subsequent influences. She gives two passages that supposedly speak to the issue: Acts 19:18–19 and Ephesians 4:28.

Note: After examining the passages cited above, it is difficult to see their connection with any supposed need to examine and deal with "generational sin." Acts 19:18–19 relates the burning of occult materials in the aftermath of the Ephesian awakening, and Ephesians 4:28 has to do with a thief no longer stealing but working with his hands.

This reminds me of the fad having to do with repressed childhood memories that was popular during the 1980s and early 1990s. The generational sin concept seems to be quite similar. Perhaps Cindy is clearing up the charge that she would be a good medium by attributing that to generational sin on her father's side.

Chapter Four: Is That You, God?

Cindy does not shy away from the fact that the prophets and prophetesses are not always correct. She writes, "Although these false prophecies do happen at times, the benefits of the prophetic gifts far outweigh any problems that are caused" (p. 64).

Cindy is aware of the occult connection and knows that divination, or fortune telling, is definitely an occult practice, "so it stands to reason that it might not always be easy to discern its practice when it seemingly is coming from a Christian" (p. 71). The test to determine whether a word is from God is if "the word" brings glory to God.

Note: This then clears it up, at least in the mind of Cindy Jacobs, who seems able to easily determine if God is glorified or not. It appears to me that in this chapter Cindy is defending herself against the charge that she is little more than a fortuneteller in Christian disguise.

Many of the NAR prophets commonly admit that only 20–40% of the prophets' predictions are accurate or even close. It is said that to learn to prophesy, mistakes and failures must be accepted. What about the person who receives false words from God, of all things? What is the point of telling people about what they did or what will happen? Is this healthy, normal, and biblical? The psychics and mediums do this sort of thing for a living; are the NAR prophets in competition with these occultists?

As time has passed, Cindy has been called to an even higher mandate, to "gather the 'generals of intercession' to pray for the nations." Though the "generals" are not named, Cindy assures the reader they are "Christian household names."

CHAPTER FIVE: REDEMPTIVE PROPHECY

Cindy continues her attempts to justify her means of prophesying by quoting Wayne Grudem, a recognized New Testament scholar in the general charismatic/Pentecostal wing of Christianity. Wayne Grudem says the following about New Testament prophecy: "Not as 'predicting the future,' or 'proclaiming a word from the Lord,' or 'powerful preaching'—but rather as 'telling something that God has spontaneously brought to mind'" (p. 90).

Note: This understanding of prophecy is exactly what one would expect, as it fits in neatly with Cindy's conceptions about her own ministry. My view is that genuine prophecy is in fact "powerful preaching," when the subject is the person and work of Jesus Christ.

We must then ask, just how does one know that God is the author of what is brought to mind? We all have notions that enter our minds throughout each day as we hear speaking on television, in videos, or in conversations around us. How confusing it must be to sort out what is what, and no wonder Cindy previously referred to the mentally and emotionally unbalanced state of weird prophets. I have met a few of these, and it is saddening.

I will skip over these chapters:

CHAPTER SIX: MENTORING THE PROPHETIC GIFT

CHAPTER SEVEN: SPIRITUAL PROTOCOL

CHAPTER EIGHT: RELEASING THE PROPHETIC GIFT

CHAPTER NINE: DREAMS, VISIONS, PROPHETIC STYLES AND GIFTS

Cindy is convinced that God attempts to speak to many by means of dreams and visions. She supports this by referencing dreams and visions experienced by biblical characters. It is interesting that God "tries" or attempts such a thing: Is this a God who cannot get things done?

Note: This last chapter takes a toll on me personally. It is stunning and disheartening to see this coming from a Christian. Having to take a stand in opposition to the NAR is something I have avoided for years, and I now see why. It is not pleasant to confront brothers and sisters in Christ. However, it must be done. With each one of the authors I have been reading and discussing here I identify and feel a kinship; they are doing what they think God has called them to do. Some may be in it for the glory, the attention, the power, or the money, and some have simply been deceived by the master deceiver.

It does no one any good to refrain from speaking out; it is part of the role of the pastors in the Church. Sheep are being harmed.

A Critique of

When Heaven Invades Earth: A Practical Guide to a Life of Miracles

Bill Johnson, Treasure House, 2003

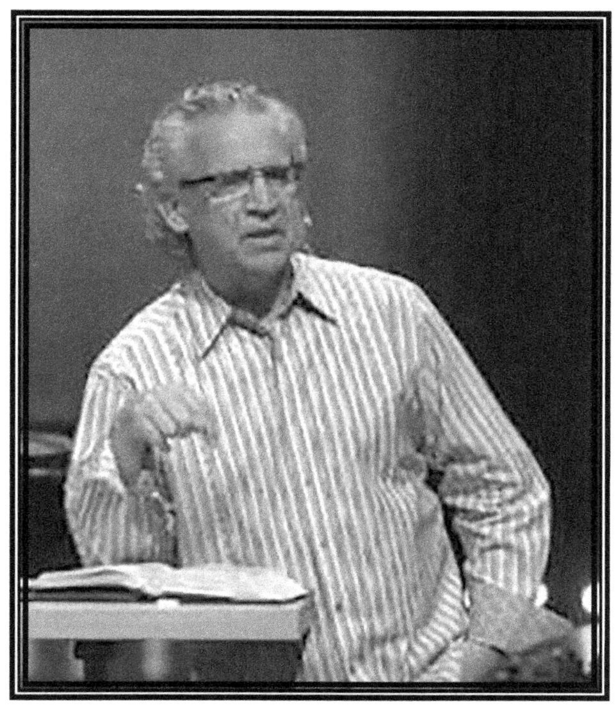

The book is endorsed by John Arnott, Wes Campbell, Ché Ahn, Stacy Campbell, Jim W. Goll, Dick Mills, Larry Randolph, Heidi G. Baker, Ph.D., Cal Pierce, and Todd Bentley, with two forewords, one by Jack R. Taylor and the other by Randy Clark.

CHAPTER ONE: THE NORMAL CHRISTIAN LIFE

"We will no longer make up excuses for powerlessness because powerlessness is inexcusable. Our mandate is simple: raise up a generation that can openly display the raw power of God. This book is all about that journey . . . the quest for the King and His Kingdom. The kingdom of God is not a matter of talk but of power" (pp. 27–28).

Note: Bill Johnson lays out the substance of his book clearly enough. It is all about power, and as we will see, that power comes through faith, faith in the unseen realm—bringing heaven to earth, which is something that we should be able to do.

Healing is the center of attention; faith to be healed and that God will heal is foremost. Pastor Johnson cannot seem to help but berate and belittle the lack of such faith and throughout the book says the same thing over and over. The basic message is, What is the matter with you? You should grasp more of the Kingdom and put it into action here and now.

This is essentially the sum and substance of this book. I will continue to expose chapter by chapter, but I could stop here.

My primary concern is that Pastor Johnson changes the meaning of biblical faith. Faith is not seeing miracles or bringing the kingdom into the present; it is trusting in Jesus for our salvation. Certainly he knows this truth. He wants more, however: he wants to see Christians acting powerfully, and this requires faith, a faith that the power in the heavenly realm can be activated here and now, mostly through healings.

CHAPTER TWO: COMMISSION RESTORED

Speaking about Jesus, Pastor Johnson states: "He performed miracles, wonders and signs as a man in right relationship to God . . . not as God. If he performed miracles because He was God, then they would be unattainable for us. But if He did them as a man, I am responsible to pursue His lifestyle. Recapturing this simple truth changes everything . . . and makes possible a full restoration of the ministry of Jesus in His Church" (p. 29).

Note: "Recapturing" what was lost is the focus of chapter 2. Pastor Johnson says that Jesus came "to seek and to save that which was lost" quoting Luke 19:10, but that is his rendering, which serves to support his thesis. The English Standard Version, along with all others I consulted, renders the passage, "For the Son of Man came to seek and to save the lost."

Jesus came to save the lost for sure, but Johnson makes the verse say that Jesus meant to restore man's "dominion over planet earth" as well (p. 31). The whole point of the book has to do with this issue—lost dominion—which is the primary point of the NAR.

On page 32 is the heading, "We Are Born to Rule." Pastor Johnson says we were born to rule, and in chapter 3 "we'll see how to use a gift to manifest His Kingdom—causing heaven to touch earth" (p. 35).

Note: I am struck by the term "causing," which means there is something we do to bring the realm of heaven to earth. This is clearly magical thinking.

CHAPTER THREE: REPENT TO SEE

Pastor Johnson knows the key Greek word usually translated "repent" means to change our way of thinking. Instead of seeing this as a change in thinking about who Jesus is and what Jesus did on the cross, he says, "The focus of repentance is to change our way of thinking until the presence of His Kingdom fills our consciousness" (p. 38). This is the way dominion will be realized.

Note: Pastor Johnson realizes that not everyone is on board with his thinking. The "opposers" need to change their way of thinking. He is not out of step with the core biblical agenda; others are. This is a constant mantra of the NAR advocates.

CHAPTER FOUR: FAITH—ANCHORED IN THE UNSEEN

Under the heading of "Seeing the Invisible" is this: "The invisible realm is superior to the natural. The reality of that invisible world dominates the natural world we live in...both positively and negatively. Because the invisible is superior to the natural, faith is anchored in the unseen" (p. 45).

He warns, "When we submit the things of God to the mind of man, unbelief and religion are the results. When we submit the mind of man to the things of God, we end up with faith and a renewed mind" (p. 47).

Pastor Johnson asserts that the "Holy Spirit lives in my spirit. This is the place of communion with God. As we learn to receive from our spirits we learn how to be Spirit led." And then in the same paragraph, "Your spirit received the life-giving power of the word from the Holy Spirit. When we learn to receive from our spirit, our mind becomes the student and is therefore subject to the Holy Spirit" (p. 47).

Note: While this may sound Christian-like, with mention of the Holy Spirit several times, I am probably not alone in thinking there is something decidedly amiss here. It sounds more like something one would find in a book written by a Wiccan witch or a shaman than a Christian pastor.

If I were to take Johnson's admonitions to heart, I would be confused and frustrated. Is it a version of mind over matter or positive thinking he is presenting?

Not only would I be puzzled, I would be discouraged. How could a person do this? My faith is not anchored in the unseen; it is centered and anchored in Jesus Christ, His person and work. Pastor Johnson is closer to the thought of Christian Science than it is to biblical Christianity.

Chapter Five: Praying Heaven Down

Chapter Six: The Kingdom and the Spirit

Note: In these chapters Pastor Johnson's emphasis on prayer and the importance of being filled with the Holy Spirit are very biblical. He does speak in ways that may be somewhat over the top, but overall the material is helpful.

"The hands that are surrendered to God can release the power of heaven into a situation. In the spirit world it is released like lightning" (p. 58). "Hands that are surrendered to God" is a peculiar phraseology. To me the words seem more magical than Christian. Perhaps it is nothing more than insider language to which I am not privy. And once again I detect the acquiring of power by means of prayer and being submitted to the Holy Spirit.

Pastor Johnson, and others like him, seems to live out an extraordinary, super-spiritual existence. Miracles are commonplace for them. Is it possible that his readers will feel they are not properly living out their lives, not living up to their potential?

Over the years I have read many biographies and autobiographies of Christian leaders, evangelists, and missionaries, and a few remind me of Bill Johnson but most do not. My own Christian walk has been much less exciting with far fewer miracles. I press on and have my highs and lows, often with more lows than highs.

These chapters for me are a mixed blessing.

CHAPTER SEVEN: THE ANOINTING AND THE ANTICHRIST SPIRIT

Speaking of Jesus, Pastor Johnson says, "it was the anointing that released the supernatural" (p.80). The anointing was by the Holy Spirit on the day when Jesus was baptized by John in the River Jordan. And it is this anointing, the experience of being filled with the Spirit, that we are to long for.

Note: Christ as a designation means Messiah, the one who was filled with and empowered by the Holy Spirit and became the King, the Savior, the Redeemer, the Prophet, and much more.

In the Old Testament kings were anointed with oil, with nothing supernaturally empowering about the oil itself, but it was a sign that such a person was recognized and set aside as the king. The Father made it clear that day at the Jordan River that Jesus was set aside as the Messiah and King. And yes, the action and then the person of Jesus was empowered by the Holy Spirit.

The phrase, "anointing," is a key concept among NAR folk. Their apostles and prophets are specially anointed for the last day's movement.

At the same time as God is anointing with power, "the spirit of the antichrist is at work today, attempting to influence believers to reject everything that has to do with the Holy Spirit anointing" (p. 81). "It is the antichrist spirit that has given rise to religious spirits. A religious spirit is a demonic presence that works to get us to substitute being led by our intellect instead of the Spirit of God. Being led by the Holy Spirit is an ongoing God encounter. Religion idolizes concepts and avoids personal experience" (p. 81). And then again, "To make matters worse, many unknowingly reject Him because He either shows up in a way that they are unaccustomed to, or He failed to come as He has in the past" (p. 83).

Note: It is clear enough that Pastor Johnson is reacting to criticism received from the Christian community about the nature of what was (and is) taking place. At the date of this book's publication in 2003, the "laughing" revival and the Lakeland, Florida, event with Todd Bentley were still in full swing. The pastor's Bethel Church was moving in the same direction, and much of what outsiders saw disturbed them. So his defense is understandable, and the focus of it is this: You Bible-only, doctrinal folk, you wrongly reject experiences, which are of course happening under the power of the Spirit.

"Fear of deception has opened the door for a tragic movement among believers. It states that because we have the Bible we are emotionally unbalanced and in danger of deception if we seek for an actual 'felt' experience with God" (p. 83).

Pastor Johnson insists that Jesus did not say, "My sheep will know my book." It is His voice that we are to know. "We can and must know the God of the Bible by experience" (p. 84).

As the chapter closes, we are given the goals the antichrist has for the Church: "embrace Jesus apart from the anointing" (p. 84). Those who follow the antichrist spirit want a safe Jesus who does not challenge or offend. Then 2 Timothy 3:5 is quoted: "having a form of godliness but denying its power. And from such people turn away!" (p. 85).

"How can people who love God be offended by the anointing of the Holy Spirit? Three reasons are given: (1) He moves like wind—apart from our control; (2) His thoughts are very different from ours; and (3) He refuses to be restricted by our understanding of His Word.

Note: The title of this book you are reading is carefully chosen: *False Prophets Among Us*. Mine is far from the first warning given out; dozens of books, numbers of blogs, and hundreds of videos have been presented to the public. Therefore, it is understandable that the apostles and prophets become defensive. And rightly they should be; the hope is that some of them will apply critical thinking as time goes on and more of the core error comes to the surface.

Chapter Eight: Teaching Into an Encounter

Pastor Johnson notes, "in this post-denominational era we are seeing an unprecedented movement of believers gathering around spiritual fathers (not gender specific)" (p. 90). He follows this statement with, "But now this gravitational pull toward fathers is happening even within denominations. Such a gathering of believers allows for differences of nonessential doctrines without causing division. Many consider this movement to be a restoration of the apostolic order of God" (p. 90).

He also contrasts "fathers" against "teachers," with the fathers having power and the teachers having only words (p. 91).

Johnson calls for a tour guide rather than a road map. Road maps are for the teacher types, but the tour guide, the Holy Spirit, is for fathers with power. About the road map, meaning the Bible, Johnson says, "But in reality, the Bible is a closed book. Anything I can get from the Word without God will not change my life. It is closed to insure that I remain dependent on the Holy Spirit" (p. 91). The pastor has a tour guide; thus he testifies, "Revelation that doesn't lead to a God encounter only serves to make me more religious" (p. 94).

Note: This is what we would expect—a not-so-subtle devaluation of those who love the Bible and teach it. And those who do so tend to criticize the NAR and have done so since the early 1990s. Pastor Johnson made a commitment to God that he would never go back to the old ways before he had the anointing—no going back, no possibility of taking a critical look at all that has transpired.

Chapter Nine: The Works of the Father

If the works of the Father are not evident—those are signs, wonders, and healing miracles—then the Father is not involved. Pastor

Johnson wants and expects the works of the Father to be evident in his work. "I hunger for the day when the Church will make the same statement to the world. If we're not doing the miracles that Jesus did, you don't have to believe us" (p. 97).

Note: It is possible that Johnson takes his cue from Jesus' statement in John 14:12 that, "Truly, truly, I say to you, whoever believes in me will also do the works that I do; and greater works than these will he do, because I am going to the Father." The issue here is that Johnson makes the presence of miracles a litmus test for faith and that the miracles produce the faith. As almost afterthoughts at the end of reports of healings in this and many other NAR books, people are said to be saved. I wonder about this. If there are healings—and maybe there are, or maybe there are not—the core of each report is about something elating or embarrassing. Can such a conversion testimony be trusted? Are the people involved just going along with the young and excited ministry team in order to please them? Why is the cross of Jesus and His forgiveness not the story?

If we consider Romans 10:17 that says, "So faith comes from hearing, and hearing through the word of Christ," we learn nothing about miracles being the causative agent for faith, although Paul himself saw and experienced many of them. Jesus performed thousands of miracles for the feeding and healing benefit of all who came to him, but not all became His followers. Miracles may or may not accompany the Gospel mission, but center stage is the proclamation of Jesus Christ and Him crucified, as Paul wrote in 1 Corinthians 2:2: "For I decided to know nothing among you except Jesus Christ and him crucified."

CHAPTER TEN: POWERLESSNESS: UNNECESSARY AND UNBALANCED

"Some Christians actually have considered it to be more noble to choose character over power. But we must not separate the two. It is an unjustifiable, illegitimate choice. Together they bring us to the only real issue—obedience" (p. 107).

"Is it possible the reason there are so few miracles in North America is because too many before us thought they had to become better Christians before God could use them? (p. 108).

Under the heading, "The Anointing, A Key to Personal Growth," Johnson says, "Christlike character can never be fully developed without serving under the anointing. Anointed ministry brings us into contact with the power needed for personal transformation" (p. 108).

Note: Pastor Johnson knows that some who operate in signs and wonders have tarnished the movement in various ways. Thus he argues that character is important, but it is better to see the power gifts in operation.

Certainly we are all sinners; no one is clean, considering all that is in our heart and mind. Johnson's ideal is "obedience," and it is expressed in carrying out the Holy Spirit's gifting.

I agree that the answer is not to throw out signs, wonders, and miracles because some have clearly lacked character. Yet the issue for many is not character but the validity of the extreme focus on miracles. Even if everyone involved with the NAR lived exemplary lives, it still does not authenticate all that is part of the NAR movement.

"The critics of the revival are unknowingly attempting to separate me from my first love. I will not give them place" (p. 116). Pastor Johnson simply will not even read books that criticize the movement characterized by signs, wonders, and miracles. Speaking of those who do, he says, "I respect them for their ability to stick their hands in the mire without getting their hearts dirty. I don't care to do it" (p. 116).

Note: Power and anointing for power is Johnson's emphasis, and it misses the central biblical truth. Paul spoke of power: "For Christ did not send me to baptize but to preach the gospel, and not with words of eloquent wisdom, lest the cross of Christ be emptied of its power" (1 Corinthians 1:17). Paul was clearly less interested in sophistry, or miracles, for that matter. The power is the blood of Jesus to cleanse from sin and bring the sinner into a saving relationship.

Pastor Johnson would not disagree with me on this point. However, Gospel preaching is not at the forefront of the revival he speaks of. And this is true across the board with NAR-aligned leaders and ministries, despite their claims to be evangelical.

CHAPTER ELEVEN: THE HIGH COST OF LOW POWER

Listed below are this chapter's sub-headings:

» Signs and Wonders Reveal the Nature of God
» Signs and Wonders Expose Sin and bring People to a Decision
» Signs and Wonders Bring Courage
» The Supernatural is the Key to the Sin Cities of the World
» Miracles Reveal His Glory
» Signs Direct People to Give Glory to God
» Signs Themselves Give Him Glory
» Miracles are a Unifying Force for the Generations
» Signs and Wonders Affirm Who Jesus Is
» Miracles Help People Hear From God
» Miracles Help People Obey God
» Miracles Validate the Identity of Both the Son of God and His Church

Speaking of the days leading up to the Day of Pentecost in Jerusalem, Pastor Johnson says, "Even though they had been with Him, even though they had experienced His power through their own ministry, they were to wait for Dunamis—the ability to perform miracles" (p. 128).

Note: Acts 1:8 reads: "But you will receive power when the

Holy Spirit has come upon you, and you will be my witnesses in Jerusalem and in all Judea and Samaria, and to the end of the earth." And when the Holy Spirit came in power, 3,000 were converted, and not one sign or wonder or healing was in evidence except the speaking in multiple languages at the same time, but that was only to facilitate the hearing and understanding by so many Jews who came from different nations speaking different languages. The power is to preach Jesus not perform miracles. And here is the major error of Bill Johnson and others like him. At great lengths Johnson defends the power gifts not the preaching of Jesus. He would bristle at this, if he ever read it, but he won't, since he will not look at critical remarks about the movement.

Chapter Twelve: Our Debt to the World: An Encounter With God

"The anointing of the Holy Spirit is His actual presence upon us for ministry. The purpose of the anointing is to make the supernatural natural" (p. 133).

Note: Pastor Johnson changes the meaning of the term "anointing." God has certainly indwelt us by His Spirit, but He has not set us aside to be the Savior or the King or the Messiah. Jesus is the Anointed One, the Messiah, the Christ. Christians are indwelt by the Spirit at conversion; Christians will be baptized or filled with the Holy Spirit but not set aside like Jesus and announced to be God with us.

Anointed, for Pastor Johnson, means to be "smeared" and is "God covering us with His power-filled presence" (p. 134). The point is we are to give this anointing away, this power that makes the supernatural a reality through signs and wonders. Yet, there is more.

"Through the shedding of His blood, it would be possible for everyone who believed on His name to do as He did and become as He was. This meant then that every true believer would have access to the realm of life that Jesus lived in" (p. 138).

Note: The words Pastor Johnson chose above may not have adequately expressed what he was trying to communicate. I hope not. It is a New Age concept that humans can become gods or godlike, or discover that they are godlike. Certainly NAR style authors like Judy Franklin, Ellyn Davis, Anthony Welton, and a host of others suggest the idea that becoming godlike is entirely possible.

A retort might be, didn't Jesus say that we would do greater things? Well, is there anything greater than raising the dead, as Jesus did on at least three occasions? Maybe the idea of doing greater meant greater in quantity and not quality.

What does "access to the realm of life" mean? This is another example of concepts being imported into the Christian vocabulary that I must state are shamanistic in nature.

"While God has provided angels to assist us in our commission, I don't take the posture that we are to command angels. Some feel they have that liberty (p. 139). And then, under the heading, "Entering the Twilight Zone," Pastor Johnson says, "Angels await the people of God speaking His word. I believe angels pick up the fragrance of the throne room through the word spoken by people. They can tell when a word has its origins in the heart of the Father. And, in turn, they recognize that word as their assignment" (p. 140).

Note: I agree with the first statement from page 139, but with the second from page 140 I utterly disagree. Angels are a big deal with NAR folk. They speak with them, are assisted by them, and too much more. Pastor Johnson obviously knows those who delight in commanding angels. He knows this is a violation of Scripture. Where he gets the authority to make the statement from page 140 is anyone's guess. Perhaps from experience or perhaps from a direct communication—the source is not stated. This is a most dangerous concept and one that will, and likely has, led many down a dangerous path, a path of deception. When a Christian embraces notions like angels picking up the fragrance of the throne room, then every wicked deception is ready to pounce.

"Signs" figure large for Pastor Johnson, who believes they must accompany the ministry of the anointed ones. By signs he means healings, knowing about the future, fragrances that can both be smelled and tasted, gold dust falling from the ceiling, oil falling on the hands (including on children's hands), feathers falling on worshippers both in worship times and even in restaurants, and clouds of the actual presence of God being observed over the heads of worshippers (pp. 141–143).

Note: I have expressed this before, but in the 1970s at The People's Temple in San Francisco where Jim Jones ministered, many of the same phenomena mentioned above were often present, and I myself experienced it twice. Later this congregation, at least a high percentage of them, committed suicide by drinking poison. After it was all over, I did funerals for some of these poor, deceived people. In speaking with their loved ones, I heard over and over the stories of the miracles. They were real; it is just that they were not of God. Satan, we do know now, is able to counterfeit signs.

CHAPTER THIRTEEN: OUR IDENTITY IN THIS WORLD

Pastor Johnson quotes from 1 John 4:17: "As he is, so are we in this world." He points out that Jesus is the risen, glorified, King of the Kingdom, seated at the right hand of the Father. "He is Lord" is one of the oldest confessions of faith.

We have been forgiven of all our sin, we have been born anew, we have been indwelt by the Holy Spirit, our names are written down in the Book of Life, our salvation is secure, and we have the blessing of God. So then we should mirror and model that in our living.

Note: This chapter's description will be short and sweet—I agree with Pastor Johnson here. We do understand we still have a fallen nature and are not perfect. We do not always walk in our victory, but most of us realize we are the most fortunate people on the planet. This is how I do see things; it is pleasant to be in concert with brother Bill.

CHAPTER FOURTEEN: WARRING TO INVADE!

Christians have been given the keys to the kingdom. We have conquered through Jesus' victory over sin, death, and the devil. We have nothing to fear. And Christians need to stand as victors and invade the Satanic kingdom. We are in warfare, plain and simple, and we do not shrink back from it. We have, in fact, already won.

Note: The title of the chapter may be a little over the top, but I embrace the content. Once again I am with brother Bill.

CHAPTER FIFTEEN: HOW TO MISS A REVIVAL

One way to miss a revival is to not be desperate for God. A hunger for God is essential. "There is something about desperation for God that enables a person to recognize whether or not something is from God" (p. 158). "Every Christian is supposed to maintain a desperate heart for God. We are in great need! Jesus addressed that fact with these words: 'Blessed are the poor is spirit, for theirs is the kingdom of heaven.'" (p. 159).

Note: The point seems to be that those who hunger for God, whatever that looks like, are those who want revival. The previous chapter focused on the victory stance of the believer, so the two chapters seem to be in contradistinction to one another.

Is Pastor Johnson saying that the Church, or that part of it that resists the revival, though stated by experts as being genuine, are those Christians who do not hunger for God? This seems to be the idea.

As a pastor for almost forty-seven years, I have noticed that desperate-for-God folks have generally been unconverted and do not have the peace of God in them. They keep trying harder, want more and more, and are attracted to wild and exuberant forms of worship. They seem to require regular affirmation that they are okay with God through healings and seeing what they think are miracles from God. "More, More, More!" is craved, even demanded. Demonstrations, experiences, feelings, visions, voices, out-of-body journeys to heaven, feathers, gold dust, angelic appearances, heavenly fragrances, clouds of glory—desperate for more and more and more.

Those who look to the Second Coming instead of wanting heaven now help quench the present move of God. Pastor Johnson says, "I believe the desire for the Church to be in heaven now is actually the counterfeit of seeking first the kingdom" (p. 161).

Note: This sounds like a criticism of the theology called Dispensationalism, which teaches that the Church will be taken away to heaven (raptured) before the tribulation and second coming of Jesus. A departure from this theology divides Johnson from most mainstream, American, evangelical denominations, although such belief is waning in recent years.

Expressive worship is not accepted by all, and such will quench the Spirit and prevent revival. "For the most part, expressive worship, ministry in spiritual gifts, and the like only turn off Christians who have had the unfortunate experience of being taught against them" (p. 163). This is followed by, "The Church has an unhealthy addiction to perfection: the kind that makes no allowances for messes" (p. 163).

"Our God-born desire for revival must keep us desperate enough to recognize Him when He comes. Without such desperation, we get satisfied with our present status and become our own worst enemies at changing history" (p. 164).

Note: The worship services at the Bethel Church in Redding, California, tend to be expressive. I personally have witnessed things that I found offensive, and this comes from a guy who once was a "wild-eyed" Pentecostal. In many instances, I was convinced what I saw had nothing to do with the Holy Spirit. I would not call

all I witnessed to be demonic necessarily, but it was not holy or honoring to God. People did the craziest things and yelled out the most outrageous silliness, yet it was all okay. There is no need for being decent and in order when the main rule is, the Spirit must not be quenched.

Chapter Sixteen: Infiltrating the System

Pastor Johnson tells the story of a pastor's conference he spoke at in a European country. He spoke about the "infiltrating Power of the Kingdom of God." He talked about the kind of ministry strategies his Bethel Church uses. The story Jesus told about leaven formed the backdrop for the sermon. After the teaching time, a group of pastors determined that "leaven" in the Bible stood for sin, and that the parable of Luke 13:20–21 meant that the Church would be filled with sin in the last days (p. 165).

Pastor Johnson goes on to speak of how the church in Redding infiltrates the system resisting the invasion of the Spirit.

Note: The rest of the chapter stays with the theme of the energetic ministry strategy employed by the Bethel Church. To read it one can only praise God. There is no question about the sincerity on the part of these brothers and sisters. I happen to know something of the kinds of outreach practiced by this church in Redding. There are fans and the detractors in the city itself. Things happen and people love to fix blame and point out excesses. I cannot help but applaud the zeal shown, though I have major misgivings about the basic concepts that fuel everything from the worship services to the kinds of outreach going on that are less focused on Gospel presentation than they are on signs and wonders.

Chapter Seventeen: This Present Revival

"Without Him we don't have enough insight even to know what to ask for in prayer" (p. 177).

Note: After some period of reflection I think I know what Pastor Johnson meant by the above sentence. That it is true is obvious. Still, I couldn't let it go. Then it came to me: What about the Bible? I could have taken that as an impression from the heavenly realm, to use NAR speak, then I realized that this is only obvious to most Christians, even those in the Church who do not operate in this last days movement.

The Scripture teaches us about prayer, Jesus Himself, the apostles, and the prophets, all who have something to say about prayer as found recorded in the Word. We have plenty of information to go on. So what was brother Bill trying to say?

Could it be he is arguing for the current revival to be the answer to it all? Is it only when "heaven invades earth" that all becomes clear? Is he saying that outside of what God is now doing in this great movement, we are left in the dark, so to speak? Is this what Bill means?

Pastor Johnson's use of the word "religion" is interesting: "Religion (which is 'form without power') will be more and more despised in the hearts of those who truly belong to Him. Revelation creates an appetite for Him. He doesn't come in a 'no frills' model. There's no economy class Holy Spirit. He only comes fully equipped. He is loaded, full of power and glory. And He wants to be seen as He is, in us" (p. 178).

Note: Evident here is a theme that runs throughout the book, the we-they formula. There is the "we," those who embrace the revival of which Bill and his church are very much a part, and there is the "they," those who have "religion." And I would be cast in this last class. The definition, "form without power," is certainly a put-down. Bill and his kin have power because they embrace the new move of the Spirit. The rest have religion without the power of the Holy Spirit. Is this coming from a defensiveness posture or a revelation from God? I have never come across such a definition. In fact, I like to say, in contradiction to the popular phrase, "I am not religious, I am spiritual" spouted by the progressive, practical atheists in Marin County where I live, I say, "I am religious, not spiritual." What I mean is that I take my faith seriously and practice it with discipline.

The remainder of chapter 17 I have little quarrel with, as it is mostly standard Christian material.

End Note: "And the Word became flesh and dwelt among us, and we have seen his glory, glory as of the only Son from the Father, full of grace and truth" (John 1:14).

When Heaven Invades Earth is the title of the book under critique. The passage from John 1:14 above talks about heaven invading earth. There is something that bothers me about the title of the book by Bill Johnson. Heaven, or Jesus to be exact, has already invaded earth, and His body, the Church, which is known only to Him, is in fact constantly on the advance despite setbacks and appearances to the contrary. The mission plan is intact.

It is a fact that Christians hold differing views about the end of history. Some see a decline toward the end or an outbreak of antichrist activity; others see the reverse, and some like me have no opinion that would need defending. As we say, it will all work out in the end.

Since we Christians can get stale and tired, there are local revivals, and there are the great outpourings of the Holy Spirit many refer to as awakenings. Enough information flows in to let us know that the Gospel is not shackled. Millions of us are busy engaged in kingdom work, which is the proclamation of salvation in Jesus Christ. And we do not worry or fret over it; no, we keep on with the work.

A Critique of

The Supernatural Power of a Transformed Mind: Access to a Life of Miracles

Bill Johnson, Destiny Image, 2014

Introduction

Bill Johnson clearly states the purpose of his book. He says of his cause, "that the kingdoms of this world would become the kingdoms of our Lord" (p. 21). He also says that it is to gain access to God's supernatural lifestyle.

Note: We can all agree with the first sentence above, but the second sentence about gaining access to the supernatural lifestyle sounds strange. At its foundation, this notion it is not anchored in Scripture.

Chapter One: Change Your Mind

Pastor Johnson sees the normal Christian life as one abounding in miracles, spiritual intervention, and revelations. The trouble, he thinks, is that the mind gets in the way. We think too much and examine things too much; instead we should experience the renewing of our minds.

We are the gatekeepers of the supernatural, which means we must bring heaven to earth. To accomplish this we must think differently; we must experience a transforming of the mind. Therefore, we must expect miracles as always possible, regularly anticipating signs and wonders.

Note: If one were to agree with Pastor Johnson, then what? How would we bring heaven to earth? Is there a passage in Scripture that points the way? Where are others through the long history of the Christian Church who have been writing about this? Since there is no help there, we can count on Brother Johnson to show us how it is done.

Chapter Two: Becoming the Dwelling Place of God

Unity among church leaders is necessary to pave the way for their congregations to enter into the "miracle realm." However, the reality is that there are pastors and elders who disagree with Johnson's call.

Note: Unity is a major theme in the NAR, and lack of it means that the supernatural events are not as abundant as they should be. As I have discovered in a number of NAR-oriented books, lack of unity comes from and on account of the segment of the Christian Church that is not in line with the NAR. Thus, there will always be a convenient excuse to explain the absence or slowness of fulfilled prophecies. Also note that "becoming" in the chapter title means that God's dwelling with us is dependent upon actions taken by Christians; thus Christians control the process of where and how God dwells.

Pastor Johnson says that, with the restoration of the offices of apostle and prophet in this last day movement, we see more clearly that God is with us. What we are seeing and experiencing now is unprecedented.

Like many NAR proponents, he talks about an "Open Heaven." It means that the demonic realm is broken and that God's will is operative much more than when heaven is closed. The job of Christians now is to see that heaven remains open, with the angels coming and going, and "angels are necessary to complete the assignment of the Lord" (p. 48). Then he says, "God is actually ushered into a situation by riding on angelic presence" (p. 48).

Note: Here Bill Johnson tightly focuses his sight on angels. A fascination with angels is typical of NAR literature, and these beings seem to regularly appear to the apostles and prophets, as though God is signaling that He has set them aside as major leaders in the last days battle. While there are angels in Scripture, they do not play such a large role as is found with the NAR. We must remember the warning Paul gives in 2 Corinthians 11:13-15:

> For such men are false apostles, deceitful workmen, disguising themselves as apostles of Christ. And no wonder for even Satan disguises himself as an angel of light. So it is no surprise if his servants, also disguise themselves as

servants of righteousness.

The implication from Johnson is that, if you have not seen and/or talked with an angel, you probably don't belong in the club. Dare one ask, "Bill, how do you know this is true?" Where in the Bible do we find anything close to this? Yes Bill, you may counter that God has revealed this to you, but we need more than your word, which does not trump the Word of God.

Pastor Johnson chides Christians that they are not bringing heaven to earth. There are no angels ascending and descending to bring heaven to earth, because God's people are not taking the risk or tapping into what heaven has for them.

The trouble, he asserts, is that the gates of hell are present in people's minds. Jesus told Peter at one point (Matthew 16:21-23) that he was "not mindful of the things of God." That the mind needs to be transformed is the center message of the book.

Johnson says the solution is to "agree with heaven" all the time, and open our minds up to be the gate of heaven, so that the angels can ascend and descend upon us and bring revelation, signs, wonders, and miracles. When we agree with heaven and the angels, the miraculous is released.

Johnson's use of released is a recurring theme in NAR literature. When the mind becomes a gateway for the angels to operate, then heaven truly comes to earth. It depends upon the Christians transforming their minds so they agree with what God is doing. Once one is in agreement, then the supernatural becomes natural. When we are aligned with heaven, we can bind and loose on earth what has been bound or loosed in heaven. There it is, and there must be revelation of this so the Christian is not working in the dark.

CHAPTER THREE: REVELATION AND UNDERSTANDING

Pastor Johnson teaches that the key to being tuned into God's revelation is to be spiritually discerning, which means to "open our spirit man to direct revelation from God" (p. 60). But one must be "listening."

Recognizing revelation is of major significance. How does one know he or she is listening to God? Bill says that one knows this because of the "freshness to it" (p. 60). The revelation will be "fresh" and better than anything anyone else could imagine. And the receiver of the revelation will be overwhelmed with it.

Note: One must hunger and seek for revelation, Bill counsels. Such counsel is easy to give, but it is vague and unstructured; it is lacking clear and solid information about what one has to do. Of course, he falls back on admonishing that the transformed mind is necessary.

CHAPTER FOUR: UNDERSTANDING IS AN EXPERIENCE

The mind must be transformed before supernatural power can be experienced. An experience is necessary in order for there to be proper understanding about the supernatural.

Pastor Johnson quotes John 5:39, where Jesus says that the Scripture (the Old Testament) points to Him. From this Johnson deduces that revelation is meant to result in encounters with God. This way of thinking is necessary to have the mind transformed. It is not enough to merely read Scripture; it must be experienced.

Johnson's essential premise is that the way is open for people to have experiences with God. This is the "Eastern mindset" rather than the "Western mindset," he writes. Much of the emphasis has to do with healing—praying for it, claiming it, or speaking it into reality.

Note: The subtitle to chapter four is, "We must require an experience from what we believe." The words "must" and "require" are rather strange. This reminds me of the road one must take in order to become a shaman. A shaman is one who, while in a trance or out-of-body state, enters into a world of spiritual entities who guide and give revelations. His or her belief has resulted in an actual spiritual encounter with spiritual entities.

When one experiences the supernatural, it is indeed life transforming, and the shaman, the Zen master, the Wiccan witch or warlock, the sorcerer, and the diviner also seek this. Ask any of these practitioners of Eastern and occult spiritualties. When the spirit beings interact with a person, real life-transforming, spiritual experience does take place.

CHAPTER FIVE: BECOMING STUDENTS OF MIRACLES

The next step in putting "revelation into practice" is to become a student of miracles. Unless one does this, he or she will fall prey to "Herod's Leaven," referring to those Christians who do not believe in an "active" God.

Ministries and churches that do not move in the miraculous are referred to as having the leaven of the Pharisees; they belong to the "religious system" category. The Pharisaical leaven yields theory without practice and experience.

In substantial contrast is the "leaven of the Kingdom." This kingdom is the expression of the final move of God in the last days, of which the author is a part. The correct spiritual leaven is sown within it.

Note: The subtitle of this chapter reads, "We must learn to 'see' by observing the effect of the unseen world on all that is visible. Miracles provide that opportunity more than any other Christian activity."

This seems contrary to walking by faith. Do miracles and signs and wonders become vehicles to prove the reality of God? My research shows that the desire to see the miraculous is a big draw to venues related to the NAR. The miracles have to keep coming, and "more" and "more" are required.

Johnson charges that unless one is engaged in the miraculous there is something missing in one's faith. I believe in the miraculous, but I do not have to be in an NAR church or ministry to do so. Our Miller Avenue Baptist Church folk pray for healings and engage in the casting out of demons as well. There are many such churches and ministries that are not involved with the NAR at all.

CHAPTER SIX: GUILT-FREE AND FORGIVEN

The subtitle is "Jesus got what I deserved so that I could get what He deserved." The focus here is on false humility, and here Pastor Johnson speaks of a problem most of us have. We may see ourselves as unworthy, thinking about all the sin in our past and present, rather than relying on the fact that Jesus took our sin upon Himself at the cross and that we are forgiven.

This biblical truth should lead us to live a guilt-free life.

Note: Pastor Johnson has it correct here. We do wallow in our guilt and shame rather than seeing "that our sin, not the part, but the whole has been nailed to the cross, and I bear it no more," as the great old hymn proclaims. This laudable chapter, printed out, would make an excellent tract to be given out to Christian and non-Christian alike.

CHAPTER SEVEN: REMEMBERING

Christians tend to forget we belong to the Kingdom and instead focus on that which is worldly; we become earthly minded. Pastor Johnson speaks of the difference between Eastern occult meditation and biblical meditation, which is a conscious thinking and reflecting on biblical things; it is "filling the mind with God's truth" (p. 104).

Note: Yes, we need to remember the truths of God and bring them into our lives, meditate on them, and live them out. Pastor Johnson is right here again. He goes on to give practical ways of making this happen.

Chapter Seven: Enduring Uncertainty

For the most part again, Pastor Johnson's counsel about overcoming adversity is sound. There are times in every Christian's life when things happen that may cause us to question who God is and our relationship with Him.

Note: My suspicion is that circumstances cause some to wonder why healings and miracles do not materialize when we need them, as when a loved one dies though there were prayers for a miraculous recovery. This wondering makes sense in an environment such as Bethel Church in Redding, with its School of the Supernatural and its tremendous focus on healing and other miracles. Is Pastor Johnson concerned with those who may be tempted to engage in critical analysis?

Chapter Eight: Learning From Your Body

This chapter opens with the story of a person who, in the midst of a worship service at the Bethel Church, began to act in a strange way. Pastor Johnson did not think the person's movements were of the Holy Spirit. He writes, "I tried to discern what was happening in my spirit man—the location of the indicator that tells you something isn't right" (p. 121).

Note: I am struck by the language because of its unbiblical manner of expression. "Spirit man" seems strange. What did he really do? Was there some form of meditation attempted? The "location of the indicator"—what is this?

Pastor Johnson was waiting for "spiritual signals," but there was nothing at first. Then the air around him grew cold, ten degrees or so cooler. He then walked into another part of the building, but it was not cold. This was an indication to him that the devil was involved. At that point he spoke to their "main dancer" and asked her to "worship before the Lord in dance on stage in order to break something in the spiritual realm." The point Johnson makes is that there are "physical indicators of spiritual realities" (p. 122).

A little later in the chapter we find a significant assertion about how the "spiritual realm" interacts with the body. "He communicates with us in various ways, through impressions of the heart, mental pictures, feelings, emotions, and physical sensations" (p. 124). The lesson is that we are to fine-tune our ability to detect such messages.

He confesses that, in his own body, when someone begins talking about revival or healing, his left hand gets hot (p. 126). Others at Bethel Church have similar experiences. Physical indicators, Pastor Johnson assures us, are not always sure indicators, but God sometimes will use them.

Note: The subtitle of the chapter is: "The human body was designed to live in the glory of God. . .made to recognize God." Now we know what he means. The door is open then to phenomena that are utterly unbiblical and which are often seen in occult healing practices.

CHAPTER TEN: DREAMING WITH GOD

God, Pastor Johnson assures us, is very interested in our desires: "He wants to know what makes us tick" (p. 134). Part of this means dreaming with God. Most churches, he believes, "lockdown" on paying any attention to desires and dreams. The point is that we should pay attention to these desires and dreams, because God may communicate to us through them.

Note: The door has indeed opened even wider here—now the mind, our dreams, our feelings, and our bodily sensations may all be means by which God speaks to us. He is straying further from biblical categories.

CHAPTER ELEVEN: INHERITING THE SUPERNATURAL

Now Pastor Johnson informs us that moving in the supernatural can be inherited, that we pass on this ability to the next generation. And this is what we see generation to generation, at least in a physical sense, through our DNA. Therefore, what is true in the natural and physical realm is true also in the spiritual realm.

We are now in the season called "accelerated growth," and we are experiencing a recovery of what was lost for hundreds of years, a time when God is now bringing something new to earth and which may pass on to future generations.

Note: This concept, passing on the new revelations now being received, seems to clash with the revelation that these days right now are the last days. Of course, there is no way to test this, so it is a concept that is difficult to challenge.

CHAPTER TWELVE: THE DIVINE YES

Here is an appeal to enter into what God has said "yes" to. God is looking for people who will build as He intended. The transformation of the earth happens from within, from within those who have their minds transformed.

A Critique of

THE FINAL QUEST

RICK JOYNER, MORNINGSTAR PUBLICATIONS, 1996

INTRODUCTION

In early 1995 Rick Joyner had an extraordinary dream of a major spiritual battle. *The Final Quest* is the result of that dream. He first published the contents of the dream with the title, "The Hordes of Hell Are Marching." Subsequently, he received a number of other visions and "prophetic experiences."

Rick describes many levels of revelation. The first is "impressions," which he claims are actual revelations from the Holy Spirit, often needing interpretation by others who understand this means of revelation. Visions may also be experienced in this impression level. He advises a person to be careful about announcing these revelations, because they might be influenced by various human factors.

The next level is "a conscious sense of the presence of the Lord, or the anointing of the Holy Spirit" (p. 12). Here again, error or misinterpretations may confuse the revelation, so humility is required.

"Open visions" is the next level, which has the quality of watching a film or a television program. Rick says these visions are "external," and there is less chance that they might be misinterpreted.

The highest level of revelation comes in the trance state. Here the prophet has moved from viewing the film from the outside to actually being inside the film itself. At this level, the prophet has great confidence in the veracity of the revelation.

The Final Quest records revelations Rick received while in a trance, but they began with dreams. While in the dream/trance state he was acutely aware, discerning, and knowledgeable. He knew things that he had not known before. "At times I would look at things or people and know their past, present, and future all at once" (p. 15).

Rick says there are essentially two purposes for prophetic revelation. The first is when the Lord reveals His "present or future strategic will." The second is for making clear the doctrines found in Scripture that may not have been previously understood.

Note: In the process of doing research for my book, *The Soul Journey: How Shamanism, Santeria, Wicca, and Charisma are Connected,* I read book after book, spoke with practitioners of each of the above spiritual practices and religions, and found virtually the same descriptions of how adherents experienced spiritual knowledge and spiritual entities. Reading *The Final Quest* reminded me of the visions shamans receive and the occurrences Wiccan witches and warlocks encountered while in a trance state.

Though Rick uses plenty of biblically oriented language, there is little of anything that can be identified as Christian in the book. The question must come to mind—How is it possible that a mature Christian like Rick Joyner could become victim to demonic influences? The answer, in my opinion, is that it happened in the same way as for the shaman, the witch, or the Santerian priest or priestess—they were overwhelmingly convinced by what they encountered while in the trance state.

Those in the NAR who engage in "deep worship" or spend hours in "soaking prayer" or undergo "Sozo Ministry" will often see visions and have dreams. They uniformly but erroneously conclude that these manifestations must come from the Holy Spirit, since it is so very spiritual and because many others confirm to them the rightness and goodness of the experience.

Surely we are now engaged in a spiritual battle—though not one we haven't faced before—but now the door to deception has swung wide open with the emergence of all that is the NAR.

PART I: THE HORDES OF HELL ARE MARCHING

This first of Joyner's five high level revelations occurred while in a trance, so he was actually right there inside the action. He sees the demonic horde advancing, but rather than riding on horses they are astride the backs of Christians. He knew that what he was seeing in his dream/trance was the "Great Christian Civil War" (p. 28). His essential message is that Christians are leading the warfare against God's truth, so the "civil war" that is currently underway is between the NAR movement and other Christians who do not accept it or even oppose it.

Note: I can testify that this is exactly what I encounter when talking with those who have embraced the alleged final season and the revelations God is supposedly bringing to his angelic and Joel's army. Those who oppose the NAR, as I do, are labeled as foot soldiers in Satan's army.

Toward the end of the first dream/trance story is a theme that runs throughout Rick's book: how heaven—meaning the angels, departed saints like the Apostle Paul, and even Jesus—honor and show deference to Rick.

Note: While Joyner concludes and tries to convince the reader that this honor is supposed to be a revelation set in real time and space, it smacks of exaggerated egotism. It is actually quite peculiar.

PART II: THE HOLY MOUNTAIN

"What you see with the eyes of your heart is more real than what you see with your physical eyes," Rick was told by an angel in a second dream/vision sequence after he had spent some undetermined amount of time—minutes, days, or months—with Jesus, in person, all in the throne room of heaven.

Wisdom, whether an angel or some other entity, was now with Rick. Wisdom instructed him that he was dreaming and in a state more real than what he usually considered reality. Rick realized that it is in the heart where God dwells and can be found. And angels often appear as actual men in people's dreams, for in the heart people are able to bypass the mind.

Note: A shaman or a Wiccan witch might have written this, because here Rick's angel lifts up the dreaming of the heart rather than the conscious mind as the place one enters in worship. Turning the eyes inward is the key. Such a phrase is found in countless books on contemplative prayer, meditation of all types, and manuals that teach how to reach an altered state of consciousness.

At one point Rick said to the angel named Wisdom, "What a great companion you are. . . . "You really will keep me on the right path." And the angel replied, "I will indeed" (p. 56).

Note: The shaman has a spirit animal; the Wiccan has a spirit as well as an animal guide. These entities always appear when the dream journeyer moves into the state of ecstasy or trance or dream. The meditators, after learning how to blank out the mind, are often met by an angel, pixie, or fairy. Is what Rick Joyner advocates even close to biblical Christianity?

Wisdom gave Rick a rather drab looking mantle, a piece of cloth to drape over his shoulders. At first Rick felt a little insulted by the look of the mantle, perhaps because he ranked himself more highly, but the angel said the mantle was humility. The trick is that humility causes others to look to him as one having authority. And, Rick will be leading in the great battle that is coming!

The last heading in Part II is "Rank in the Kingdom." Rick reports that angels, as he passed by them, bent a knee to him and showed him great respect. When he questioned the angels about their behavior, they responded that the mantle Rick was wearing was the symbol of humility, and it was the highest rank in the Kingdom.

Note: Rick fully believes what he saw in his dream was actual. A real angel, real angel companies, Jesus fully bodily present and speaking with him, battles being fought on different levels of the mountain, and all with no evidence of any sort of critical analysis. He assumed that the entire experience was all of God. And those under his ministry, one would assume, must do the same.

PART III:
THE RETURN OF THE EAGLES

An eagle landed near Rick. He had seen eagles earlier, and this one he describes as having a presence that was very awesome. This eagle asked, "Do you want to know who we are?" Then it proceeded to say, "We are the hidden prophets who have been kept for this hour" (p. 73).

Rick is one of the NAR prophets, probably an apostle also, but the eagle before him knew all about the final battles that will be fought before the kingdom of God is fully established.

The eagle also pointed out that only those people who receive the prophets will receive a prophet's reward and are then able to avail themselves of the eagles' services.

The eagle wanted Rick to know that he needed the eagle as much as the eagle needed him. As an eagle, he does not have the gifts that Rick does, and vice versa, but the eagles as a group know the secrets of God. The eagles have been given to Rick until the end.

After a time of instruction and encouragement, the eagle departed. Rick says, "I already loved the eagle so much that I could hardly stand to leave him" (p. 83).

Next Rick took a walk, only to find a great company of angels following him. Rick asked why this was so and received the answer, "We have been given to you, to serve you here and in the battle to come" (p. 84).

Indeed, Rick's status had become so elevated among the great eagles and angels that he could speak with them as though they were his equals.

Near the conclusion of this dream/trance, Rick opened his eyes to find another eagle standing before him. The eagle had three stones—one blue, one green, and one red. Rick was instructed to eat them. These stones had a renewing kind of effect upon him. But there was more—he noticed that the three stones were set into the handle of his sword and they were also upon his shoulders. It is difficult to make sense of this imagery.

Then came one last word from the angel leader: "Listen to your heart. That is where these great truths now abide" (p. 91).

Note: During research for my Soul Journey book, especially the material on shamanism, I came across similar accounts. Some entity—an angel, a power animal, or a spirit guide—would speak to the shaman while in his trance state and say words almost identical to what the eagle said to Rick. Somehow Rick's followers do not or cannot question the reality or the veracity of the things he reports. One can understand why they withhold critical questions, since the NAR prophets tend to be sensitive to people's reactions to them to the point of rather serious defensiveness, almost crossing the line into paranoia.

PART IV: THE WHITE THRONE

Inside the mountain, Rick found himself in a huge room. An eagle stood there, and this time Rick noticed his scars and broken feathers—battle wounds—indicating that the eagle was preparing Rick for battles that are coming and therefore the need to be courageous.

At one point Rick entered a great hall, so wonderful, so magnificent, that words cannot express it. At the far end of the room he saw such glory that it must be the "glory of the Lord." As he moved toward the glory he found multitudes of others there with angelic appearance—they were departed saints now resurrected to heaven, the great cloud of witnesses. On Rick's approach they bowed in greeting "as though they recognized me" (p. 106).

Rick asked how it was that they knew him. The answer was, "You are one of the saints fighting in the last battle." Everyone in that great room knew who Rick was. They not only knew him but also watched everything he did. Rick even recognized some whom he had known on earth.

Strangely, Rick spoke with some saints who were not as faithful as they should have been while on earth. They were like the foolish virgins of Jesus' parable; they did not keep full of the oil, or the Spirit, and so one said, "We wasted our lives on earth" (p. 109).

Note: There is no hint that what Rick experienced is anything but actual; he takes the symbolic descriptions in Scripture about heaven literally. The "heaven" he describes is like a grand palace humans might build. This scene reinforces my perception that Rick needs to be admired as a great personage in God's final plan. Though the drab mantle is supposed to represent humility, I find little of this attitude in any part of this book.

Venturing further into the grand room, Rick encountered people he knew or had known about. He was surprised to find that some whom he presumed had a high status on earth had a low rank or position in heaven. They had fallen due to pride after achieving great victories or were jealous of others who had great success in ministry. Indeed, some had fallen due to lust, discouragement, or bitterness. And some of them "had to be taken" before they fell into "perdition" (I assume by perdition he means hell) (p. 139).

Those he found of higher rank emanated unspeakable glory.

Rick came next into the throne room; he passed the "judgment seat of Christ" and continued down the row of thrones. There were even thrones for those who "ruled over the affairs of the physical creation, such as star systems and galaxies"(p. 140).

Note: The throne room is a really popular place to go to for a number of the NAR apostles and prophets. Years ago few spoke of this, but now almost anyone is allowed in. By throne room is meant the place where God dwells, and Jesus has a throne to the right of the big one, and there are thrones for the Twelve Apostles as well. I am shocked that so many assume the factualness of this portrayal and hope to get there themselves. Apparently it does not take that much.

At one point Jesus assured Rick, "You are worthy to sit on one of these," meaning thrones set-aside for overcomers (p. 142). Jesus emphasized that the thrones are for those who wear the mantle of humility and have His "likeness." And Rick will have that likeness, if he keeps his mantle throughout the coming battle.

Note: This battle, sometimes described as the Final Civil War or the Christian Civil War apparently has to do with the battle that does go on now, between those Christians who embrace the apostles and prophets and those like myself, who do not. One unfamiliar with the language of the NAR might think of Islam, or secularism, or something else, but no, this is a battle going on in the Church and among Christians. Other NAR authors hint that the battle will be fought for real, including actual physical violence.

As Rick was led away from the throne of Jesus, who had stood up, an angel spoke to him: "Now that He has stood, He will not sit again until the last battle is over. He has been seated until the time when His enemies are to be put under His feet. The time has now come. The legions of angels that have been standing ready since the night of His passion have now been released upon the earth. The hordes of hell have also been released" (p. 147).

Note: Is it important to be reminded that this book was copyrighted in 1996?

PART V: THE OVERCOMERS

In this last dream/trance sequence is the most incredible account I have ever read at any time. I am tempted to give it just as Rick does, but I will instead shorten and paraphrase it.

Rick walked down the row of thrones and passed in front of the Twelve. Jesus was walking and talking with him. Rick saw who he thought was the Apostle Paul, but Paul did not look happy. Rick glanced at Jesus whom Rick felt gave him permission to talk with Paul.

Rick thanked Paul for his ministry, but Paul berated himself while also praising Rick. Paul told how much "we" have looked forward to meeting those who will lead in the final battle. Rick protested, but Paul stated that he himself was the worst of the apostles for all the bad things he had done when he persecuted the Church. Paul also told Rick that he had fallen short of what he was called to do. The Apostle mentioned that despite his letters in the New Testament, there are still many who pervert them. Again Paul reminded Rick that he was the greatest of sinners but that he, Rick, "can walk in much more than I did" (p. 161).

Jesus expressed to Rick that there is little real ministry and preaching going on in the world today "except for a few places."

Rick was assured he will be mightily used in the final battle. The Church today would, in fact, succeed where the Church of the first century failed. Jesus even told him, "I will make more of My grace and power available to the last-day church, because she must accomplish more than the church in any age has accomplished" (pp. 165–166).

Jesus told Rick something of His great power and said, "To resurrect all the dead who have ever lived on earth will not even cause Me to strain" (p. 171). At one point, toward the conclusion of Rick's visit to the throne room, Jesus smiled at him and put his arm around him "just like a friend" (p. 177). Then Rick pulled aside his cloak of humility and found that he wore armor of the same glory that Jesus was wearing (p. 178). There were even more strange and weird exchanges between Jesus and Rick, but the preceding probably is enough to provide insight.

Note: So much for the mantle of humility; it must have fallen off to be replaced by glorious armor, armor just like what Jesus was wearing.

I am not trying to picture Rick's account in a false light. In fact, I left many incredible events and statements out. This process of making summaries of the books of some of the leaders in the NAR has been painful, but it seemed better to do this than merely speak generally about the contents.

Several times during the preparing of this particular summary I wondered what it might be like to be part of Rick Joyner's Morningstar ministries there in South Carolina. I wonder if I would be able to voice criticism or even question what came out of the mouth and from the pen of Rick Joyner. If not, then it has all the marks of a toxic, even dangerous ministry.

A Critique of

A Time to Triumph: How to Win the War Ahead

Chuck Pierce, Chosen Books, 2016

On the front cover is depicted two angelic looking creatures with swords raised in the air. On the back cover are the words, "You are part of GOD'S PLAN for the Days Ahead. RISE UP and join the fight!"

Chuck Pierce took over the leadership of Global Spheres, Inc. from C. Peter Wagner in 2010.

Bishop Bill Hamon, Dutch Sheets, and C. Peter Wagner provided endorsements for the book.

The dedication reads, "To the Triumphant Reserve that is now rising throughout the earth!"

CHAPTER ONE: A PROPHETIC PORTAL INTO THE FUTURE

Pierce claims that God does not move unless He informs His prophets first. On January 1, 1984, God indeed began to reveal "shifts" in world events, and this came via "a peculiar visitation" to Pierce (p. 12).

Two years later, after God saw that he could trust Pierce with revelation, He began to lay out in detail events that would occur in ten-year cycles all the way to 2026. The major theme of the revelations in 1986 was that a great war was coming and that America was a key player in this war. But when prophet Pierce began sharing these revelations, he met with resistance.

Note: It is characteristic that NAR apostles and prophets like to establish themselves as major players from early on—over thirty years prior to this book's publication for Chuck Pierce. In charismatic/Pentecostal circles, it is generally frowned upon to question the words of prophets. I had the same mindset in the early 1970s, because questioning "words" given from God was seen as tantamount to committing blasphemy against the Holy Spirit. This understanding had a chilling effect on many of us at the time.

The core of the revelation Pierce received concerned a coming war, and to win that war the people of God had to map out a strategy. God began to reveal to Pierce the plan that would win the war: He would close the gap between heaven and earth, which would result in a "third-day Church" having power never seen before (p. 22). And to become this Church, it would be necessary to grasp the heavenly realms. God revealed this to both Pierce and Rebecca Wagner Sytsema.

A key concept is "the Third Heaven." This is where God literally sits upon a throne with Jesus on the throne at His right hand. From the Third Heaven, God is "releasing" revelation, giving gifts to bring unity to the Church of the last day as mentioned in Ephesus 4:11.

The First Heaven, Pierce says, is the universe in which we live and from which we have access to the Third Heaven. The Church is being established in the First Heaven, whose army has great power, and "the Church is in place to enforce His headship"(p. 23).

The Second Heaven is where Satan rules and prevents God's will from being done in the First Heaven by means of the principalities, powers, and rulers of the darkness of this age" (p. 23).

But at the right time, "portals of Glory" will be established so that God can "express Himself" (pp. 24-25). A portal is an opening through which God comes down to reveal His presence and His will to His anointed ones. This revelation comes by means of dreams, visions, and miracles given to those whom He has called into His army.

Chapter Two: Shifting into the War Ahead

Pierce announces a "kingdom shift" taking place right now. He seems to refer to the NAR, of which he is very much a part. He announces that the end does not come until after the war, which will be fought for generations.

He urges his readers to make the shift over to those things being revealed and released. He uses the phrase "church structure" to refer to those in churches of all denominations who have not or will not make the shift.

Prior to this present restoring of the apostolic gifts there was the period of the evangelist during the 1950s, the period of the Jesus Movement in the late 1960s, and the period of the charismatic manifestations of the 1970s and 1980s known as the Third Wave. The restoration of the prophetic gift was added to this period, and finally the apostolic gifting was restored in the 1990s. This present period is the "third great reformation in the earth realm" (p. 36).

Note: Pierce speaks of a person's "spirit man" being a conduit for the Holy Spirit. This is common NAR language, but it is not New Testament language. This is the language of psychic mediums and fortunetellers.

Pierce's understanding of the last days seems to differ from others of the NAR worldview. I have to say seems, because he is not always clear.

So far he has not specifically said who the enemy is, but it appears the enemy is in the Church—those who do not make the shift over to the new move of God, who refuse to embrace what God is doing right now.

For one to make the shift into what God is doing now, he lists the following:

1. Develop His mind
2. Learn to express His heart
3. Change your atmosphere
4. Optimize resources for doing exploits
5. Watch for the "suddenlies"
6. Learn to cross over
7. Develop a Kingdom mentality
8. Find your new river of joy
9. Experience a shift even if it creates a rift

Note: He is convinced the Kingdom is ours for the taking. The above list describes things Christians in the new move of God can do. I decided not to include the few sentences Pierce uses to illuminate each of the nine ways to make the shift, because they are ludicrous to the extreme and utterly unbiblical.

Under the heading, "The Church of the Future" (p. 42), he gives a prophecy he received about what this church would look like: "God said, 'This is the government of the Church of the future! The people of this government will arise and spread My light throughout the world in the days of the latter wars. This government will overcome all other governments'" (p. 43).

Another word given was that "China is the apostolic Church, and she is now arising."

Pierce describes himself as having received the "Issachar Anointing" and says of himself, "I am probably best recognized for this anointing for time in the Body of Christ, and I have attempted to study to show myself approved" (p. 44).

The characteristics of this Issachar Anointing are:

1. Prosperity
2. Intercession
3. Divine alignment
4. Ability to ascertain seasonal and immediate changes in time
5. Awareness of the anointing
6. Understanding of war and political change
7. Possession of the power to bless

Then there are things to watch for in the earth realm, and those in the war will be given their assignments by the Spirit of God. Here is the list of what to watch for:

1. We must watch Israel.
2. We must watch the rising conflicting kingdoms.
3. We need to watch as a triumphant reserve arises.
4. We must watch as war is declared against an unseen, undefined enemy.
5. We need to watch as God gathers His scattered sheep.
6. We must watch our emotions.
7. We must watch David's Tabernacle manifest today. [This is explained as watching God's people transferring from a Word understanding to a glory demonstration.]

8. We must watch as new sounds create a new movement.
9. We must watch the war of the sons of Greece vs. the sons of Zion. [Pierce believes this means the "enemy will be against the vineyards that produce wine for Shabbat. In every war, a certain beverage will be key" (p. 53)].
10. We must watch the rising war of provision.
11. We must watch the choices of a maturing new generation.
12. We must watch for our divine escape.

Now then is the list of some of the battlegrounds that will be fought.

1. Manipulation of time and law
2. Root wars
3. Trade iniquities
4. The redemptive blood and glory of God
5. Worship
6. Kingdom mysteries
7. Healing and unusual workings of miracles
8. Strategies of harvest
9. Communication wars
10. Border wars
11. New paradigms for a new generation

Note: In regard to # 5 Worship, the focus is music. So much depends on worship music, which is designed, deliberately, to bring worshippers into a relaxed and joyful state of mind. As music sequences move on, the base and drum dominate. Few can resist moving to the beat. After a time, skillful worship leaders combine dancing with the music and altered states of consciousness are often the result. Here is where the deception takes the forefront. It is thought that it is a state of mind where one is more open to hearing from God or an angel, or that one enters into the third heaven.

Chapter Three: A New Mindskin for a New Wineskin

Note: Pierce's book reminds me of Bill Johnson's book, which speaks of the need to have the mind transformed.

This new period when God is doing incredible new things calls for a new mind, one that can receive the new wine. The present church structure will not have the new mind but will be part of the enemy forces.

Pierce is clear that the new wine is being poured out, and now a new dawn is breaking, and we are shifting from Church to Kingdom. Here then are the differences between Kingdom and Church:

1. Kingdom has a government.
2. Kingdom is ruled by a king.
3. Kingdom has administration.
4. Kingdom has a culture.
5. Kingdom is good news.
6. Kingdom is connected through generations.
7. God's heavenly Kingdom is not based on worldly patterns.
8. God's Kingdom is beyond man's natural thoughts.
9. Kingdom cannot be obtained by ambition.
10. Kingdom should never be postponed.
11. Kingdom has provision.
12. Kingdom has territory.
13. Kingdom has an atmosphere.
14. Kingdom has prophets.
15. Kingdom has war units.
16. Kingdom has gatekeepers.
17. Kingdom has treasurers.
18. Kingdom has music and sound.
19. Kingdom has people who serve as the priests and Levites did.
20. Kingdom has chief ministers.
21. Kingdom has power.

Note: Given the high place Pierce has in the NAR, his prophecies and revelations cannot be dismissed—they must be embraced. The above revelations do not paint a picture of what we see of heaven in Scripture but more closely resemble an earthbound structure.

"Touch not my anointed" is a phrase used by NAR advocates when one of their prophets or apostles is questioned about a prophecy or interpretation of a prophecy. And this is surely a hallmark of the cultic mentality.

War is openly addressed, and it is obvious that the enemy is the "church structure" meaning people like myself who directly and openly oppose the "Kingdom."

CHAPTER FOUR: WHY CHRISTIANS MUST LEARN WAR

There is a war against an enemy, and Pierce puts out the call for warriors. It is war such as found in the Old Testament—a real war. To understand this war it is necessary to understand the Kingdom. Much of this present chapter is found in his earlier book, *A Field Manual for Advancing the Kingdom of God*.

Pierce makes the point that death in war is not murder. Murder is "premeditated sin against life" (p. 89). But this kind of war "is a manifestation of God's character against injustice. There are times when we must go to war" (p. 89). He finds support in Jesus' statement, "Do not think that I came to bring peace on earth. I did not come to bring peace but a sword" (Matthew 10:34). Therefore, Pierce concludes that warfare is in the New Testament as well as the Old.

The enemy, according to Pierce, is a combination of Satan, the flesh, those who delight in evil, the world, and death (p. 98). The antichrist system operates in five areas: anti-Semitism, abuse of the prophetic gift, oppression of women, ethnic domination, and mammon and iniquitous thrones (pp. 101-102).

In the conclusion of this present chapter Pierce provides over five pages of prophecy that he received prior to a prayer meeting.

He said, "the Spirit of God spoke to me," then came the prophecy. In the prophecy God is doing fantastic things, bringing miracles that are beyond description into the present.

Note: There is no simple way of understanding what Pierce is saying. Is this real war, or is it a spiritual war? The latter seems to be the correct viewpoint, but such is not entirely clear. The NAR speaks of the Civil War, and it is a Christian Civil War, meaning a war among those who identify with Christ. NAR identifiers see themselves as the new warriors God has called into being, and the enemies are those who oppose them. Will there be actual physical warfare between the Church Structure and the NAR army? Pierce will not be decisively pinned down here. The bulk of the evidence points, however, to real warfare. No date about when the prophecy was made is provided, but even if it were recent, where is the fulfillment? I wonder how it is that he was able to reduce the very long prophecy to writing.

CHAPTER FIVE: AUTHORITY TO OVERTHROW INIQUITOUS THRONES

A recurring theme in NAR-oriented literature is found on pages 126 and 127: "He wants us to commune with Him, listen carefully to His voice, gain prophetic revelation and decree that revelation into the earth."

Note: After examining Pierce's presentation it is clear that he is talking about people prophesying. "Commune" has to do with being in a state of mind where one is able to hear God's voice. After receiving words from God, they are to be proclaimed to others, which is necessary for the will of God to come from heaven to earth. To me Pierce's God is limited and not sovereign. He depends upon His ultimate will being accomplished through prophets.

CHAPTER SIX: A TRIUMPHANT ARMY ARISING

"When people try to communicate the war ahead to those who are not aware, sometimes they find much resistance" (p. 139). This is apparently what Pierce has experienced since 2007, when he says God called him away from the "prayer movement" and into calling out the triumphant army that will lead in the great last war.

The triumphant people, God showed him, had these characteristics:

1. They were infused with a victorious attitude.
2. They were aligned for victory.
3. They occupied a high-level aptitude to adjust quickly.
4. They were creative, cunning (more shrewd than the enemy) and confrontational.

Note: So much of the content of this book has to do with what the last day Christians must accomplish. It is more than a full time job, to say the least, and all dependent on what people must remember, think, decree, practice, focus on, and on and on. All the principles that must be mastered are extensive, confusing, unclear, and overlapping. To take this book seriously would be to enter into a burdensome ordeal.

CHAPTER SEVEN: OVERCOMERS OF THE COVENANT WAR

CHAPTER EIGHT: THE WAR OVER ONE NEW MAN

CHAPTER NINE: THE WAR OF RELIGION

Chapters seven, eight, and nine cover much of the same ground, mostly a series of "musts" for the triumphant army arising, the overcomers, the new man, and all who will do battle against the enemy.

It is in chapter nine that Pierce gets more to the point. "Religious spirits are demonically empowered philosophies that narrow our expression of the God of heaven and prevent Him from displaying free, expressive worship in earth" (p. 209). He is not thinking here of the many world religions; he is using the word "religion" to refer to those who do not embrace the NAR—people like me. He experiences resistance, because people reject his gifting. He explains this by saying, "I have always been a creative thinker and an expressive worshiper. In addition, I have been known throughout the Body of Christ as a modern-day prophet who expresses the heart and mind of God" (p. 210).

The religionists have God tightly locked in a box, he insists, and this prevents the releasing of what He is doing now. He sees religion as loosing condemnation and being judgmental.

Note: Pierce experiences what others do who are associated with the NAR. They are very aware that not everyone is on board and that more critics are coming forward. I would even say that Pierce and others are becoming defensive to the point that they accuse questioners of being part of the enemy.

In *God's Super-Apostles*, by R. Douglas Geivett and Holly Pivec, (Weaver Book Company, 2014), pages 140-141, is a list of terms NAR folk use for those who oppose them: critical spirit, Greek mindset, Jezebel spirit, legalist, old wineskin, Pharisee, religious spirit, spirit of Saul, and unanointed.

By claiming to speak God's words, the NAR prophets and apostles have boxed themselves into a corner. And by attacking those who criticize them, they have created enemies of a sort. How does one back away from this? This remains to be seen.

Chapter Ten: What Will Become of Me?

The title of the chapter refers to what will happen to "us" and how "we" will be during the last days, which are now upon us. To be ready for the final season, to be part of the victorious army, one must essentially embrace what he has laid out in this book. Choices must be made, he cautions, as there are two sides to every war—one triumphant, the other vanquished.

AN APPENDIX: AN ANALYSIS OF THE SEVEN CHURCHES OF REVELATION

Pierce takes the reader to the book of Revelation and sees in the seven churches of Asia seven different types of churches. Below are the titles or descriptions he gives to each of the seven churches:

Ephesus	The Church That Lost Its Fervent Love
Smyrna	The Persecuted Church
Pergamon	The Unfaithful Church
Thyatira	A Church Invaded by a Religious Spirit
Sardis	The Comfortable Church
Philadelphia	The Church of God's Favor
Laodicea	The Lukewarm Church

A Critique of

Angel Armies:
Releasing the Warriors of Heaven

Tim Sheets, Destiny Image, 2017

CHAPTER ONE: VORTEX FIRE

Sheets describes a vision of two submarines—the old one is the charismatic movement, which has submerged into the culture. The new one is "His remnant," the New Testament church. "It will now emerge from the culture to rule and reign" (p. 25).

"The season of the Third Great Awakening has now begun" (p. 25). The first two are Pentecost and the charismatic movement. He says, "We must prepare our regions, bathing them in prayer."

Tim has an angel, Mahanaim, "who accompanies the apostolic assignment on my life" (p. 27).

Note: Tim's having his own angel apparently does not bother those associated with the NAR, because a number of other apostles and prophets have them, too, so they would not be willing to object to the unbiblical nature of such an arrangement. Others, such as William Branham, have claimed to have angels hovering or standing with them; Branham's angel was named Emma and controlled the healing part of his ministry. Are these angels or demonic spirits impersonating angels? Paul helps us with this in 2 Corinthians 11:13-15.

My experience and research reveals that demons appearing as angels is age old, older than the Scripture and very convincing. Here is one of the traps set for those who expect to talk with Jesus, hear the audible voice of God, or enter into a 'third heaven' and speak with the Father, the Son, or apostles sitting on thrones. Once a person experiences something of this nature, he or she is convinced that a direct experience or contact with heaven has actually taken place. However, the same is true for the Wiccan witch, the shaman, and the Santerian priest when he or she, while in a trance state, goes on a soul journey and makes contact with spirit guides, spirit animals, dead saints, fairies, and other sorts of spiritual entities. One is never the same afterward.

Chapter Two: The Holy Spirit and Angels of Fire

Sheets refers to "Holy Spirit" not "the Holy Spirit" (p. 33). "Holy Spirit talked to me about another Pentecost He would soon steward upon the earth. He revealed that a new move of God would soon begin, a move that He described as an 'awakening surge greater than the world has ever seen.'" This came to him in the fall of 2003. It was revealed "This time I am coming with far more of the angel armies" (p. 33). He goes on: "Greater Kingdom power than has ever been seen will now flow from Christ's New Testament church. Enlightenment came that there is now an alignment of heaven's Angel Army with the Remnant Warrior Army and with what I now call the War Eagle Army from the coming generation" (p. 34).

"There are millions of these angel warriors, fellow servants who are assisting us" (p. 37).

Under the heading, "The Trinity and the New Campaign," Tim writes, based on John 14:7, "These verses show that the Father, Son (Jesus), and the Holy Spirit are one and the same" (p. 41).

"I would often see flashes of light everywhere. I now know that is a sign by which we can discern angelic activity" (p. 45).

Chapter Three: Angels Minister to Us

Sheets "began to think about the potential of all the networks partnering with the angel network under Holy Spirit supervision and how it has never been done to fullness" (p. 51). He lists several networks, such as evangelism networks in the 1950s established by Billy Graham, Oral Roberts, and T.L. Osborn; pastoral networks and great churches in the 1960s under Jack Hayford and Tommy Barnett; teaching networks in the 1970s with Kenneth Hagin, Kenneth Copeland, and others; and prophetic networks in the 1980s "all over America and around the world with mean and women of God like Churck Pierce, Dr. Peter Wagner, and Cindy Jacobs." Finally, in the 1990s, apostolic networks began, and "all of these were brought into existence for this season" (p. 51).

He then switches to the work of angels: "Some angels are assigned to regions, while others are assigned to churches. These ministering angels rescue us and provide safety. They preserve and protect us, the heirs of Christ. They minister certain aspects of salvation to us, assisting our deliverance and destiny. They are present-time deliverers. Now-time deliverers" (p. 52-53).

The "heir force" or armies of angels—"They are organized to open up the heavens, to scatter powers of darkness encamped in regions, to thwart the strategies of hell, and to partner with apostolic teams" (p. 54).

He knows this because of words spoken to him by prophets such as Prophet Mark Chironna: "You will be wooed by My Spirit into the depths of My presence, and you will be awakened into the awareness of angel ministry" (p. 54). He also listens to Prophets James Goll, Barbara Yoder, Jane Hamon, Chuck Pierce, and Ann Tate, who have all visited his church.

His conclusion and summary of the angelic work: "When we declare the dominion of King Jesus over a region, angels begin to assist in establishing it. Fellow servants begin to patrol the boundaries. They will war in the natural realm or the spirit realm. Fellow servants will then begin to administer the covenants we have declared there in Jesus' name" (p. 58).

Note: One must ask, how does he know this? Certainly this information does not come from Scripture except in the most imaginary sort of way. It is extra-biblical, but for Tim it is indisputable since it comes by prophetic revelation. I am surprised that Tim is not more apologetic with his incredible announcements. He assumes it all must be true, and demands, maybe expects would be more accurate, the same must be so for other Christians.

CHAPTER FOUR: THE INTRINSIC NATURE OF ANGELS

"Angels have hands, feet, heads, mouths, hair, faces, and voices. This allows them to appear in our three-dimensional realm of length, breadth, and height, looking exactly like us" (p. 67). Angels are meek beings, joyful beings, powerful and mighty, obedient, holy, have wills, have spirit bodies, need no rest, eat food, travel at inconceivable speeds, ascend into heaven, and descend back to earth.

Note: How he knows this is not spelled out.

CHAPTER FIVE: HOW ANGELS ASSIST YOUR DESTINY

"An amazing benefit of the ministry of angels is how they assist the releasing of destiny" (p. 73).

Note: Tim thinks it essential to know all about angels. Many do not, because such has not been revealed to them.

CHAPTER SIX: WAR EAGLES AND ANGELS

The "heir force" is the angel network, and the Lord spoke to Tim to "release" this network (p. 85).

Note: Wow, this shows what a major player Tim is.

Here is the prophesy Tim received: "The Lord said, 'It is time for a fresh release of My Holy Spirit. Power will be poured out, and the King's anointing and authority will increase in unprecedented, delegated proportions. The angel network is assisting the Holy Spirit in exalting heaven's King. Now the young and the old will participate together in the greatest movement of the Kingdom in history'" (p. 86).

In another prophesy, "My 'War Eagles. They will make up My eagle force, and eagle force will partner with My angel force and My remnant warrior champions" (p. 87).

CHAPTER SEVEN: ANGELS HELP CHANGE REGIONS

"A major benefit of angel assistance is how they help apostles, pastoral leaders, and five-fold ministries shift their regions into divine alignment. It is time for a major shift in our nation and in the church. It's time to shift into harvest mode, seeing millions come to Jesus" (p. 95).

Note: Most of these words came to Tim in 2006.

In regard to the biblical day of Pentecost, Tim says, "Jesus sent His Other Self, the Holy Spirit, to begin a brand new campaign on the earth" (p. 104).

Note: Another confusion of the Trinity? Is this coming from the "Jesus Only" segment of Pentecostal Holiness?

CHAPTER EIGHT: BATTLING FOR THE THRONE OF A REGION

"Clearly, Christ Jesus expects His ekklesia to declare or make rulings in His name" (p. 111). Tim sees this ekklesia to be essentially the prophets and apostles, those directing the move of the Holy Spirit.

Like the battle for the Throne of God in heaven, which battle Satan lost, there is a new battle taking place right now. He says, "This is happening in the real, not imaginary, spirit realm right now" (p. 114). Tim has in mind that the regions or territories and the angelic forces are battling Satan for control. He goes on, "It is time for Christ's church to follow His lead and cast out hell's dominions and powers" (p. 115).

CHAPTER NINE: WHAT ATTENDING ANGELS DO

To begin the chapter, Tim gives a summary of what has been said prior: "King Jesus is on a new campaign upon the earth. An outpouring has begun—a Third great awakening—and according to

Holy Spirit, it's going to be very similar to what occurred in Acts 2. Holy Spirit is coming with His angels who will partner with the remnant warriors and with the war Eagle generation [the coming generation] to implement this new move of King Jesus" (p. 127).

On page 136, Tim speaks of a message an angel gave him in 1975: "In 1975, I received insight for healings and miracles through an angel in a dream. I believe today that it was an angel assigned to me because of my apostolic calling. Years ago, when I accepted the apostolic calling for my life different angels were assigned to me, and I often hear those angels in healing services telling me of people with a particular sickness or disease that I'm to minister to. It's not unusual for someone in the service to tell me later that they saw the angel standing beside me" (p. 136).

Note: The same was true for William Branham, who had the angel, Emma, and Todd Bentley, who called his angel Emmie.

CHAPTER TEN: MOBILIZING ANGELS WITH YOUR WORDS

"How do you mobilize angelic armies? With words of faith that decree what God says. Words of faith activate angels; unbelief stifles angels. Angels are watching and listening" (p. 159).

"The church today has millions of angels available. We need to give them plenty to do. We need to put them on assignment with decrees of faith" (p. 163).

Note: Tim actually thinks we command angels, thus God, to do our bidding.

CHAPTER ELEVEN: ANGELS CONNECT US TO GREAT PROSPERITY

"Angels connect God's people to places, people, events, businesses, sales, and material property that will prosper them" (p. 166).

Under the heading of "The Principle of Giving and Receiving," we have, "If you are going to get more in return and God has guaranteed it, then why would you refrain from giving?" (p. 171).

Chapter Twelve: Making Angels Angry

Angry angels are to be avoided, and apostles can assist in this—they can settle disputes and put things right. "Apostles are called to confront such wrongdoing and bring change. They are called to challenge people to live in such a way that angels are content" (p. 179).

Note: For those who accept this concept, apostles such as Tim will have extraordinary power and authority in the lives of those who see them as apostles and prophets.

Tim warns: "We must guard how we live because angels are watching" (p. 179).

Note: We must please the angels, then, rather than pleasing Jesus.

Angels and Prayer Decrees

In the book's last section, Tim provides 303 prayer decrees. He prefaces the list with, "The heirs of God and the joint heirs with Christ have authority to decree words of Scripture, words of promise, words of prophecy (which are also words of God given through Holy Spirit enlightenment)" (p. 189)

Note: A decree is something spoken and releases or activates, according to Tim. These are spoken out loud for heaven and the angels to hear. They resemble commands more than appeals. It is similar to what shamans do: magical incantations.

"When you decree a word, you are prophesying into the course of your life. You are prophesying your future. Angels will hearken to bring it to pass. It is vital that we pray what God says. It is vital that we declare our faith, speaking His words over our lives. Hearkening angels will begin building them into our future" (p. 190).

He then says, "I encourage you to stir your faith and speak these decrees out loud over your life. Doing so will loose angels sent to assist you" (p. 190).

Here is a sampling of decrees:

#25: (in regard to angels) "In Jesus' name we deploy them."

#30: "Holy Spirit, execute God activity right here and right now."

#43: (in regard to angels) "In Jesus' name, we loose them now. Work for us. Assist us."

#51: "We loose angels to bring us messages in dreams."

#52: "Dreams, be loosed to provide guidance in Jesus' name."

#68: "Angels who bring messages from the Godhead—be loosed in Jesus' name."

#85 "Anointing for increased dreams and visions—be released to us."

#127: "New things never done before will now be done."

#132: "In Jesus' name, we loose angels to assist us in gathering harvest."

#138: "We decree our faith—delay no longer."

#297: "Angels are orbiting to hearken to God's Word that we decree."

#303: "We, the remnant church, will declare what God says. Angels will hear it and together we will fight hell and win."

Note: This is nothing more than a series of magical charms, a literal ordering of God around. The deception here is startling.

Clearly Tim Sheets has made significant contact with angelic type beings. This book I am critiquing Tim signed for me personally at the International Christian Retailers Show in Cincinnati, Ohio, in June of 2017. I spoke with him briefly about it and he was very pleasant with me. That something has unalterably convinced him of the reality of angels is without question. My conclusion is he did encounter angelic-like entities, but they were demons in disguise. I do not say this easily, but there can be no other conclusion.

A Critique of

Planting the Heavens:
Releasing the Authority of the Kingdom Through Your Words, Prayers, and Declarations

Tim Sheets, Destiny Image, 2017

CHAPTER ONE: WORDS ARE SEEDS

When we made the shift from a local church to an apostolic hub, there were quite a few who chose not to shift with us. They either didn't have a full understanding of where we were headed or they preferred a regular church. As a result, we lost a lot of people. During a time frame of several years, we had staff pastors leave as well as many people who had been with us from the beginning" (p. 31).

Note: Naturally, Tim needs to justify why people did not get on board with the shift from the ordinary local church to an "apostolic hub." This would have been the start of his aligning with the apostles and prophets of the NAR. This statement describes what has been happening in countless numbers of churches today. There are strong attractions to become an apostle or prophet or for the local church to come under the cover of an apostle or prophet. It is causing quite a divide as churches all over America face whether or not to go along.

"We need to reprogram our minds to think like children of God. . . .We must think like one living the mandate of God to exercise dominion upon the earth in His name, activating real Christian living . . . Your DNA reads Overcomer. Your DNA says Dominator. Your DNA declares Rule with my Father. . . . God's seed in you energizes you to create God's will by decreeing His Word" (p. 36).

Note: This is far too close to a magical view of Christianity. The message is that those who oppose moving into "what God is doing now" requires a reprogramming of the mind. The last sentence above is akin to becoming a shaman or Wiccan.

Sheets continues in this vein: "We can see the heavens with the Words of God, creating change and releasing His power. We can extend His rule on the earth by planting the heavens with energized, activated words" (p. 37).

"The world is crying out for the manifestation of the sons and daughters of God." "It's time we use our Word seed decrees that disciple a nation" (p. 38).

CHAPTER TWO: PLANTING THE HEAVENS

"I am also seeding the atmosphere of a region. I'm preaching a message, but I am really planting revival seeds everywhere. I'm planting God's will into the region. I am setting the foundations in the spirit realm. Sometimes I feel like I am laying a foundation in the spirit realm or into the atmosphere so that there can be productivity. I am preaching and planting the heavens. I'm preaching and planting the earth, in and around this country, for reformation and awakening" (p. 46).

Note: One is reminded of Jesus' parable about the sower. However, in that parable, the sower does not have the power that Tim does. His role in the new order of things is astonishing. He is the "agent of God's will." What he preaches is the will of God. Amazing!

Under the heading, "Building a Firewall," Sheets writes, "This has helped me with the Awakening Now Prayer Network, which we began in Ohio in 2008 and is spreading into the surrounding states. This network now has hundreds of churches in the region. The word from Prophet Chuck Pierce was, 'Build a firewall around the entire state.' . . . I didn't know how to build a firewall around the whole state, but in prayer the Holy Spirit said, 'Go to all eighty-eight counties and hold prayer assemblies.' We are currently doing that—we take apostolic teams and worship teams to the prayer assemblies and we make 50 or 60 decrees into that county. . . . Without this understanding of words as seeds or praying into the atmosphere, there is little doubt that I would not be doing what I am now doing" (p. 47).

In regard to the above-mentioned prayer, Tim says, "That's a different kind of prayer because it's not really a petition—it's a declaration. It's not a foretelling of the future—it's a commanding decree" (p. 48).

"When the sons and daughters of God open their mouths and decree God's Word, it can change the atmosphere of a region. . . . Our decrees attract angel armies to ascend and descend and assist the heirs of salvation in the region" (p. 49).

"We should expect deliverance, freedom, prosperity, harvest, miracles, healings, signs, wonders, favor, strength, restoration, satisfaction, fullness, preservation, ways provided for us, help provided for us, abundance to come our way, rest for our souls, and wisdom for answers" (p. 55).

Note: To decree something, declaring it into the atmosphere, is dramatically close to speaking out magical charms. One wonders how Tim could consider this activity to be biblical. Where in all the Word is there such a thing? Yet, because his followers know "Do not touch God's anointed," few will verbalize any doubts. A mass cultic mindset is at work here. The voices of dissent would soon be pressured, even in loving ways, to leave the fellowship or church.

Chapter Three: The Dominion Mandate

"We see that God says His born-again ones who decree His Word as seed are given dominion." "When God's sons and daughters plant His Word, the seed's dominion is activated and it will break out of all confinements and produce" (pp. 57–58).

Note: It is shocking that statements like the above go unchallenged. To "decree" is hardly a biblical concept. It is far more than being faithful; it is playing God.

Sheets cites Genesis 1:26–28 as containing the mandate to dominate all that God has created. "It was His will for His imaged ones to rule and reign on the earth." "Christ's death and resurrection reactivated God's original intent for His born-again ones." "He commanded us, 'You, disciple nations. Become My Kingdom government upon the earth'" (p. 59).

"The truth that America is a Christian nation is being suppressed, even though there are thousands of documents that say otherwise." "Sadly, sound doctrine is also being suppressed in nominal churches everywhere" (p. 61).

"God wants us to rule territories, nations, countries, lands all across this earth. . . .We have allowed the myths of the separation of church and state to confine us and distort our doctrine. . . . Christians are continually told, 'Stay out of governing.'" (p. 64).

"Even though I believe that Jesus is coming and we will be taken out of here at some point, an escape mentality stops us from occupying or taking care of God's business until He comes" (p. 64).

"Jesus said to make disciples of all the nations, teaching them His commands. Most believers today read that with a worldview that suppresses truth. They read it as, 'Go and win souls for Christ.'" (p. 65).

"When you buy into the lie of separation of church and state, you empower liars every time" (p. 66).

"The dominion mandate is a message of truth that must be restored to the Body of Christ, while the whole world may not see it, the remnant will see it" (p. 68).

Note: There is a strong political agenda here. Tim does not think America should be a democracy; he wants it to be a theocracy ruled over by God's anointed apostles and prophets. This is old time postmillennialism or Dominionism dressed up in modern guise. One wonders if the members of his group are able to swallow this. America is at the center of the globe and the movement for many like Tim—but not all.

CHAPTER FOUR: THE REIGNING CHURCH, CHRIST'S EKKLESIA

"The church is to be **a** ruling and reigning branch of His Kingdom upon the earth" (p. 72).

Note: Jesus said His kingdom was not of this world. However, Tim sees things otherwise, since God is directly speaking to him of the new things He is doing. We note that this is the same goal that Islam embraces—to rule the world, not just America, where one either converts to Islam, submits to Islam, or is terminated. The similarity is way too close between what Islam teaches and Tim says is the will and purpose of God.

Notice in the above quote Tim writes the church is to be a ruling branch and I have bolded the "**a**". He throughout implies that the church is to be the ruling branch but apparently cannot go all the way with stating it directly here.

"He expects His Kingdom to rule and reign with Him on this earth right now. . . . He expects them to, in His name, forbid some things and permit some things" (p. 74).

Note: Again, he uses the words "forbid" and "permit" in the same manner Islam does. His concept of the kingdom of God has come to him through personal conversation with the Deity, or so he thinks.

"The word *ekklesia* first occurs in the 5th century before Christ. Again, it was a political term, not a religious term" (page 80). "Jesus said, 'My ekklesia is to set the cultural standards for a region.' He understood what it meant" (p. 82).

Note: This last sentence from page 82—Is this a prophecy Tim received? It must be since Jesus never said anything close to this in any of the Gospels. It is absolutely foreign to the New Testament's concept of the coming kingdom of God. Most Christians see that the kingdom began with Jesus' earthly ministry, in His calling out His people, the church, but that kingdom in its fullness is yet to come.

"Jesus said, 'The body who stewards this for Me is My church, My ekklesia, My called-out ones. The born-again citizens of My Kingdom will worship Me as their King, represent Me as their King, and in My name they will steward their territorial or geographical boundaries. They will steward the laws and commands to ensure they are biblically based. They will steward societal and cultural values to conform to and be shaped by My ways and Word. They will call to account political governments. They will decide official positions and remove some from official positions by voting. Some have got to go. It's the church's responsibility. They will, in My name, steward economies, insisting on ethical financial behavior by voting over what is acceptable" (p. 86).

Note: What is the difference between what Tim says above, purportedly spoken by Jesus, and what we find in The Course of Miracles or The Book of Mormon, and so on. If I were to speak in such a way at Miller Avenue Baptist Church where I am pastor I would be summarily dismissed—and rightly so.

CHAPTER FIVE: DECREE YOUR AUTHORITY

To support the notion that we are to make decrees, and with authority, Sheets looks to a passage from the book of Job. The verse is Job 22:28: "Thou shalt also decree a thing, and it shall be established unto thee."

Note: He says it is something Job said when in fact one of Job's friends said it, namely Eliphaz. Tim is not a careful expositor of Scripture. For instance, on page 93 he states that Job is the oldest book in the Bible and was written by Moses. It is anyone's guess as to where he received this information.

"It is time to release authority language into your atmosphere. Until it's decreed, the seed is dormant. It's time to plant the heavens" (p. 99).

Note: Apparently God is limited to this decreeing; certainly Tim's God is not sovereign.

Under the heading "Decrees," we see a series of items that are apparently Tim's own wording, things he thinks need to be decreed. I have pulled several sentences from them. (Pages 100-104):

"Lord, You made so many promises to us, one after another

after another. We declare every one of them is coming to fullness right now in the name of Jesus."

"We speak against those who will not."

"We decree that we are receiving fresh power from an open heaven."

"Enabling power, come. Creative power, come. Tipping point power, come."

"We declare all generational curses are broken off of every life in Jesus' name."

"We decree abundance, prosperity, and plenty is now being released."

"We decree the wealth of the sinner is being laid up for the just, as God's Word says."

CHAPTER SIX: SPEAK LIKE A KING

"As a word of encouragement I want to share a prophetic word the Lord recently gave me. No more delay, says Heaven. Darkness will now be penetrated and dispelled by glorious light . . . Demon thrones will be toppled by glorious authority, dominating authority, supreme authority, ruling, and reigning authority . . . The surge of Heaven has now begun" (p. 115).

Note: Other prophets in the movement have been saying similar things now for years. When will the prophetic words be fulfilled? How will anyone recognize a fulfillment? Will it be literal and tangible or hidden and mystical? Should Tim be held accountable for his words of prophecy? Will new and different things be revealed that will supersede previous dramatic prophecies?

CHAPTER SEVEN: COME HERE

"Decrees create. They can create ideas in your heart. They create things that are not seen with the natural eye. They can create changes in conditions and in the atmosphere physically, spiritually, emotionally, materially, governmentally, politically, vocationally, and provisionally. Decrees are a creative force and they release a creative force that will bless us abundantly" (p. 121).

Tim is aware that his decreeing idea has problems. His answer: "I often hear someone who is believing for a promise say, 'But I don't see any evidence of this.' Exactly! That is the point! You don't see any evidence because *it is suspended in time*" [emphasis mine] (p. 125).

Note: Tim is more entertainer than prophet. His followers could not imagine that he would speak error. And he provides a cover for all the prophetic words that have not been fulfilled—"It is suspended in time." If you believe in that one, well, I have some ocean front property in Arizona . . .

"As believers, we need to begin to declare, 'Come here and come here now.'" . . ."You can easily see the commanding authority language that we are supposed to be walking in" (p. 128).

"You are to arise and speak in this manner, 'In Jesus' name, come here and come here right now'" (p. 129).

Note: This now is perhaps the most blatant of all the magical charms Tim has presented. He states we are to command whatever in "Jesus' name." You will find the same in books that deal with what is called "white magic."

CHAPTER EIGHT: DON'T GET NAILED

"If you speak the right words, you will live life well." . . . "This New Testament principle says we are destined to live the life we speak from our mouths" (p. 141).

"Every promise in the Bible is conditional upon whether or not we believe it and decree it" (p. 142).

"I wear a signet ring; in the last fifteen years, I haven't preached without wearing this particular ring." "I like to discreetly tap the document with my ring as a seal stating, 'Done, in the name of our Kingdom'" (p. 143).

Most of the rest of the chapter contains decrees that Tim endorses, and one of the most unusual ones is found on pages 147–148. He says about it, "That is a decree based upon the Word of God, and it is so easy to do. Just follow along and declare it, and when you do, the Word will reset you for what is ahead."

Note: After reading chapter eight there can be no doubt that Tim has abandoned Christianity and is now a sorcerer and a magician. I wish it were not so, and I am saddened to consider the many he is deceiving and leading astray.

CHAPTER NINE: THE FORCE OF WORDS

Tim employs a popular understanding that positive views promote health rather than the opposite. He uses this simple illustration to support speaking decrees. Also, there is good chemistry occurring in the body when we laugh and sing.

Note: This material apparently is meant to support the speaking of decrees, the planting of these in heaven where the angelic forces are then able to use them according to our purposes. He shows awareness of how close he is to unbiblical worldviews.

CHAPTER TEN: BUILDING BLOCKS

Tim uses Mark 11:22-24 where Jesus, encouraging trust in God, says, "That whosoever shall say unto this mountain, Be thou removed, and be thou cast into the sea, and shall not doubt in his heart, but shall believe that those things which he saith shall come to pass, he shall have whatsoever he saith." The point of the passage, according to Tim, is that "what you decree will be done for you" (p. 166).

Note: It did not take Tim long to return to magical thinking.

CHAPTER ELEVEN: MOUNTAIN MOVING FAITH

The thesis here is to repress doubts and questionings and trust God that what you decree will come to pass.

Note: Tim knows the danger of his followers practicing critical thinking. Imagine a Christian leader saying to repress doubts! Never mind thinking through things or seeking answers elsewhere, just decree and trust it will all work out. Does he really think this is true biblical faith?

A Critique of

SCHOOL OF THE PROPHETS: ADVANCED TRAINING FOR PROPHETIC MINISTRY

KRIS VALLOTTON, CHOSEN BOOKS, 2015

PREFACE

Bill Johnson, senior leader at Bethel Church in Redding, California, writes in the preface concerning Kris Vallotton's ministry, "The focus of his ministry is on what God is doing." Johnson contrasts that with the focus of many prophets who mainly deal with what is wrong with the world or the Church.

Note: The key error vividly illustrated here is that Kris, along with other NAR prophets, unequivocally states he knows what God is doing. And this is not in reference to biblical passages but based upon revelations he receives supernaturally.

INTRODUCTION: NAVIGATING WHITE WATER

In speaking of his experiences with God as a young person, Kris claims these were in answer to a prayer for his mother's healing: "A moment later, an audible voice said, 'My name is Jesus Christ, and you have what you requested!'"

Concerning the Jesus People Movement and the charismatic movement in general he states that the Jesus People were moved by experiences or feelings or the excitement that they found in Christ, which set the stage for wanting more of the same.

Note: As a Jesus person myself from 1967 to 1972 and pastor of a charismatic church during the decade of the '70s, I can testify that he is correct in identifying the reason for so much error that penetrated so deeply among us. Direct personal experience with "entities"—and there are all sorts of entities to encounter—led so many of us astray. We constantly wanted that initial joy and followed the promise of it wherever it led.

Kris describes his work in the School of the Supernatural at Bethel as akin to "herding cats," as these people are "extraordinarily sensitive and can easily feel misunderstood and/or rejected."

Note: Might this be due to the constant failures of what is prophesied to come true? Or, might it be the need to see miracles and experience close spiritual encounters?

Chapter One: Discovering Your Divine Call

Kris speaks of the time of his "call" to prophetic ministry. During a time of personal worship, while soaking in a bathtub, he saw Jesus actually walk through the wall and stand right in front of him. Jesus then said to him that He had called him to be a "prophet to the nations." Toward the end of this book, Kris refers to himself as a "father to the nations," with entire countries becoming his sons and daughters.

Jesus' commissioning ended with, "History will tell us if you believe Me!" Kris is shocked by such an incredible pronouncement reminding him that it had only been two years since he had suffered a "serious nervous breakdown" (p. 24). He was indeed shocked that he was called to guide the nations and present to world leaders revelations that came directly from the throne of God.

The calling was confirmed by other "prophets," and Proverbs 18:16 was a key passage: "A man's gift makes room for him and brings him before great men." In 1998, twenty years after the call, he joined the staff at Bethel Church under the lead pastor, Bill Johnson.

Toward the end of chapter one he writes of the "countless congregations" who suffered under false prophets who attempted to establish their ministries and gain a standing by drawing congregants after them and away from their pastors.

Note: After reading book after book by and about NAR apostles and prophets and viewing their videos on YouTube, such infighting and confusion is plain to see and understand. The typical scenario is that the local church pastor is often the obstacle in preventing so-called apostles and prophets from gathering followers to themselves. Now that it only takes the announcement that Jesus has personally appeared to the candidate, with a few already accepted apostles and/or prophets vouching for authenticity and paying of the annual fee, almost anyone can earn the exalted and coveted designations.

CHAPTER TWO: NEW VERSUS OLD TESTAMENT PROPHETS

This chapter presents a fairly biblically oriented though not complete view of the differences between Old and New Testament prophets. Kris characterizes the difference as being that the Old proclaimed judgment and the New proclaimed freedom, with Jesus taking judgment upon Himself at the cross.

Note: Once again I am speaking of an intramural not an extramural debate. Those who fit into the NAR movement are by-in-large brothers and sisters in Christ. However, as church historians understand, heresy may arise from within the Christian family. The error need not be theological; it may have to do with methodology or ecclesiology—that is, our way of viewing others and ourselves. From within the movement, the view is that, if one is not embracing the NAR, the new season where God is establishing his end time apostles and prophets, then one is standing directly against God. Most NAR adherents would see me as definitely opposed to their views and thus would label me as confused or even resistant to the Holy Spirit.

Note: Missing in Kris' contrast of the two testaments is the fact that there is also judgment in the New Testament. The Gospel is two-sided: all have sinned and fall short of the glory of God—and we find grace and mercy through the sacrifice of Jesus on the cross. God does pass judgment on those who are not safe in Christ.

CHAPTER THREE: TWO DIFFERENT DISPENSATIONS

The point of this chapter seems to be that Kris objects to the preaching coming from some NAR-aligned prophets who preach judgment not reconciliation.

He admits that early on his prophecies were of a judgmental nature, though accurate, but they came from a "wrong spirit." By this he means the words he thought he was receiving from God were aimed at calling out people's sins rather than speaking peace and forgiveness.

Then, some time later, he experienced what I guess is a common designation—he had a "revelation bump" that served to set him in a New Testament mode for the prophet.

Note: The idea that a New Testament prophet speaks directly to individuals regarding personal things is problematic. Hebrews 1:1–4 teaches that God spoke of old to "our fathers" by the prophets Elijah, Isaiah, Jeremiah, etc., "but in these last days He has spoken to us by His son . . . ." Now we have in Scripture all we need; therefore, to prophesy is to proclaim the finished work of Jesus Christ. The prophet is the Gospel preacher. Though there were some New Testament prophets who predicted coming events, like Agabus in the Book of Acts, we observe that this sort of thing disappeared once the New Testament books were gathered together.

This is not to say I am a "cessationist," that is, one who believes that the charismatic gifts of the Holy Spirit are no longer experienced. No, and neither am I a "continuationist," believing that the charismatic gifts of the Holy Spirit continue normally. I follow the position of David Martin Lloyd-Jones, Iain Murray, and others, that the gifts of the Spirit, as we find them in Romans 12 and 1 Corinthians 12, are seen in many awakenings when God pours out His Spirit—for instance, in the Jesus People Movement. But we do not see them normally or at all times.

CHAPTER FOUR: PROPHETIC PERSPECTIVES

A startling statement is made in terms of contrasting biblical and present day prophets: "I used to believe that prophecies were supposed to come completely from God, but I no longer believe that is possible" (p. 80).

Kris is saying that the contemporary prophet puts his or her own "accent" into the prophecy, meaning that the prophet imputes context into the words from God. Feelings, understandings, agendas, and so on, flavor the messages. He then goes on with means to help the prophet learn to keep himself or herself out of the way, to evaluate what goes into their words. And this would be sound counsel given his views regarding the call to prophetic ministry today.

Note: After reading hundreds of prophecies spoken to people, individuals, or congregations, I discern a typical pattern. The messages can usually apply across many situations using language that is easily bent or adapted in many different ways. At the conclusion of this present book, Kris gives some quotes from prophecies he delivered to the leader of some "nation." These are different in nature, as they describe events that had occurred in the past or were in the process of occurring. I was struck by how similar these sounded to fortuneteller and palm reader assertions today.

Chapter Five: Prophecy Versus Prophets

Kris intends to distinguish between the "office of the prophet" and the gift of prophecy. The NAR's prophets do more than prophesy; they occupy the office of the prophet. This is a position of authority, like a government office. The same is true for apostles, and the two—the apostle and the prophet—are in place to rule.

Note: The position of the NAR leaders is that in these last days, this final season, God has established the five-fold ministry, that of apostle, prophet, evangelist, and pastor and teacher in order that these might bring the kingdom of God down to earth from heaven to prepare for the return of Jesus. And on what basis do we know this to be the very truth? Definitely not from any biblical passage but rather on the basis of what the apostles and prophets themselves say has been revealed to them by God. There it is, and to question such is to be considered a legalist, a Pharisee, or to have a Greek mindset, a critical spirit, a Jezebel spirit, a religious spirit, the spirit of Saul, to be unanointed, or to be clinging to the old wineskin.

Kris has been the senior prophet at Bethel Church in Redding since 1998, which is earlier than when C. Peter Wagner thinks the final season began, which was around 2001.

According to Kris, even young children, in the toddler age range, are receiving revelations from God.

In the heading, "A Holy House for Two," Kris says that the Christian has two spirits dwelling inside—the human spirit and the Holy Spirit. This two-spirit indwelling can cause confusion to the prophet and is one reason why the prophet's words are not always accurate. He admits that sometimes prophetic words are not words from God at all.

The office of prophet is the gift, the gift of God to the Church. The prophets may be imperfect in many different ways, but despite that, they are God's prophets given to the Church to lead and guide it.

Note: This doctrine is questionable, yet so much he teaches is based on it. This is unusual language. The Bible does speak of soul, spirit, mind, flesh, and heart—five aspects of the human being made in the image of God. But they are not separated and distinct entities. We are one person with all of these aspects to us. The Christian is only indwelt, upon conversion, by the Holy Spirit, so there are not two "spirits" indwelling us. The seeming aim of all this confusion is to make allowance for false prophecies. Otherwise, according to the Law of Moses, there would be a whole lot of dead (stoned) prophets lying around.

Kris admits prophets may be a bit strange, since they live in a multi-dimensional world; it can even make them feel crazy.

CHAPTER SIX: THE ROLE OF THE PROPHET

The NAR prophet is to be a builder for the Kingdom of God. Kris largely ignores the so-called office of apostle. He is a prophet, and the prophet is the one who makes the Church in the last days shine out in the darkness to bring people to the King. It is only God who calls people to be prophets; the Church does not and churches do not. Only God does this, so the office of prophet is sacrosanct and should be held in the highest honor.

Note: His opinion of the role of the prophet is extremely high, as though others, say apostles, evangelists, pastors and teachers, have an almost insignificant role to play. In other NAR materials I have read, pastors and teachers seem to be nothing more than obstacles to bringing in the Kingdom of God. I suspect such is the case, because pastors of local churches would and do likely resist prophets provoking chaos. Pastors may also come into conflict with self-proclaimed apostles who claim authority. It is "first" apostles and "second" prophets in Scripture (see 1 Corinthians 12:28), but this does not mean there are rankings of positions of authority. Apostle is first because of passages like Acts 1:8, where the emphasis for the Church is on sending out apostles (Grk., apostolous), a word which means "sent ones." It is an activity and a mission, not an office, and the NAR's misunderstanding of the biblical meanings of apostles and prophets is where it makes a most serious error.

"Mantles for Missions" is the title of a sub-heading in the chapter. Kris writes, "When God commissions His leaders such as Joshua, He *releases* [emphasis mine] mantles over them" (p. 147). The mantles are what give the prophets the power and authority they have. The prophet, however, does not have the power; the calling or anointing is the power. He says it is similar to a mantle for the president of a country. The president does not own or possess the mantle; the mantle belongs to the office and is passed along to the next president. Basically the prophet has been given a mantle, and this is what makes it all work.

"God's Secret Service" is a rather interesting section in chapter six. The prophets, Kris says, know secrets from God that God does not want everyone to know. This is based on Amos 3:7: "For the Lord God does nothing without revealing his secret to his servants the prophets" (ESV). The rest of what Kris believes about prophets keeping God's secrets highly elevates the power and prestige of the prophet, and he is one. Kris thinks or wonders if the level of anointing a prophet has is directly related to that prophet's ability to keep secrets.

God protects His prophets, but God calls prophets to protect nations. He says that God has woken him up on occasions to prophesy words against terrorism.

Note: It is as though God cannot act on His own but is dependent upon the words of authority from His prophets.

Chapter Seven: Building a Prophetic Community

Kris describes his role as a coach in the community of prophets at Bethel Church's School of the Supernatural. As a person with considerable experiences he outlines principles that might guide the development of many different types of work and ministry. He is rather complex, interpersonal, and thorough.

He relates that some of his students act as though they are "prophetic superheroes." As such, they make errors, perhaps by means of exaggeration. They may become super- or hyper-spiritual, in that they report an angel under every rock and commonly experience heavenly visitations, visions, and dreams. He admits some students "often live in fantasy so long that it becomes a way of life, a way to cope, a way to escape their agony" (p. 182).

Students learning to prophesy—and taking classes in how to prophesy is not considered strange—are considered to be doing well if they can utter something like, "God loves you. He really, really loves you. And he thinks you are amazing."

Note: I do not want to make fun of these dear people who want to think they are prophets and prophetesses, as at the School of the Supernatural at Bethel, but such a curriculum will not serve them well. For me, it is a sad thing. For nearly ten years I was the senior pastor of a group in the charismatic/Pentecostal branch of Christianity that I realized had become errant. We thought we were doing what God wanted, but we were harming quite a number of others. For six years—1988 to 1994—I put together a cult recovery support group for those who were either bounced out of or voluntarily left cultic groups. My thinking is that the NAR will one day implode. Many are already walking away, and what about those who are very damaged? This is why the third section of this book offers some hope and comfort to those who will need recovery.

Chapter Eight: Standing Before Kings

A major theme of this book is that prophets and prophetesses are called by God to "help transform nations" (p. 189). He even refers to the prophets as "fathering the nations," as though the nations were sons and daughters.

On page 208, Kris even says, "Like Joseph and Daniel, God has called me as a prophetic father not just to the nations, but as a father of many nations." He refers to "international sons and daughters of mine."

These prophets and prophetesses are secretly placed in high levels of authority in nations to help guide according to God's planning.

Note: These images or metaphors, if they can be called such, make a major break with anything biblical. Where does Jesus, Paul, Peter, John, or anyone else in Scripture open the door to such megalomaniacal thinking? How does one who is a Christian and who loves the Lord move to such a position as this? Indeed one is reminded of Matthew 24:24: "For false christs and prophets will arise and perform great signs and wonders, so as to lead astray, if possible, even the elect" (ESV). We must notice that the phrase "if possible" is a first class conditional phrase and means that it is possible to lead astray the elect. "Lead astray" does not mean salvation is lost, rather that the elect are not immune to being deceived.

Chapter Nine: Noble Prophets

In this last chapter, Kris describes his meeting with the leader of a certain country. No details other than this are revealed. By way of an intermediary, Kris is presented to the country's leader as a "futurist" rather than as a Christian prophet.

After preliminary protocols were observed, Kris began to prophecy to the leader things that only God and the leader would have known. Kris reports that the leader was visibly shaken, with the result that his authority as the futurist was established. More was then revealed, which further cemented Kris' status. He reports that whenever he is in this leader's country, the leader will meet him wherever he is to learn more. Kris says this leader is only one of many who do the same.

Note: Here now is revealed the most troubling part of the book, because in my estimation as someone who knows something of the occult world, Kris is operating as a fortune teller, palm reader, or sorcerer and not as a biblically oriented prophet. Neither the subject of Jesus, nor the Bible, nor the Gospel ever came up. The leader did not even know Kris was a Christian. There was only a glance into the crystal ball and the revealing of things in the past and present—this is hardly Christian ministry.

A Critique of

The Passion Translation New Testament: With Psalms, Proverbs and Song of Songs

Dr. Brian Simmons, BroadStreet Publishing Group, 2017

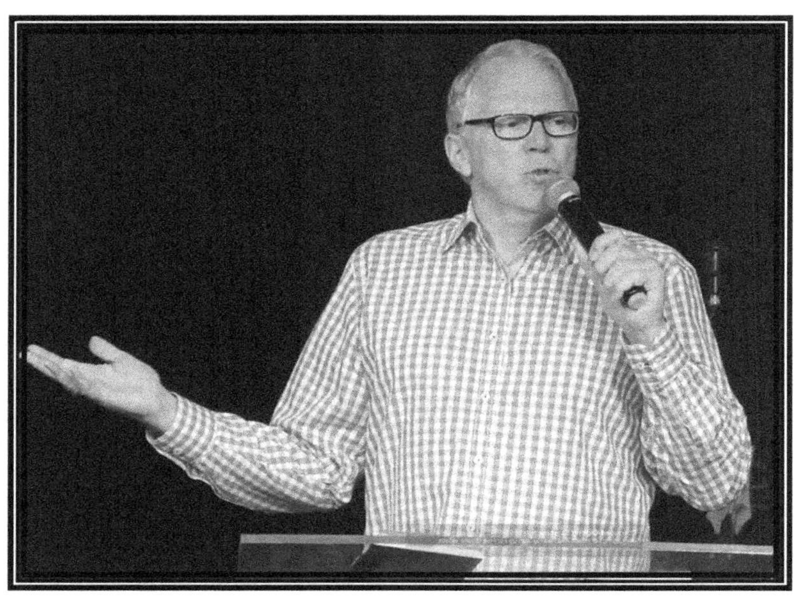

It is tempting to react harshly to *The Passion Translation* (TPT) , because it is a bold and direct violation of the warning of Revelation 22:18-19:

> I warn everyone who hears the words of the prophecy of this book, if anyone adds to them, God will add to him the plagues described in this book, and if anyone takes away from the words of the book of this prophecy, God will take away his share in the tree of life and in the holy city, which are described in this book.

The apostle John's copyright infringement warning, for that is the essence of it, is not an uncommon admonition found at the conclusion of documents in ancient days. In addition, it's purview is the Book of Revelation alone, but since it occurs at the end of the Bible, the warning is most often taken to include the whole of the Bible—and that may be the intent of the Holy Spirit. Because of the extent of strange interpretations throughout the TPT, the Revelation passage above applies to its entirety.

The question comes to mind—why would anyone attempt to create a version of the Bible that so strongly begs to be judged in this way?

Following is only one instance showing how Dr. Simmons has added to Scripture: Philippians 1:1: "My name is Paul and I'm joined by my spiritual son Timothy, both of us passionate servants of Jesus, the Anointed One."

In the Greek text there are only six words: Paul, and, Timothy, slaves, Christ, Jesus. The ESV, and most other Bible versions, translates these words as "Paul and Timothy, servants of Christ Jesus."

Dr. Simmons carries forth his agenda by adding "my spiritual son" and "both of us passionate" and using one of the key phrases of people in the New Apostolic Reformation (NAR), "Anointed One," in place of Christ. Christ means Messiah much more than "Anointed One," but the NAR apostles and prophets consider themselves under the anointing of God and thus must be accorded the highest honor and authority. Therefore, they subtly elevate their own status in comparison to Christ's.

TPT—THE BIBLE OF THE NAR-ALIGNED APOSTLES AND PROPHETS

A number of the apostles and prophets of the NAR endorse the TPT and regularly use it in preaching and teaching. Apparently, Bill Johnson of Bethel Church in Redding, California, preaches from it as well as James Goll and many others. It becomes another mark of NAR orthodoxy and helps to create a division in the broad Christian community. I am reminded of the many discussions I have had with Jehovah's Witnesses who disregard my use of the New International Version translation or the English Standard Version, saying their New World Bible is the only rightly translated Bible. I cannot help but equate the TPT and the New World translation of the JWs.

THE TPT IS A PARAPHRASE AND NOT A TRANSLATION

The Living Bible is a paraphrase of the Bible and does not claim to be a strict translation. Dr. Simmons, however, claims his is a translation. He claims to render the text's "emotional" content and not simply deliver a word for word translation.

This approach certainly serves his purpose. He is part of the NAR network and does his best to boost the ideas of the NAR through his rendering of what he believes is the original language of the New Testament—Aramaic.

While there certainly are ancient manuscripts of the New Testament in Aramaic, the bulk of the ancient documents are written in Greek. The numbers are not even close; Greek manuscripts outnumber Aramaic by a wide margin. Claiming that the original documents are in Aramaic helps Dr. Simmons disregard most church pastors and the overwhelming majority of New Testament scholars whose work shows that Greek is the original language of all the books of the New Testament. Consider the problems that would have ensued if Paul had written in Aramaic to those in Graeco/Roman churches like Thessalonica, Rome, Philippi, and Corinth, those who knew and spoke Greek and not Aramaic!

Dr. Simmons claims that Jesus spoke only Aramaic, a claim that cannot be substantiated. Growing up in Nazareth of Galilee, it is possible he spoke both Aramaic and Greek. Regardless, the vast evidence points to Greek as being the language of all of the New Testament books—gospels, epistles, and apocalyptic writing—regardless of what language Jesus spoke.

The claim about Aramaic being the language of the original New Testament leads to Dr. Simmons' resulting license to change as much Scripture as he wishes. He sees in the Aramaic the Eastern mindset that is, according to him, more passionate and emotional and much freer and exuberant than a Greek mindset. He assesses the Greek mindset as too introverted, emotionless, literal, and bound. But, is this division of mindsets applicable or even accurate?

All of Scripture, Old and New Testaments, is written from the Eastern mindset. What makes the difference regarding mindset is how one interprets what is written. And yes, it does make a difference from the reader's point of view. The Greek mindset tends to a more literal understanding of biblical phrases, words, and images, but that does not imply or lead to modern translations being blind to the letter and intent of Scripture. In my preaching I characteristically distinguish between the two different ways of interpreting Scripture, and yes, it is important to see the difference.

At issue is that Dr. Simmons uses the difference to cast doubt on translations of the Bible other than his own. "Greek mindset" is one of the labels NAR adherents use for those outside the NAR—a clumsy attempt to dismiss opposers. But the Eastern mindset, Dr. Simmons somehow conjures up, is more open to the moving of the Spirit and thus preferable.

All of this is without any real evidence. But, mind you, he is either an apostle or a prophet or both, and he merely has to claim divine revelation.

HOW IT ALL STARTED

Characteristic of NAR phenomenon, the TPT began with a visit from Jesus. In 2009, Jesus entered the room in which Dr. Simmons was sitting, breathed on him, and told him he was to write a new translation of the Bible. Dr. Simmons received the "spirit of revelation" at that moment, which would equip him to make the translation.

Immediately, Dr. Simmons began to experience what he calls "downloads" likened to a computer chip given to him that would help him do the work. This means that the TPT is given directly by God—to one person. Multiple scholars working in tandem accomplish most translations, though evidently Kenneth Taylor of The Living Bible acted pretty much alone on his paraphrase. Dr. Simmons did not include anyone else in the translation work, nor did anyone else edit or examine it.

THE TWENTY-SECOND CHAPTER OF THE GOSPEL OF JOHN

More of the TPT is to come, apparently. Dr. Simmons claims knowledge about a twenty-second chapter of the Gospel of John, but it will be given at some later point. Jesus showed it to him in a large library-like room on one occasion when Jesus took him out of his body. Dr. Simmons was invited by Jesus to take only two books back to earth. Then he spied a book entitled John 22 and was tempted to steal it, but he refrained from doing so. Jesus then pacified Dr. Simmons with the news that he would be receiving the last chapter of John at just the right time. How exciting!

I suppose if one believes this, one would believe almost anything. The trouble is that, "touch not my anointed ones, do my prophets no harm" (1 Chronicles 16:22) is the NAR's favorite phrase that seems to stifle any and all critique.

So, what did Simmons' sneak peek of John 22 reveal? It is an unpacking of the "greater works will you do" referenced in John 14:12. Of course, the NAR apostles and prophets claim that this is happening right now through the offices of the apostles and prophets. My guess is that John's last chapter will be about signs, wonders, and miracles being "released" upon the last day's church. Or, might it be instructions for waging the great Christian Civil War?

All of this began in 2009, and the NAR claims that the supernatural is already upon us—so where is John 22?

Section Two

Essays

Section two consists of essays I have written on NAR-related topics over the years. In some of the early pieces I had no real awareness of the size, depth, and significance of the movement. It has only been in the last few years, from about 2010, that the impact of this movement around the world became clear to me. Surely, this is the largest and most dangerous cultic movement by whatever measurement in the history of the Christian Church including that of the Arian controversy. And I say this because of such large numbers involved with a very high percentage of those engaged being brothers and sisters in Christ. Indeed, I consider it to be the most harmful of all demonic deceptions poured out on the planet.

Permission is given to anyone who would like to use any of the essays in whatever manner desired. Consider using them as tracts. In the Jesus People Movement handing out gospel tracts was routine; I estimate that I have handed out tens of thousands of tracts over the course of decades, most of which I wrote and printed myself. Anyone can do it.

We are forming "The Jesus People Tract Society," hoping to reinvigorate the practice. Many would like to actively engage in evangelism, but due to fear or not knowing how to get started, do very little if anything at all. Here is an invitation to get started handing out gospel tracts and become a part of our society.

Please email me at kentphilpott@comcast.net, and I will include you in the Jesus People Tract Society and send you a link to download and print any numbers of tracts for free. Perhaps you have some tracts you have written yourself. Please send them along. No guarantee that we will print them or that we will not edit them (with your approval), but it is all without cost or money flowing in any direction. So then, let's get out there and start doing the work to which we are called.

Essay One

I Am a 'Flaming' Pentecostal

Yes, I am now a 'flaming' Pentecostal, but I was not always one.

A Brief History—Establishing My Credentials

During the late 1960s through the 1970s, I was a charismatic with a Baptistic, Arminian theology. Yes, I was a tongue speaker, I guess, and was somewhat noted for my 'gifts' to the point I was even a guest on Pat Robertson's 500 Club, in that program's early days. Spirituality was measured then by the clearance when doing back flips over the pews. (This is not really true—only an old joke of mine.) And yes, the length of the lines of those waiting for the laying on of hands was also considered a reliable measure of just how much anointing of the Spirit one had.

I am not making fun of my charismatic/Pentecostal brethren either—this is simply part of my history.

During that period, I was considered a full-out charismatic if not a wild-eyed Pentecostal. One of my publishers in those days was Logos International, when Dan Maluchuk was president. Logos was for years a leading publisher of charismatic authors. (Logos published three of my books in the 1970s. I am only establishing my credentials here.)

A Different Sort of Pentecostal

In the church calendar we are in the longest stretch of the year, Pentecost, and I have been preaching on the work of the Holy Spirit at Miller Avenue. Doing a series of sermons on one subject tends to focus the mind on the one subject, and I think for the first time I see the working of the Holy Spirit in my life more clearly than ever before. When I step back and look at it I can say that I really am a 'flaming' Pentecostal—now.

You might be, too.

Consider: (The following list is not necessarily in proper order.)

1. It is the Holy Spirit who revealed to us our huge need of a Savior. Jesus said this would be the case; the Spirit convicts us of sin—personally, clearly, showing us our desperate situation.

2. The Holy Spirit, after showing us the state of condemnation we are in, then reveals to us that Jesus is the Savior who died in our place, taking our sin, guilt, and condemnation forever away. Only the Holy Spirit can do this, because we can never figure this out on our own. We only excuse, compare, deny, hide and lie to ourselves—the Holy Spirit's testimony is true and accurate.

3. The Holy Spirit is powerful and persuasive and cannot be resisted—which is a very real measure of God's love for us. Even when we deliberately turn away, even blaspheme His name, He yet pursues us, searches us out, and saves us despite ourselves.

4. The Holy Spirit indwells us, doing the work of regeneration, whereby we are born again, repenting of sin and trusting in Jesus as Savior and Lord. This is so huge, so incredible, it can only be the work of the Triune God.

5. The Holy Spirit places us into Christ. This is very mystical and spiritual; no one can fully explain or appreciate it. Placed into Christ by the Holy Spirit, one is part of His Church, the invisible Church of God.

6. The Holy Spirit seals us, puts God's stamp of approval on

us or in us, makes us His own without qualification, and does so absolutely permanently.

7. The Holy Spirit prays for us in a way we never can do, and with 'groanings' expressing what we are unable to convey.

8. The Holy Spirit empowers our witness, teaching, and preaching. This 'baptism' of the Spirit we depend on for all the tangible fruit that comes from our labor in His vineyard.

Here is a liberating truth: the Holy Spirit does the work of conversion from beginning to end—it is not me. Therefore I am not burdened with results and success; rather I go about my work of teaching and preaching, as carefully and energetically as possible of course but all the while believing in the ministry of the Holy Spirit.

9. The Holy Spirit, additionally, gives us gifts of grace so that we can do the work we have been called to—everything from wisdom to acts of mercy.

10. The Holy Spirit so works in us that we grow up into the fullness of the stature of Jesus, to maturity. If we have learned anything from the Scripture, the Holy Spirit has done this. If we learn to be like Jesus—gentle, loving and merciful—the Holy Spirit is responsible for these as well.

11. The Holy Spirit must be credited when there is honor and glory given to our Lord Jesus Christ—this is His work, to glorify God the Son.

A Correction

It would be presumptuous on my part to say I am a 'flaming' Pentecostal. It seems though that I am moving in that direction, however haltingly, and every flicker of fire comes from the one who baptizes with the Holy Spirit, our Lord Jesus Christ.

September, 2009

Essay Two

Not Only Am I a 'Flaming' Pentecostal, I Am a 'Flaming' Evangelist

I am a full-gospel Pentecostal. By that I mean I rely upon the whole gospel, the good news that though I once stood condemned because of my sin and rebellion I have been rescued by God through Jesus Christ from certain and everlasting destruction in hell. And this all accomplished by the Holy Spirit's applying the finished work of Christ and His cross to me, causing me to be regenerated, born again, forgiven, clothed with the righteousness of that same Christ, indwelt by His Spirit, seated with Christ at the right hand of the throne of God in heaven, and a whole lot more.

Now then, I am no longer under condemnation but I am in Christ. And by virtue of being in Christ I belong to Him, I am His disciple, His follower, sitting at His feet as His servant. And as His servant I hear His command to make disciples of all nations (Matthew 28:19), to proclaim forgiveness of sins in his name to all nations (Luke 24:47), and be His witness starting at Jerusalem, then Judea, Samaria, and to the end of the earth (Acts 1:8).

It is very clear

It could not be any plainer—I am a witness, a proclaimer, a disciple maker, or it might be said, I am or am supposed to be a flaming evangelist.

You understand I am having fun with 'flaming'. The word has been used to negatively describe religious type nuts and other outlandish behavior. I admit I have used it in a derogatory fashion of any number of zealots I thought were beside themselves—nuts.

It is the Holy Spirit who makes me a flaming evangelist—it has to be the work of the Holy Spirit, because it is not naturally in me. There was a time when I considered becoming a hyper-Calvinist, one who figured I had no responsibility to evangelize because God didn't need the likes of me running around making a fool of myself. He would call whom he would and it didn't make any difference what I did or didn't do.

That wouldn't do, however. The commands are too clear to be a witness, a proclaimer, a disciple maker—in short, an evangelist with Holy Spirit empowering, as Jesus said He would do (see Acts 1:8—the part about receiving "power when the Holy Spirit has come upon you"). Flaming it is.

A FAVORITE VERSE

Yes, I believe in election, all the way. I also believe in obeying the commands to evangelize that Jesus so clearly gave His Church—that is you and I. There is no contradiction.

Paul resolves the tension in a favorite verse of mine, Romans 10:17: "So faith comes from hearing, and hearing through the word of Christ." I preach, the Holy Spirit inspires, applying the word of Christ as He will, and faith is the result. So then, I am as a preacher of the Gospel both a flaming Pentecostal and evangelist. These two are inseparable. And what's more, I love the labels, though once I would have shunned them. So what do I care how adjectives are thrown about—I am the servant who cares to be about his master's business.

September, 2009

Essay Three

Saints and Angels

Christians are worshipping saints and angels like never before—what's going on?

The worship or adoration of angels and saints is nothing new for Christians—it goes back many centuries. The Roman Catholic Church and the Eastern Orthodox Church both have extensive histories of honoring, adoring, and praying to angels and saints, the saints being purified believers now present with God in heaven. It is thought that each person has a guardian angel who is actively engaged in guidance and protection through granting answers to prayer and miraculous intervention in real time. Additionally, there are those who believe "holy saints" in heaven are able to interact with people alive today.

Though the Christian Scripture does not endorse or promote the worship of angels or saints, the traditions of these churches do, and they trump whatever proscriptions might be found in the Bible itself. Therefore, if the church sanctions angel and saint worship, then it is permitted for the individual believer.

The foregoing is well understood. However, some Protestants (maybe the term should rather be "neo-Protestants") are beginning to embrace the concept that angels and saints now in heaven are or should be involved in the lives of believers.

When Heaven Invades Earth

Bill Johnson, pastor of Bethel Church in Redding, California, wrote a book with the above title and believes that heaven has invaded earth by means of purified saints. No, he is not talking about the incarnation, nor is he talking about "the Word become flesh" (see John 1:14); he means that saints in "these last days" are engaged in empowering Christians to do mighty things, particularly healings.

It is all about power. A key phrase from Johnson is, "The kingdom of God is not a matter of talk but of power." As he describes it, saints, who are a part of the "mystical body of Christ in heaven," are eager to be joined with the "mystical body of Christ on earth," as in a marriage of a man and a woman. And when such a union occurs, then real kingdom power is unleashed and manifested with virtually unlimited scope and power. When this is "realized," then the great branches of the Christian Church will be united.

Christians, Johnson teaches, may now avail themselves of the power of the Spirit, the angels, and the saints. He envisions the great cloud of saints in heaven becoming one with the believers on earth. Part of the authority for this doctrine comes from Hebrews 12:18-24 where in verses 22 and 23 are the words, "But you have come to Mount Zion and to the city of the living God, the heavenly Jerusalem, and to the assembly of the firstborn who are enrolled in heaven, and to God, the judge of all, and to the spirits of the righteous made perfect" (ESV).

There is not space here to adequately expose the passage, but the interpretation that departed saints are eager to engage with believers on earth now and empower them is certainly unusual and has nothing in common with the vast majority of commentators and scholars. The general theme of the passage is that God, in Christ, has established a kingdom that is complete, perfect, and which cannot be shaken or destroyed.

The Great Cloud of Witnesses

The purified saints—that great cloud of witnesses—have been rewarded by God and given authority to intervene in or invade the affairs of Christians living today, or so writes Bill Johnson. The invaders have the ability to work great power miracles in the ministries of Christians who both understand the empowerment and who seek it. The Christian living today should seek this out, Johnson urges, seek this gifting, impartation, or anointing—and then be able to bring healing and words of knowledge or prophecy to the body of Christ on earth. Very heady indeed!

Pastor Johnson of Bethel Church appeals to Matthew 10:41: "The one who receives a prophet because he is a prophet will receive a prophet's reward, and the one who receives a righteous person because he is a righteous person will receive a righteous person's reward." The context of the passage is plain enough. Jesus outlines the fact that those who will receive or hear the message of His representatives or followers are then receiving He Himself and will be rewarded with hearing the message of the Gospel. But Johnson makes the passage mean something else entirely. It is his way of encouraging Christians today to seek out the empowering of the "great cloud of witnesses"—the departed saints.

Dare I ask, "How is this any different from what the psychic medium practices?"

Johnson's Warning

Bill Johnson certainly knows that his view is not broadly shared in the Christian community, so he therefore issues a warning. He understands that most biblically based Christians will have been taught that communicating with the saints in heaven is demonic in nature, that it is a deception perpetrated by the devil. The resultant fear of the devil's tricks, Johnson warns, would then cut one off from having faith in communion with the saints and the benefits available through the powerful working of these saints. A clever tactic indeed, bringing up and negating the argument Johnson knows will be used by biblically based Christians.

Certainly, the Scripture is the barrier that Johnson must overcome. In chapter 6 of his book, Johnson concludes with this most revealing statement: "Those who feel safe because of their grasp of Scripture enjoy a false sense of security. We all have the Holy Spirit, but to follow Him, we must be willing to follow Him off the map—to go beyond what we know" (p. 76).

For Johnson it is not the Word of God but the new move of the "Spirit" that matters. It is all about power and not faithfulness to the Scripture. Christians who adhere to the Bible are then belittled as being stuck in old revelation and not able to follow the leading of the Spirit into new regions. So, let the Scripture go, follow the new anointing, receive the new impartations, be empowered by the purified saints.

Luke 16:26 Nullifies Johnson's Position

In the parable found in Luke 16:19-31, usually titled "The Rich Man and Lazarus," Jesus puts into Abraham's mouth a truth that clearly nullifies the theology behind Bill Johnson's idea that purified saints interact with living Christians. "'And besides all this, between us and you a great chasm has been fixed, in order that those who would pass from here to you may not be able, and none may cross from there to us'" (Luke 16:26).

Christians have long understood, based on such passages as Deuteronomy 18:9–14, that mediumship and necromancy are both forbidden by God and are abominable practices. Yet Bill Johnson celebrates such and encourages others to enter into this very thing. Of course, he does not frame it in occult terminology, but it is impossible to view it any other way. Yet, persons who claim Christ as Savior and hope to be biblically correct are falling into error on this point. One is reminded of a passage in Galatians where Paul referred to a moving away from Gospel truth into error, a "turning to a different gospel" (Galatians 1:6).

How Did It Come to This?

For people who have accepted the idea that God is doing new

things in the "last days," any new direction is possible. Everything then appears to have changed, because the end is near, and it is by a display of power that the kingdom will come. Christians must then travel "off the map" if they really want to tap into what God is doing—and Johnson, among others, positions himself as a direction-giver on that new map to tell us exactly what God is doing now. Amazingly, thousands believe this, and the numbers are growing. These concepts have exerted considerable influence not only in America, and not only among charismatics and Pentecostals, but in Latin American, Asia, and in Africa. It is impossible to underestimate the influence of these ideas.

One note: How is it that one can be certain that the last days have come? Declarations that the end of history has come are nothing new. There is simply no way to know what God has determined by His own counsel. Anyone can make a claim or utter a "prophecy," but experience and wisdom teach us that it is better to wait and see and not be pushed into adopting ideas that have a proven failure rate, which is 100%.

Why are these non-biblical ideas taking hold? Power, new anointing, new improved truth—the same old errors are at work once again. It is heady and it is powerful, for there is real power; miracles do happen—there is a real spirit at work, and when you see the power, you may well be convinced. What is crucial to understand here is that not all spiritual power is from God. The power gurus of Hinduism, like Osho or Muktananda, performed amazing power miracles. Power is deceptive. The magicians of Egypt were temporarily able to imitate the power of God demonstrated through Moses.

Are those who propound communion with departed saints in order to acquire their power evil persons bent on misleading the people of God? Not necessarily. But, demonic deception and human error are both real, and most often these two go hand in hand.

Angel of Light

In the church at Corinth Paul realized there were men who had a ministry that was running counter to that which he had been commissioned by Christ to preach. From the reports that Paul had received he understood the dangers involved. Here is how Paul described the situation:

> For such men are false apostles, deceitful workmen, disguising themselves as apostles of Christ. And no wonder, for even Satan disguises himself as an angel of light. So it is no surprise if his servants also disguise themselves as servants of righteousness. (2 Corinthians 11:13-15)

"Angel of light"—who would not be deceived, especially if one thought that the last days had come and everything had changed and we were "off the map"? With angels of light you can imagine there would be amazing knowledge and power. It may be that those who are sure they cannot be tricked are most vulnerable to being tricked.

Summary and Conclusion

Realizing the need to write this has not been pleasant, but as a pastor I am obligated to warn and protect the flock God has given me. I intend this also for a wider audience, because our part of the world has already been impacted by the false teaching described in this article.

We are not to be united with departed and perfected saints in heaven. As born-again followers of Jesus, we are indwelt by the Holy Spirit and have the written Word of God to instruct us. We have all we need. And God will bring in His Kingdom in His own time.

To be clear about this, my conviction is that communication with so-called saints in heaven is actually trafficking with demons. It is a base deception to suggest that Christians are to seek empowerment from the saints in heaven.

We are not to seek out departed saints or pray to or worship angels (see Colossians 2:16-20.) In addition, recall that when Jesus taught His disciples to pray, the key words were "Our Father in heaven" and not an "Our angel" or "Our saint." No, we are to be faithful followers of Jesus who are already empowered with the Spirit to proclaim the Good News of the cross and resurrection. This is our work, whether Jesus will return for us tomorrow or in a thousand years.

November, 2009

Essay Four

Healing, Healing, Healing—Is It All about Healing?

A significant part of Jesus' ministry involved healing. The motive for Jesus' healing ministry was compassion. "When he went ashore he saw a great crowd, and he had compassion on them and healed their sick" (Matthew 14:14). In John's Gospel, healing, along with other miracles, were also signs confirming that Jesus was the long-awaited Messiah.

It would seem that an emphasis on healing has taken center stage in many American churches. Some even think that if a church does not have a healing ministry, even specific healing rooms, it is deficient and that there must be something wrong with that church. This does not apply to all Christian churches in the USA, since the healing focus is still largely among Pentecostal and charismatic churches, but healing ministries, along with prosperity teaching, seem to be spilling over into churches that are neither Pentecostal nor charismatically inclined.

Why is this so? The most obvious reason may be that healing draws large numbers of people. It certainly did so in the ministry of Jesus. Many passages from the Gospels could be quoted to verify this. However, simply because an emphasis on healing may attract crowds is not sufficient to justify a healing ministry. No, adhering to biblical precedent and faithfulness is foremost. Our work as Christians cannot be driven by seeming success in terms of "nickels and noses."

Whatever we do must clearly conform to established biblical methodology. My point is that the current popularity of healing ministries is not grounded in Scripture.

MIRACLES, MIRACLES, MIRACLES

People have traversed the globe hoping to see a miracle. This has long been known, and it is not to be associated only with the past. Places like Lourdes in France have been internationally famous for centuries and provide millions of pilgrims with the hope of a cure. Today thousands flock to churches and ministries that focus on healing, often with nothing other than a desire to witness a miracle. Certainly, many either have a need for some sort of healing or have loved ones who do. This is understandable.

Why do people like me then caution against seeking the miracle of healing? Notice the word "caution," as it is not wrong to seek God for healing.

One reason is that abuses may easily occur under such circumstances. People are so eager to be healed that such will be claimed when, in fact, no healing took place. This can be dangerous. Based on what I have found, miracles are claimed without any verification that an actual healing corrected an actual injury.

Another reason is that healing ministries are vulnerable to what I call "mind bending." Healings will be reported when none occurred, simply to support a healer and avoid the emotional conflict associated with cognitive dissonance. Few are able to protest in front of a congregation that is rooting for both the healer and the subject of the healing. Most will simply go along. Standing in the midst of hundreds of people, I would likely "bend" to the obvious will and need of those watching.

And then, not all healings are from the Spirit of God. Jesus warned, "False christs and false prophets will arise and perform great signs and wonders, so as to lead astray, if possible, even the elect (Matthew 24:24). "Signs and wonders" is a phrase often used in the New Testament and included physical healing (see John 4:48; Acts 4:30; Acts 8:4–13). This warning came toward the end of Jesus' earthly ministry, and something akin to it came at the beginning. Consider what Jesus said in Matthew 7:21–23:

> "Not everyone who says to me, 'Lord, Lord,' will enter the kingdom of heaven, but the one who does the will of my Father who is in heaven. On that day many will say to me, 'Lord, Lord, did we not prophesy in your name, and cast out demons in your name, and do many mighty words in your name?' And then will I declare to them, 'I never knew you; depart from me, you workers of lawlessness.'"

Paul spoke similarly in 2 Thessalonians 9: "The coming of the lawless one is by the activity of Satan with all power and false signs and wonders." This depiction of the end of history and the working of Satan would likely involve healing, since we see the phrase "signs and wonders" used here in the very same manner we see it used to describe actual healing by God's Spirit. Satan indeed is a counterfeiter.

A last reason to be cautious about the present, renewed emphasis on healing is that it is a distraction from the central ministry of the Church. Jesus commanded His followers to preach the Gospel in what we call the "Great Commission." He did not command us to go about healing (see Matthew 28:18–20 and Acts 1:8), although the longer ending of Mark 16:9–20 does contain these words: "they will lay hands on the sick, and they will recover" (Mark 16:18). The longer endings of Mark are clearly later additions to the Gospel and not original, but most editions of the King James Version of the Bible do not reflect the lack of early manuscript evidence, so many who rely on that version believe the ending is authentic.

Those who challenge churches that focus on miracles and healing will do so on the basis that there is little or no Gospel proclamation involved. And those intent upon a healing emphasis have dismissed the criticism by insisting that the Gospel is indeed preached along with the healing work. However, after reading the literature, attending meetings, and surveying the many blogs covering the healing efforts, I would deny that the presentation of the Gospel is anything more than a casual mention, and even then it is, in my opinion, not the purpose of the minister to preach salvation.

The primacy of preaching Jesus, His person and His work, is what marks an authentic Christian ministry. One may be healed and yet be unconverted. Witnessing a miracle or being healed is not the same as being born again. However many times someone might be healed, he or she will one day die. Then there is the judgment, and heaven or hell will be the final outcome. Healing is of significance, but, as Paul understood, it is at best secondary: "For I decided to know nothing among you except Jesus Christ and him crucified" (1 Corinthians 2:2).

THE HUNGER FOR MIRACLES

Miracles are addictive—seeing one is not enough. The miracle work of Jesus produced some untoward attention as well. In John 2:23–25 are these very revealing words:

> Now when he was in Jerusalem at the Passover Feast, many believed in his name when they saw the signs that he was doing. But Jesus on his part did not entrust himself to them, because he knew all people and needed no one to bear witness about man, for he himself knew what was in man.

Though many "believed," it is apparent that the believing was not of a saving nature. Saving faith is trust in Jesus alone for salvation and not a cognitive acknowledgment that Jesus is a miracle worker. Thus Jesus, knowing the great desire humans had to witness the supernatural, refused to be caught up in the inordinate excitement.

Ah, to Be a Miracle Worker

During the Jesus People Movement of the late 1960s and early 1970s, many of us did witness miracles, and healing was included in that mix of signs and wonders. For a period of several years I prayed for people to be healed, accompanied by anointing with oil and laying on of hands. The problem for me with the healing ministry was the notoriety it brought. It was overly intoxicating, but it was also short-lived. We watched the healings and other miracles wane, even cease, as the Jesus People Movement ebbed away. The experience of seeing these miracles disappear caused many of us to question ongoing charismatic claims, but I now think that one could even be a cessationist—believing that the charismatic gifts did not survive the apostolic period—and yet believe in healing. (I identified at that time as a charismatic, but I no longer would be considered such in the sense that the word is used today.)

Let it be noted that I am one who is very aware of the power of the devil to imitate miracles and produce counterfeit healings. In addition, I am aware of the power of suggestion, the placebo effect, and the fact that nearly 50% of all doctor's visits have to do with psychosomatic complaints rather than true disease. Even still, I will attest to being a witness to real miracles, including healings.

My concern here is that we do not throw the proverbial baby out with the bath water, that we keep what is biblically faithful and reject that which is not. My view of it is that the instruction of James 5:13–15 is normative for the Church in all ages:

> Is anyone among you suffering: Let him pray. Is anyone cheerful: Let him sing praise. Is anyone among you sick? Let him call for the elders of the church, and let them pray over him, anointing him with oil in the name of the Lord. And the prayer of faith will save the one who is sick and the Lord will raise him up. And if he has committed sins, he will be forgiven.

Some have argued that the letter of James is sub-Christian, a "right strawy epistle" as Martin Luther thought. However, even after considering the historical context lying behind the letter of James, my view of it is that it is not error that we have the small letter included in our canon of inspired Scripture.

Could it be that many biblically oriented Christians have ignored anything to do with healing, de-emphasized it at least, because it has been hijacked and abused by the wealth and health preachers?

Must We Be Charismatic Faith Healers?

When requested, I will yet pray for people to be healed, basing my action on James 5 and the general compassion-based ministry of Jesus. Very few, if any, are healed in these current times. In fact, I rarely even speak of healing. But it is often in the back of my mind that dear people in the congregation are ill and need attention.

Is there a format for healing ministry? Must one anoint with oil and lay hands on the person to be healed? Whose faith is operative, the person who needs healing or the one(s) doing the praying for healing? These questions are difficult to answer. Jesus used no set pattern in healing. Sometimes He healed from a distance, sometimes He simply commanded it, and sometimes He touched, spit, made clay, and so on. If we think certain procedures must be carried out, like oil anointing or hands laid on, we are coming dangerously close to magical thinking. This occult-oriented notion must be strictly avoided. Regarding whose faith is operative or how much is needed, we simply have the words, "the prayer of faith will save the one who is sick" (James 5:15). There is a mystery here, but the one who is prayed to is the One who heals. That much is certain.

Whether or not people are obviously, verifiably healed must not motivate my decision to pray for them to be healed. In the same manner, I will proclaim the grace and mercy of God in salvation, whether people are converted in front of me or not.

A Plea

A simple plea: It is important for me not to break fellowship with my Reformed brethren who may not view things as I do. I am hoping that my willingness to engage in praying for people to be healed will be seen as an intramural debate among brethren, rather than an extramural dispute involving serious breaches of established biblical doctrine.

No one is a healer. I am not a healer. I would not be numbered among the charismatics. But I will pray for healing, because it is God alone who heals. Sometimes, especially in outpourings of the Spirit in awakenings, there are healings. Even in the Jesus People Movement some, but not all, were healed. We did not know why, nor could we predict outcomes, and we refused to blame the minister or the one who needed healing if there was no healing. I repeat, some were healed. That is my testimony. In the years since the Jesus People Movement, during what might be referred to as "normal times," compared to times of awakening, few are healed. Over the last three decades I have prayed for about twenty people, and to my knowledge not one was healed. Maybe it is better to be faithful, biblical, and hopeful than successful; in any case, in light of the current confusion and error regarding healing, I am beginning to reflect on my views and ministerial practices. Thus I am considering including an opportunity for any who would like to have the elders of our church pray for them along the lines of James 5. If I do so, it will not make me a charismatic healer or a quack. And if a healing should occur, then to God be the glory. And if healing is not given, then to God be the glory.

January, 2010

Essay Five

AN 'AWAKENING' CONFERENCE HEADLINED BY STACEY CAMPBELL AND HEIDI BAKER

Venue: New Life Christian Center in Novato, California, March 4–5, 2011.

LOVE NOT FEAR

As March 4 grew near, I began considering not attending after all. I anticipated running into people I knew, and the likelihood of unpleasant encounters made me feel uneasy. This was to be a gathering of Christians who believe that God has sent another spiritual awakening to the Church, but I do not share that view, so clashes would be inevitable. I consider these people to be brothers and sisters in Christ, and for that reason a warning must be sounded. A friend of mine who also monitors the so-called awakening, especially its expression at the Bethel Church in Redding, said, "If you love them, warn them."

It was not my intention to cause trouble or do anything untoward or discourteous. I wanted to see, learn, and experience what was being proclaimed as the last great move of God, heralded by special revelation directly from Him to usher in the Second Coming of Christ. Yes, this is proclaimed as the last generation of the Church in the world, and a select few have been anointed to bring billions of people into the kingdom before it is too late. I must attend!

For twelve-plus years I have been following the leading up to what has now come to Marin County: Mike Bickle and IHOP along with the Kansas City Prophets; the laughing revival and the Toronto Blessing (among other designations) at the Toronto Vineyard Church in Canada with John and Carol Arnott; Bethel Church in Redding, California, pastored by Bill Johnson; and then Morningstar ministries in South Carolina, led by Rick Joyner. A number of times I visited longtime and close friends in Redding, and so attended meetings at Bethel. On one such I heard Rodney Howard Browne and Randy Clark, as well as Bill Johnson.

So now two of the stars of the "awakening" were coming to a theater near me. "Theater"—is this a proper word to use? Perhaps. Let the reader be the judge as I attempt to describe what I saw and experienced.

Attending the Conference

Walking toward the entrance of the church we passed several people out front who allowed us passage, or so it seemed to me. Arriving a good forty-five minutes early, we found seats toward the back. As far as I know, no one recognized me except the people at the table where we got our prepared badges. Maybe I read too much into it, but I was uneasy when one large man moved to a seat very near us and another took a seat directly behind us and did not move or make a sound for the two-plus hours we were there. According to a website, the leaders of the conference were expecting protestors.[1]

At a little after the 7 p.m. start time, the band moved onto the stage. I say stage, since there was nothing physically visible to indicate this as a place of worship. For a little over an hour the band played only two songs, so loud that my wife had to put wads

1 It seems they are expecting, maybe even hoping for opposition, which would also authenticate their being on the forefront of what God is doing with this last generation on the planet.

of tissue in her ears, and the music so repetitious, so empty of content, so boring really, that it reminded me of the music at the Hare Krishna *kirtans* during the hippie years in the Haight-Ashbury. At one point I whispered to her that the words would have fit the worship of any number of gods or goddesses. Overly critical? Maybe, or maybe not.

After the band, Wesley Campbell came onto the platform to introduce his wife, Stacey Campbell, the headliner speaker for the evening. The audience was primed to expect something supernatural.

An Awakening Context

Let me provide a context and rationale for the conference. Through revelations given to specially anointed prophets and apostles, God is supposedly doing something so unusual, so off the charts, and so new that even Scripture cannot be used to evaluate the exciting new anointing. Even the so-called five-fold ministry spoken of by Paul in Ephesians 4 has been restored to the Church, and Campbell and Baker are proclaimed (by someone) to be prophets. The awakening's anointed ones are on the cutting edge of what God is doing in the last days. God is speaking to them directly, with Baker apparently receiving revelation of great things directly from God in person. Stacey Campbell has stated that fellow prophets have estimated the Second Coming to take place in 2014, 2020, or maybe 2030, depending on which prophet you are invested in. This is big stuff, and the authentication for it all are signs and wonders, with special emphasis on healings. And there have been reports of gold fillings in teeth, gold dust appearing on skin, feathers floating down from ceilings (my good friend has one of these feathers, which looks like those used to stuff pillows), and other proofs of the supernatural presence of God and/or angels.

A Look Back at The People's Temple

Such signs and wonders are likely of a supernatural origin, but I seriously question whether these are from God. Let me illustrate this. During the 1970s I was senior pastor of a church that came out of the Jesus People Movement centered in Marin County, which is just across the Golden Gate Bridge from San Francisco. Jim Jones, pastor of The People's Temple in the city, sent a school bus to the parking lot of our church in San Rafael on Sunday mornings, hoping to pack a few more into their services. Some of our folks did take the offer and traveled to the meetings, which we heard were something special and not to be missed. This went on for some time before I learned of it, but the next time the bus driver pulled up, I told him it was his last. Sadly, I was a bit late on this, and after the mass suicide in Jones' encampment in Guiana, there followed funeral services I had to arrange for some whose bodies were shipped back.

On two different Sundays I visited The People's Temple, for much the same reason I attended the Awakening Conference to hear Campbell and Baker—I had to see for myself. To summarize, and not to exaggerate in any way, here are the highlights of what I experienced at that earlier time. One, oil dripped onto open Bibles. Two, the "sweet savor of the Lord" wafted through the air. Three, the brush of angel's wings could be felt. Four, reaching a hand into the air, an angel would grasp it as though shaking hands with you. All these I experienced both times, as did those who accompanied me. And once a young black girl from Oakland, just across the Bay, stood in front of the packed house, and the stigmata appeared—blood oozing from the hands, the ankles, and side of the girl—those places where Jesus was wounded. Signs and wonders? Yes. From God? No. But how then?

As charismatics/Pentecostals we were ill prepared for what we saw. We were taught to believe that anything supernatural was from God. Not that we did not believe in the devil—oh no, we were aware of all that—but we were Christians and therefore were not to be worried. For some reason, we were not aware of passages like Matthew 24:24, 2 Thessalonians 2:8–9, Revelation 13:14 and 16:14—ones that point out that Satan performs signs and wonders also. And we were not acquainted with the passage where Paul taught that Satan is able to transform himself into an angel of light (see 2 Corinthians 11:13–15).

At least during the Jesus People Movement, we were living in an awakening, or so we came to find out after it was all over. America has experienced three confirmed, but I think four awakenings.[2] With the exception of the third awakening, these were accompanied by signs and wonders. Observers marked the Godly nature of them with many conversions—through preaching alone and no altar calls, nor sinner's prayer, nor other mechanisms to secure a decision; and there were healings, even the multiplication of food.

THEY BEGIN AND THEY END

A common characteristic of an awakening is that they begin and they end. Those engaged in these moves of the Spirit do not generally have an awareness of anything unusual—though they are caught up in it, the discovery occurs after the outpouring has passed.[3] This is a significant point in regard to what is now being called an awakening—some assert that this awakening is a continuation of the Jesus People Movement, or if not that, then a new and completely separate awakening that saw its origin in the Toronto Blessing at the Toronto Vineyard Church in Canada.

BACK TO STACEY CAMPBELL

After some banter and generalized talking, Stacey began to defend the awakening against naysayers. She attacked, ridiculed may be a better description, those who hold to a Reformed theology, or to cessationism, or to replacement theology, which would seem to

---

2 I consider the Jesus People Movement to meet the criteria, as set forth by church historians, of what constitutes an awakening. The first, from 1734 to 1742; the second, from 1798 to a. 1825; the third, 1857 to 1859; and the JPM, from 1967 to a. 1972.

3 Soon after this article was posted Earthen Vessel Publishing released *Awakenings in America and the Jesus People Movement* by Kent Philpott. It is still available at www.evpbooks.com or other online sites.

place her and her fellow awakeners into the dispensational camp. It was blatant faction making, a clear "we versus they" mentality: we move in the supernatural; they resist it. She rejected her Plymouth Brethren and Baptist roots as narrow and stultifying. It was like David versus Michel, when Michel was offended at the sight of David's ecstatic celebrating (see 2 Samuel 6). Those who are like David, a man after God's own heart, care nothing for anything that would restrain. Inhibitions are stultifying and to be ignored. This was a common theme of the conference.

Campbell emphasized that what they were doing was big, while everyone else in their small congregations and solemn services were wimpy and to be dismissed. At this the crowd showed some life and applauded, waving their arms about.

Then the prophecies began. I suppose Stacey is considered a prophet as well as a healer. The general content of her prophecies over individuals was that they would be greatly used in the kingdom work; they would have large, national and international healing ministries. As previously stated, she reported that various prophets have determined that the present generation is the last generation, and dates of 2014, 2020, and 2030, among others, have been given for the Second Coming. In addition, those in the last great awakening will be used to win billions of people. Stacey liked to name-drop and put herself at the forefront of what God was doing in the last days. The leaders of the awakening are constantly flying all over the world, attended by large crowds with healings, healings, healings, and with multitudes being saved.

Stacey's husband Wesley joined her when she began to give individual prophecies. As is her trademark, she shook her head violently from side to side while she spoke or rather shouted the words of prophecy and healing into a microphone. (Her words seemed to move rapidly from one topic to another, so it was not always easy to follow all that was being said.) Several times Wesley shouted into his microphone, "Wow!" in reaction to a prophecy about how someone would have a world-impacting ministry.

The end of Stacey's presentation was essentially a long boast of the work of Mike Bickle and IHOP, the International House of Prayer. "Boast" is a word I am not using carelessly here. Stacey apparently is headquartered with IHOP.

HEIDI BAKER

Stacey came on Friday night, but the big anticipation being built was for Saturday night when Heidi Baker would be on stage—a prophetess who speaks directly and frequently with God—conversations which, by the way, take place in heaven. Wow.

That Saturday night, and like any big rock concert, the whole thing was late in starting, and the buzz increased as the minutes passed the seven o'clock start time. A music leader named Sean, whose below-the-shoulder-length curly hair gave the impression he was trying to look like a rock star, led the band. For forty-five minutes he played guitar and sang a song he had written, one song over and over and over with words projected on a screen via Power Point, with the band accompanying. The song was barely passable in my estimation, and less than half the crowd paid any attention to it. During the "worship" there were dozens of little conversations going on in the pews with many people wandering about aimlessly. The only enthusiasm was when Sean led another song with the lyrics "Splish-splash, I'm takin' a bath in the glory" and "I'm swimming, swimming in your love," during which all were encouraged and eager to do a swimming motion with their arms.

Heidi Baker, an attractive blonde in her early fifties, then came on stage. A stage is what it was, as she appeared to be playing the house like a performance artist for the Pentecostal circuit. She lay down or maybe crouched down—it was too dark to know—and began alternately speaking in tongues interspersed with some sort of commentary on her mood and other things that I could not understand. Several times she yelled, "No spectating," apparently to get people to stop watching (gawking?) and start participating. She is engaged in a work in Africa with disadvantaged children, and some of her words may have been from a tribal language.

"Shandababa or Shandabandai" was in every third clause or so, and either this is her favorite ecstatic utterance or it is some entity she calls on constantly.

After twenty or so minutes of this, she stood up and launched into a long story of her life and her healings. To say it was all about her would be an understatement.

"Silly" is a word my wife used to describe Heidi Baker's presentation. It was essentially void of content. She had her fans, however, and they moved up close and sat on the floor in front of the platform to be nearer to her. It was a confused and puzzling presentation over all. For me, it was down right discouraging.

What happened?

It was plain to see that a large number of people, at least two-fifths of the audience, simply sat and listened without engaging in any way. About one-fifth were really into it, waving arms, speaking in tongues, and so on. Some displayed the most bizarre bodily movements, hacking the air as though arms were swords or axes, with twisted motions or uncontrolled body shaking and strange waving of the arms as though they were trying to waft the Spirit to them. Many simply sat with sad, depressed looks on their faces.

Heidi claimed to be seeing or sensing that many diseases were being healed as she spoke. She said that God was doing brain surgery right then and there: things like dyslexia, multiple sclerosis, brain cancer, fibromyalgia, and other physical brain-centered conditions were mentioned, ones whose actual existence and subsequent disappearance would be almost impossible to prove. She offered anecdotes about previous healings of these conditions, but she offered no proof of medical corroboration; some of the stories I had heard before, but with different details. Maybe she gets better results in Mozambique.

There were no feathers, no gold dust, and not much celebration either, unless you call loud country/rock style music celebration. There were no healings announced, and no new revelations were made except to individuals. The name of Jesus was mentioned, some Bible verses were quoted, and the word "gospel" was spoken, but neither Campbell nor Baker preached anything close to the actual Gospel of Jesus Christ.

AN AWAKENING OF WHAT AND FOR WHAT?

An awakening—it was billed as an Awakening Conference—but awakening of what and for what? It seems to me the well is running dry. Getting up the enthusiasm is requiring more work, and it looks like a sort of desperation is setting in. The crowd must be satisfied, rewarded, and motivated with more, more, more. What will be next? What can done for an encore? Headliners are few and not very polished, and the old gimmicks are wearing thin.

Having lived through the Jesus People Movement, having seen many healings (I was once healed myself and without even praying for it or being prayed for), having seen signs and wonders, both of the Spirit of God and of the devil, continuing to believe the gifts of the Holy Spirit are genuine and are still being given (so not a cessationist), and having studied many of the awakenings that have occurred in the Church, I must only conclude that what is here being called an awakening is not. It is a humanly engineered enterprise and will ultimately either come to some scandalous ending or will simply fade away. I am hoping for the latter.

As Christians we do hope to see another awakening in our own time and place, when God pours out His Spirit and sweeps countless numbers into His kingdom. He is sovereign and will do it according to His own good pleasure. And when He does, it will be the real thing.

March, 2011

Essay Six

Tapping into What? Sounding a Warning

The title is intriguing: "Discover your inner superhero at Marin conference." The June 8, 2010 Marin Independent Journal article featured the presentation of speaker Jeff Kripal, a professor of religion at Rice University, at an annual conference to be held at a local Episcopal church. The theme of the conference, "The Intention of the Universe: Our Evolutionary Destiny," echoes well the audience's worldview.

Jeff Kripal has every good intention—encouraging people to step outside their inhibitions and restraints and tap into power within themselves. It sounds good, even appealing and exciting. Power—humans are anxious to have more power and control.

What follows now is one person's opinion, and I am no skeptic—there is indeed a latent supernatural power.

There is a powerful realm beyond the material; it is the supernatural. But not all supernatural spiritual power is godly. Those who are acquainted with various spiritualties know there is such power, and acquiring it is the moving force behind ancient and modern occult practices. Humans have in all ages longed for and sought after this power, sought to be superheroes, both of the good and of the evil kinds. The extreme expressions of this seeking and obtaining power is the dynamic behind so much of what is wrong with our world—the dictators, the tyrants in whatever guise who demand ultimate obedience—historically the destroyers of life and culture.

There is, in fact, a counterfeit spiritual power that is of a demonic nature, and the superhero of demonic power is Satan.

Biblical Prohibitions of Occult Practices

The dark side, also known as the demonic realm, has long worked through particular mechanisms. The most complete list of these is found in the Torah, in one of the books of Moses—Deuteronomy 18:8–14. When the people of Israel came into the land promised to them by God it was necessary to warn them not to engage in the "abominable practices" of the people who were living there. Without this warning, the Israelites would likely have been pulled into the pagan rites and beliefs of their neighbors. Therefore, God said they were not to copy anyone "who practices divination or tells fortunes or interprets omens, or a sorcerer or a charmer or a medium or a necromancer or one who inquires of the dead, for whoever does these things is an abomination to the Lord."

In the ancient Greek city of Philippi once lived a slave girl who was able to divine the future. She earned large sums of money for her masters using this supernatural power. One day a follower of Jesus named Paul, who had considerable study in rabbinic instruction, encountered this fortune teller. Paul said to her, "I command you in the name of Jesus Christ to come out of her." Paul was speaking to the evil spirit that had possessed the girl and had empowered her to tell fortunes. Once the demonic spirit was gone she was no longer able to perform her occult art. To some the psychic ability to foretell the future might have seemed like a wonderful supernatural gift, but it was not that at all—rather it was satanic. (The whole story is in the New Testament book of Acts, chapter 16 verses 16–24.)

As promoted by Jeff Kripal, tapping into latent power in ourselves so that we might get in touch with the presumed future is of a psychic nature and thus fits into what we find in the passages from Deuteronomy and Acts cited above.

Encouraging the Psychic or Paranormal?

The context for Mr. Kripal's ideas are evidenced in the futuristic writings of people like Jules Verne. He is interested in releasing and encouraging the creative juices that he suggests move people toward that which is psychic or paranormal.

The purpose of this essay is to sound a call for critical thinking. There may be more here than meets the eye. Unhappily, an obsessive hunger for supernatural power will not be of benefit in the long run. It may instead prove to be overwhelming, compulsive, and disappointing, besides being spiritually and emotionally dangerous.

October, 2012

Essay Seven

John Bunyan, the Quakers, and Prophecy

In the late 1960s I learned how to prophesy. Among my early teachers were young missionaries sent into San Francisco's Haight-Ashbury District, the center of the Hippie phenomenon, by America's largest Pentecostal denomination, the Assemblies of God. My education in the prophetic picked up by way of the Full Gospel Business Men and the ministry of the Fort Lauderdale Five, as we called them, which consisted of Bob Mumford, Derek Prince, Ern Baxter, Charles Simpson, and Don Basham.

It seemed easy. Close your eyes, lay hands on the subject's head, say "Thus saith the Lord," and proceed with whatever was in your mind, because the next words that came out of your mouth would be from God, or so it was thought. The Spirit would be released by faith.

What I found in my mind were usually stock phrases that I had heard many times: "You will be greatly used of God." "You are one of God's anointed." "You will return to your home and be a mighty witness to your family and friends." "You are to go back to college." "Seek out churches that are moving in the Spirit." "You will be healed of all your diseases." These are a smattering of the words of prophecy I heard over the course of about six months and which I incorporated into my own prophetic ministry, as minimal as it was; however, the larger part of my ministry was healing, and the two seemed to go together.

As time went on I became more specific in my prophetic utterances. "Marry the young man you are living with in sin." "Quit your job and go into full time ministry." "God is calling you to go to South America to be a missionary." "God is telling me you are to cut your hair and stop smoking dope." "You are not spending enough time in prayer." "God wants you to be playing guitar in our praise band." Strange, I thought sometimes, how the prophecies had a great deal to do with the needs of our own ministry and later, our church.

It is painful to recall the manipulating we did in the name of the Spirit.[1] Perhaps I should have known better. At the time it seemed good and right, a kind of short cut in pastoral ministry. Instead of carefully working with an individual, a quick "word of knowledge" or "prophecy" saved a lot of time. There was also an intoxicating sense of being somebody of importance in the kingdom of God—at least at first. Later on, being known as a person anointed with the Spirit meant that some were afraid of me or demanded my time and attention.

My sense of history regarding prophecy at that point was minimal at best. At seminary I became aware of some excesses identified with prophets from the second century and also something similar that happened in Munster, Germany shortly following the Reformation under Martin Luther. Because of the impact the charismatic movement was making during the 1960s, there was also a renewed interest in the history of Pentecostalism. It was not apparent to me at that point that what I was seeing differed significantly from the traditional or historic concept of the

1 At a funeral some years ago a woman I had prophesied over and told that she was to marry a certain man scolded me and announced loudly that the man in question, and with whom she had two children, was in prison for sexually molesting them. All I could say was, I'm sorry. I had by that time realized the awful consequences of my prophetic ministry.

ministry of the Holy Spirit.

I now wish I had known then something of the interaction between John Bunyan and the English Quakers.

JOHN BUNYAN

Born in 1628 in Bedfordshire, England, John Bunyan would become one of the greatest of the Baptist preachers and writers, a fact attested to by all who have read *Pilgrim's Progress* and *Grace Abounding*. He fought in Oliver Cromwell's Parliamentary Army, married after his discharge, and some time later and after a rather dramatic conversion, became known for his strong preaching.

It was in Bedford that Bunyan became acquainted with the Quakers, who believed in the "inner light"—or "inward light"—terms that were developed by George Fox.[2] Fox also would use the more biblically-oriented phrase, "Christ within." He had little respect for the organized church of his day and taught that Christians did not need to have any professionals teaching them, as they each had the inner guidance of the Holy Spirit. For Fox there was no need of any teacher but the Light, and after all, did not Jesus say He was the Light? Fox's influence upon the Quakers was such that, to this day, many Quaker meetings are without teachers or preachers. Members gather and sit in silence and are only to speak when the inner Light moves within them, causing them to "quake" as a sign of the Light's readiness to bring light and reveal the things that the Christ within speaks clearly to them.

John Bunyan, however, did not trust the voices "within." He was only too aware of the voices he had heard within him, voices urging him to sinful behavior. The Quaker response to their critic was that they could indeed trust the voices they heard as the "Christ within."

Bunyan objected that what the Quakers needed to be listening to was the story of the "Christ without," the biblical story of the person and work of Jesus, that God in the flesh had died,

---

2 For more on John Bunyan and the Quakers see *Original Sin* by Alan Jacobs, published by HarperOne.

been buried, and risen from the dead, had ascended into heaven, and was now seated at the right hand of the Father. He knew the depths of depravity in human beings, he knew that the thoughts of the heart are only on evil continually, and that unless solid Bible teaching and doctrine was proclaimed, there would only be darkness and confusion.

In Bunyan's estimation, the Quakers would indeed hear voices within, which they would carelessly assume was the Spirit—they had little or no discernment. He saw them as too credulous and lacking sober suspicion. The Quakers had ignored the fact that there is a spiritual warfare and a "god of this world" who roams about seeking someone to devour, a god who most often uses lies and deception to do his dirty work.

The Quaker response was that Bunyan placed too much importance on the written Word and was therefore guilty of stunting the working of the Spirit—tantamount to a blasphemy of the Spirit—which is very intimidating for those who do not grasp the powerful and permanent electing work of God.

WHAT IS PROPHECY?

Influenced by charismatic/Pentecostal teachers in the late 1960s while I was engaged in what would be called The Jesus People Movement, I thought that prophecy was predictive. Whenever I read "prophet" in Scripture I imagined them doing what I was seeing done and was doing—giving words or direction or encouragement to people. It did not occur to me that the primary activity was a forth-telling of the words of God that had already been revealed. Prophets were preachers, not psychics or fortune tellers. This was not a lesson easily or quickly grasped.

Old Testament prophets looked forward to the coming of the Messiah in both incarnations, the first at Bethlehem and the second which is yet to be. They proclaimed the Word of God. Now Jesus has come, we have our New Testament as well as the Old, and we have all we need. Jesus has given us every bit of direction we need to keep us about our work until that grand and glorious Day of his return.

NEW PROPHETS?

However, the idea developed, even back to the days of the second century, that God speaks words about the future by the Spirit.[3] Recently some have determined that God is raising up new prophets to guide us into the coming last days. Why such direction would be needed is not made clear, but they apparently believe that God is constantly changing strategies and plans.

The John Bunyans among us are not convinced. We hold that the Spirit of God has given us all the information we need to carry on until we see Him in the clouds. In addition, we do not trust the words that come out of the mouths of all the newly anointed prophets that direct this and that and announce this and that. We are far too aware of the error that so easily springs from the heady idea that God has called us to a prophetic ministry and that the words coming from our mouths are the actual words of God. Some of us have had enough experience with false prophecies—up close and personal—to the point that we wonder that maybe we ought to have been stoned to death for our false prophesying.[4]

POWER OVER PEOPLE

What I most enjoyed when I was a "prophet" was the power I had over people. I think it was the neo-Orthodox theologian Reinhold Niebuhr who defined sin as "the will to power."[5] If my prophecy was refused, neglected, or even questioned, these were sure signs of disobedience and lack of a heart for God and His glory. Even when a specific "word" proved by later events to be in error, I had at my disposal a number of reasons, and a "lack of faith" on somebody's part was at the top of the list. Telling people what to do, directing them and guiding them in the ways we thought they

3 Marcion, the Gnostic/Christian, considered himself a prophet with a unique role to play in the church. His movement ended in confusion and scandal.

4 See Deuteronomy chapters 13 and 18.

5 Niebuhr"s understanding of sin is presented in his classic work *The Nature and Destiny of Man*, published in 1941.

ought to go—this was heady and deceiving—however spiritual we might have fancied ourselves.

It was not until many years later that my understanding of prophecy began to change. Though I do not consider myself a cessationist, my view is that prophecy is primarily the forth-telling of the Word of God already revealed to us in Scripture.[6] Though I embrace a Reformed Theology[7] , I can find no clear passage in the Bible that demands I adopt a cessationist point of view.

GENUINE PROPHESY

But I must attest to the possibility that there is a place for prophecy similar to what we find in Acts 11:28 and 21:10. In these two passages we find a man named Agabus, described by Luke as a prophet, who told of a coming famine in Acts 11 and later in Acts 21 warned Paul that he would be taken prisoner if he visited Jerusalem. In regard to the famine prophecy, the believers took it seriously, though Paul went on to Jerusalem anyway, despite the word from Agabus. Nowhere was it reported that Agabus was not a genuine prophet.

It was my experience in the Jesus Movement that there were instances of genuine prophecy and other power gifts of the Spirit, including healings and miracles. This conclusion is based on nothing more than my own observation. In studying other awakenings, I found chronicled miracles of healing along with the presence of prophesying. The exact nature of such is unknown, but my thinking is that God will do what He will do in times when the Spirit of God is moving in power.

---

6 Cessationism says that the gifts of the Holy Spirit, especially the "power gifts," are no longer operative since the completion of the New Testament. For lists of the charismatic or Spirit-given gifts in the New Testament see 1 Corinthians 12 and Romans 12. Some see other gifts mentioned as well, among which is celibacy—1 Corinthians 7.

7 Reformed Theology is otherwise known as The Doctrines of Grace and is associated with the work and followers of John Calvin in the 16th century.

The Need for Critical Analysis

What I see taking place at Bethel Church in Redding, California and other places[8] does not seem to me to be biblically-oriented prophecy. Scanning the many words of prophecy coming out of places like Bethel in particular, but not limited to it, I see the same old patterns emerging that I am familiar with from the early days of the charismatic movement and the Jesus People Movement. It seems to me they are words coming out of the minds of the "prophets" and not words from God. Simply employing the trappings of a prophet—"Thus saith the Lord"—with laying on of hands, even the use of anointing oil, does not make for genuine prophecy.

My sense of it is that much of what we see in the guise of prophecy are misguided attempts to serve God rather than intentional manipulation. Saying that, it may be that I am being too generous. I am no judge and jury, but because I know firsthand the dangers of predictive prophecies, it is wise to be cautious and critically analytical. To do so is not to question God, which is often suggested by those who want to defend their prophetic ministries. The use of intimidation based on spiritual threatening is sub-Christian.

Fear of Men and Fear of God

How difficult it is to be critically aware in the presence of these "ministries." For one thing, there is the desire to please the prophet, especially in a public forum like a service at a church. Few would want to stand out in front of hundreds of people and not go along with what was expected. Failure to react in the right way might bring laughter, scorn, even rejection.

There is also the fear of displeasing or disobeying God. If thousands testify to the God-given prophetic gifts of a person, and all in the name of Jesus, who dares to stand against such overwhelming

---

8 Included here would be Toronto (former) Vineyard Church in Canada, the so-called Kansas City Prophets associated with IHOP, the International House of Prayer in Kansas City, Kansas, and at Morningstar in South Carolina, and other churches and ministries that have aligned themselves with the aforementioned churches and ministries.

pressure? And, however wrongly, a person may also have a strong fear that by questioning the authenticity of a prophet and/or a prophecy they might be guilty of blaspheming the Holy Spirit or at least disobeying direct revelation from God. My experience has been that people who expect God to speak to them through a prophet have little chance of being able to critique the event.

Not All Can Be Like John Bunyan

There have been times I have "gone along to get along," even when I saw that not all was as it should be. John Bunyan was able to stand up against the excesses and errors of his day, and he paid a heavy price for doing so. What if he had capitulated and embraced the messages of the voices who spoke when the quaking began?

To stand against fellow Christians is not easily done. It is more than some can do. I would not care so much, if at stake was something like politics or sports or something else equally trivial in the grand scheme of things. No, we are engaged in spiritual warfare against an implacable and murderous adversary who is relentless and merciless, the "father of lies," who wields the weapons of confusion and deception to turn away many, perhaps even professed Christians, from the Lord Jesus.[9]

With the author of *Pilgrim's Progress*, let us not be too credulous and lacking sober suspicion.

August, 2013

9 Matthew 24:24—"For false christs and false prophets will arise and perform great signs and wonders, so as to lead astray, if possible, even the elect." Also consider 2 Thess 2:8-9 and Rev 13:14 about the work of the anti-christ in the last days.

Essay Eight

The Third Heaven: The Apostle Paul versus Kat Kerr

Paul went to the third heaven. He had a vision—a revelation—and it was not the first time. Here is what he said:

> I must go on boasting. Though there is nothing to be gained by it, I will go on to visions and revelations of the Lord. I know a man in Christ who fourteen years ago was caught up to the third heaven—whether in the body or out of the body I do not know, God knows. And I know that this man was caught up into paradise—whether in the body or out of the body I do not know, God knows—and he heard things that cannot be told, which man may not utter. On behalf of this man I will boast, but on my own behalf I will not boast, except of my weaknesses. (1 Corinthians 12:1–5)

Most commentators think 2 Corinthians was written between AD 55 and AD 57. The vision he described occurred fourteen years earlier, or between AD 41 and 43. This would have been around the time of his second visit to Jerusalem and before his first missionary journey. His third heaven experience would have been, it is speculated, his third vision. A record of Paul's visions is as follows: (1) on the day of his conversion he had a vision of the glorified Christ—Acts 9:3 and 22:6; (2) a vision of Ananias coming to him—Acts 9:12; (3) a vision showing he would minister to Gentiles—Acts 22:17; (4) his vision-call to Macedonia —Acts 16:9; (5) an encouraging vision when difficulty arose in Corinth—Acts 18:9–10; (6) a vision that followed his arrest in Jerusalem—Acts 23:11; (7) a vision during a storm at sea—Acts 27:23; and (8) a vision that gave him insight into understanding the mysteries of Christ—Ephesians 3: 1-6.[1]

It is likely that the report of Paul's vision revealed in 2 Corinthians was the first time he mentioned it. He did so, because some detractors who had come into the Corinthian church were challenging his status as an authentic apostle, thereby at minimum attempting to downgrade the doctrines and theologies Paul preached. Paul's critics, as was the custom, elevated themselves by claiming supernatural knowledge obtained by means of dreams and visions. For millennia, the shamans had gained authority by claiming direct encounters with supernatural entities, and this shamanistic tradition was alive and well in the Graeco-Roman world. It is alive and well in our own day, and shamans continue to enter into a trance state, a soul journey to heaven or hell, in order to bring back information to their clients, which is mostly of a comforting nature.

Reluctantly, Paul describes a vision he had, in order to assert his status and authority as a true apostle of Christ. He does not employ typical shamanistic language, however, nor does he use trance-inducing techniques such as meditation, mind-altering substances, dance, physical deprivations, or any magical devices. His is a distinct vision that fits into what his detractors and the congregation at Corinth would find acceptable.

---

1 It has been suggested that this last vision as mentioned in Ephesians 3 is a reference to the same vision spoken of in our passage in 2 Corinthians. I will not commit either way.

PAUL'S LIMITATIONS

Paul had not known Jesus during the days of His earthly ministry. The apostles in Jerusalem, as well as the general Christian community, had been afraid of Paul, because they knew well enough of his career as their persecutor. Paul had little chance yet to establish himself, whether by personal testimony or through second hand accounts of his dramatic reformation. Being zealous for the work of Christ and for the well being of the churches that he founded, he brought to the table what he could, though at the stage in his career of AD 55 or 57, the Corinthians would have had little information to confirm Paul as a full-fledged messenger of the Gospel. But Paul had been to the third heaven.

A COMMONSENSE VIEW

The first heaven consisted of the clouds and the air that humans breathed. The second heaven held the lights above the clouds - the sun, moon, and stars. The third heaven was where God dwelt - His abode.[2] The foregoing is a generalized way that Jewish people conceived of what was above them. God was above them, far away, and transcendent over them yet with them at the same time.

Paradise was considered the same as the third heaven. Paradise is a loan word from the Persians meaning "garden" and was a reference to the garden where God walked and talked with Adam and Eve. Fellowship restored with the Creator would take place in Paradise, the dwelling place of God.

CAUGHT UP

Paul, referring to himself in the third person and therefore in a humble fashion, was "caught up" to the third heaven. He did not know whether he was in the body or out of the body. He simply did not know. Not too much should be made of Paul's inability

2 Some Jewish traditions report seven heavens, even ten. The use of numbers like three, seven, and ten have special meaning in ancient Jewish beliefs as well as in Scripture and point to completeness, wholeness, and fulfillment. "Third heaven" is surely the very presence of God.

or refusal to be more concrete. The distance between his experience and mechanisms used by shamans for vision questing is very great.

Despite the other visions to which Paul referred (see above), this is the only time he reports being in the presence of God, or in the third heaven. My opinion is that Paul's vision and revelation would be like other visions in the New Testament. For instance, John was "in the Spirit" on the Lord's day when he received what we know as Revelation, the last book of the New Testament (see Revelation 1:9–11). What "in the Spirit" means is uncertain, and it may or may not be the same as a vision.

John was exiled to the Isle of Patmos by Roman authorities. Alone in a cave on a hillside grotto on that island (tradition tells us), he saw things that were heavenly, not earthly. He reports it as though he turned and saw a real life play set before him.

Paul's experience simply happened to him; he did not seek it. It came upon him in much the same way as what happened to John on Patmos. There was no "soul journey" and no mediumistic trance, nor was there a pagan transportation facilitated or attended by spirit guides. Without warning, without expectation, without any means at all, Paul was suddenly seeing that which he would not speak of, even if he had been able. Only God knew how it all took place, which Paul emphatically asserts with the double denial, "whether in the body or out of the body I do not know, God knows."

"[He] heard things that cannot be told, which man may not utter," is one of the more puzzling statements Paul makes as he describes the vision experience. Commonly, commentators suggest four different solutions to explain Paul's meaning. One, he was warned not to speak of what he had seen. Two, he could not find words suitable to describe the incredible content of the vision. Three, it would do harm to do so. Four, to reveal the sum and substance of the vision would make him sound like he had lost his mind. Whichever it was, and the short list may miss it all together, Paul never revealed anything other than the fact of his vision.

KAT KERR AND *REVEALING HEAVEN: AN EYEWITNESS ACCOUNT*

Kat Kerr, a sixty-year-old woman living in Florida and sporting pinkish hair dyed "in obedience" to God's command (she insists), wrote the above titled book. In it she reports not on her visions but upon her direct encounters, including conversations, with "the Father" in heaven's "throne room."[3]

Kerr is radically different from Paul, in that she freely talks about what she sees and hears. There is no hesitancy on her part, unlike Paul. It is apparent that her mission is to communicate what she experienced in her visits to the "throne room."

On one occasion the Father escorted her, via time travel or what some would call 'astral travel', to the very time when Jesus was crucified. She says she was right there at the cross of Calvary; not only that, she was there at the resurrection. Wow, not even the shamans have been as brazen as that!

She visits various persons' loved ones in order to bring back reports on their status in heaven. Here is where she is closely identified not only with the shamans but also with the psychics and mediums of the occult branch of spiritism. Always she reports that the departed are securely saved and well, much to the comfort of the bereaved. In one instance, according to Kerr's testimony, a person who lost a loved one was surprised to hear of that person being in heaven at all.

She reports that every human being has at least one guardian angel that comes to be with him or her at the moment of conception. These angels go with the believer all along the road of life, helping, rescuing, and at death accompanying the faithful departed all the way to heaven. She learned that if a person had done bad things while on earth the guardian angel is owed an apology upon arrival in heaven. Sometimes, however, she says that Jesus personally does the work of escorting to heaven, at least for those

3 Kat Kerr has recorded a number of videos and has uploaded them on YouTube. In the videos she reports on her visits, not visions, to heaven.

who have been especially faithful.

Heaven, she reports, is within the created universe and has streets of gold as John of the Revelation saw.[4]

In so many ways Kerr is biblically sound and presents a standard gospel message, which is firmly in the Arminian stream. She recounts her own conversion experience at age four, then again at age five, when she prayed the sinner's prayer just to be sure.[5] She is of a Pentecostal persuasion, and her rapidly growing audience is primarily among the charismatics and Pentecostals.

A More Significant Concern

It is not necessary to continue detailing the incredible things Kerr reports about her frequent visits to heaven; these can be garnered by visiting YouTube and typing her name in the search field. There are other more significant and dangerous aspects to her ministry.

One, it is a divisive ministry. One either accepts what she says as true or one disagrees and objects. In this latter circumstance it is tantamount to declaring her a false prophet. The Old Testament penalty for 'false prophecy' is stoning; the New Testament settles for simply rejecting the message. As the issue of Kerr's veracity and authenticity is forced into discussion, it will impact congregations and relationships. In some instances husbands and wives will be divided; in others, the leadership of a church may embrace Kerr while others are duty bound to reject the whole business. This is happening right now, since Kerr has caught on in a big way.

Two, acceptance of her ministry opens the door to further connection with spiritism and shamanism, for this is essentially what Kerr is up to. We do not find mention in the New Testament

---

4 In a way, this is troubling since it reduces God to be less than transcendent and seems to violate what Peter said about the universe being destroyed. See 2 Peter chapter three.

5 There is a mystery to conversion, and most mature Christians are aware of false conversion, especially in a culture that is saturated with Christianity. I examine the possibility of false conversion in my book, *A Matter of Life and Death*, Earthen Vessel Publishing, 2014.

of congregations developing such connections or recommending them. The experiences of Paul and John are exceptional and are not anywhere the same as Kerr's.

Three, there is a mind bending process going on. Much of what she details of her visits crosses the line of that which is plausible. If one accepts that Kerr visits heaven, then one is compelled to believe what she reports to happen there despite its unusual nature. With the wide acclaim Kerr is presently enjoying, people will have to suspend skepticism in order to accept the often-bizarre nature of what she proclaims so as to go along with the crowd. Thus comes into play the toxic or cultic mindset. Little by little we can be led astray.

Four, Kerr has a not-so-subtle expectation that others should be or could be doing what she herself is doing: you, too, can visit heaven and talk with the Father, and here's how, so why don't you? Pretty soon Christians are being moved into the occult realm. Talk about a "slippery slope"!

Five, those who are critical in their analysis are ignored or shunned by the suggestion that opposing Kerr is blasphemy of the Holy Spirit. The idea is that if Kerr is critiqued, it is the same as blasphemy or rejection of what God is doing in "these last days."

THE CORE CONTRAST BETWEEN PAUL AND KAT KERR

Paul does not state that he spoke with God—not the Father, not the Son, and not the Holy Spirit—in any mention of a vision he experienced. On the other hand, Kat Kerr does. Herein is the great and telling contrast between Paul and Kerr. Kerr's description of her interaction with the Father is more akin to that of a conversation with a friend than anything else. I think this is exactly what Kerr intends to convey, that she has such an exalted status she is able to be in the very presence of God and talk directly with Him, reminiscent of how Adam and Eve spoke with the Creator God in the Garden of Eden before the Fall (see Genesis 2:15–17; 3:1–19). It is disingenuous for her to state or imply that anyone could do the same.

Paul spoke of the utter transcendent nature of God in his first letter to Timothy: "he who is the blessed and only Sovereign, the King of kings and Lord of lords, who alone has immortality, who dwells in unapproachable light, whom no one has ever seen or can see" (vv. 15b-16). It is true that the Spirit-indwelt, born-again Christian is seated with Christ in the heavenly places, indicating that the priesthood of the believer conveys access to the Father in prayer. It also points to the fact we rest in the finished work of Christ and cease from our efforts of trying to save ourselves. But it does not mean we are presently in the heavenly places. Kerr ignores this standard and historical Christian understanding and claims to actually and repeatedly be in the very presence of God, although God dwells in "unapproachable light." This contrast cannot be ignored.

CONCLUDING CONSIDERATIONS

Kat Kerr is not the first one to claim conscious contact with angels and/or deity. One thinks of Muhammad, Joseph Smith, David Berg of the Children of God, Sung young Moon, and countless others. The claiming of special revelation is standard fare in the spiritual market place.

And where will this all lead? What is next for Kat Kerr? Her reporting is firm and clear, so there are only two responses: she is either spot on or a false prophet. The general Christian community will either face compliance and acceptance or resistance and rejection of her claims. Her followers could develop a new cultic expression within the visible Christian church. She may tone it down some, but due to her published videos and book, it will be nearly impossible to move away from claiming, and reporting, heavenly visitations. Nothing short of a clear confession and repentance will suffice.

It is with a saddened heart that I write this essay. It is crucial, however, for Bible based Christians to stand up and be counted. Fortunately, I no longer identify with the charismatic and Pentecostal movement, because if I still did it would be difficult for me to write this.

We must recognize that everyone who claims spiritual experiences does not have to be accepted and believed. There will be false signs and wonders performed by the power of Satan. This we know about, and the demonic tricks are sometimes played out within the Christian community. Deceptive attacks almost always come from within.

"Watch and pray," Jesus told His disciples that last night in Gethsemane. So we are to watch and pray.

September, 2013

Essay Nine

Charismatic and Pentecostal: An Opinion

I admit it: I am a charismatic and a Pentecostal.[1]

A charismatic is a person who believes in, and/or practices, or has one or more of the "grace" gifts. The Greek word for grace as transliterated from the Greek is *charis*. The word charismatic, then, is an adjective turned into another noun built from *charis*. All but cessationists—those who deny the operation of grace gifts now that the New Testament is published and the age of the Apostles is over—would be classed as charismatics or at least persons believing that the grace gifts are still bestowed on believers today.

A "Pentecostal" usually means someone who, in the tradition of the early part of the 20th century in the Azusa Street Revival (Los Angeles in 1908) to the present, speaks in tongues. Early in their tradition, Pentecostals believed that if a person did not speak in tongues they were not really born again, since the evidence of the indwelling Holy Spirit was tongue speaking. (Some denominations still teach this while most do not.) Pentecostals generally hold that, even if tongue speaking is not evidence of salvation, it is at least something everyone will do if they are truly

1 This essay does not refer to any specific denomination with "Pentecostal" in its title or charter.

seeking after God.[2]

I spoke in tongues from 1968 to about 1980, with the frequency going steadily downhill until finally it ceased completely. During the Jesus People Movement I also received words of wisdom, knowledge, and prophecy, plus consistently had the gifts of discernment (distinguishing between spirits), healing, and miracles. This is no exaggeration; in fact, I am purposefully minimizing my experiences.

Let us look at the grace gifts:

1 Corinthians 12:1–11	Romans 12
utterance of wisdom	prophecy
utterance of knowledge	service
faith	teaching
gifts of healing	exhorting
working of miracles	contributing (in generosity)
prophecy	leading (with zeal)
ability to distinguish between spirits	acts of mercy (with cheerfulness)
various kinds of tongues	
interpretation of tongues	

Many contend, as do I, that Paul cites an additional grace charismatic gift, celibacy. 1 Corinthians 7:6–7 seems to teach this.

LET US TAKE A MOMENT TO EXAMINE THE CHARISMATIC GIFTS.

The cessationist ought to have a problem with the idea that the charismatic gifts are no longer operational, since many of these gifts seem to be in evidence today. Among them are wisdom, knowledge, faith, healing, distinguishing between spirits, service, teaching, exhorting (which means encouraging), contributing,

2 Paul made it clear that even in the Corinthian Church where there was tongue speaking, not everyone did. See 1 Corinthians 12:30.

leading, and acts of mercy. In looking at one of these, acts of mercy, it is apparent to most pastors that some have this gift while others do not. There are observable differences, then, and not only with acts of mercy. Others that I have seen are leading, contributing, encouraging, teaching, and serving.

What the cessationist actually rejects, however, are the so-called "power gifts"—tongues, miracles, and prophecy; the others are ignored or accommodated in some way or another. Prophecy, in particular, is generally misunderstood. It is essentially a forthtelling or proclamation of the Word and Truth of God, which, ever since the publication of the New Testament, is simply the preaching of the Word of Christ. In the Jesus People Movement we used to think prophecy was a "Thus saith the Lord" thing, with the prophet communicating new information. After long exposure to and experience with this form of prophecy, I concluded that the prophet would tend to announce what was in his or her own mind, however sincerely. I thought and practiced in this manner for a decade, much to my regret now.

Being an Actual Pentecostal

Whether one speaks in tongues or does not is of no consequence. If such is necessary for proclaiming the glory of God, then God will supply it.

The real problem surrounding tongues speaking occurs in a congregational setting. As a senior pastor of a fairly large church during the 1970s I ignored the teaching about the necessity of interpreting tongues for the understanding and teaching of the congregation. I also turned a blind eye to the statement of Paul's that there should be only a few tongue-speaking messages (see 1 Corinthians 14:27).

Another significant issue arises in a situation where many people are speaking in tongues during a service. Others who are new to the group may feel expected to join in. I suspect that whatever can be observed, that is, seen or heard, can be mimicked. Frankly, I have seen this hundreds of times. If one wants to be seen as spiritual and have a need to be approved by the group, he or she may well copy or mimic what the others are doing. Then the group will congratulate, approve, and welcome the new tongue speaker into the inner circle of the truly born again.

A kind of cognitive dissonance is operative. There is pressure to speak in tongues, the urging to do so, the prayers offered up for the gift to be granted, only to have nothing happen. Eventually, the tension must be broken, and the result will be either mimicry or abandonment of the whole effort.

I Am Pentecostal

This is my testimony: I am Pentecostal. In has been decades since I have spoken in tongues, but it could come back. No, I will not carry on speaking in tongues with a whole group of others doing the same thing and without interpretation, as it is a complete violation of Scripture. As I have carefully studied 1 Corinthians chapters 12, 13, and 14, I have made every effort to set aside pre-conceived views. I must be more concerned about being faithful to the Word of God than to the traditions of men.

At this present time, in September of 2013, I consider that many gifts of the Spirit abound in tens of thousands of congregations around the world, probably without many of these people even being aware of it. My experience has been that those who least suspect they are being gifted by the Spirit are, in fact, the most gifted.

Here is where I see the real evidence, the most biblically oriented evidence, of the working of the charismatic gifts: in proclaiming the Person and Work of Jesus Christ.

In Acts 1:8, Jesus set His agenda for the Church to continue until His Second Coming: "But you will receive power when the Holy Spirit has come upon you, and you will be my witnesses in Jerusalem and in all Judea, and Samaria, and to the end of the earth." Indeed, when the day of Pentecost arrived, the Apostles spoke in tongues, to the effect that people heard them telling in their own languages "the mighty works of God" (Acts 2:11). Three thousand converts came from the proclaiming of a dozen, less one, preachers.

What were the "mighty works"? They were the old, old story of Jesus and His cross and resurrection. Yes, the Messiah had come and died in the sinner's place. Nothing has changed since then, but when the babbling goes on and on, confused and clamoring, it is not the Spirit of God. It is either human confusion or demonic imitation.[3]

Another Kind of Speaking in Tongues: Prayer Language

It is characteristic of charismatics and Pentecostals to distinguish between speaking in tongues as a prayer language and the speaking in tongues in a congregational setting. It is this latter form that demands interpretation. Let me repeat: if there is so-called speaking in tongues in a group of Christians with an absence of interpretation, then something is wrong.[4]

"Prayer language" is what the lone Christian utters, words that are unintelligible to the human ear but which are supposed to be the indwelling Holy Spirit praying through the mouth of the believer. We are on murky ground here, because the material in support of a private prayer language is not perfectly clear but is open to interpretation. In 1 Corinthians 14:2 Paul writes, "For one

3 Based on Scripture it has been long understood that Satan is capable of counterfeiting the charismatic gifts of the Holy Spirit. This is sad, confusing, and alarming, but nonetheless true. The story of Simon the magician in Acts 8:9–25 is a case in point.

4 No one knows what speaking in tongues looked like or sounded like on the day of Pentecost. It is simply an assumption that what is seen and heard today is the same as what took place then. But it is only a guess, as there were no recordings made. The fact is that many religious groups, and non-Christian groups among them, claim to speak in ecstatic tongues. The phenomenon is not limited to Christianity. Some who so practice are as far from Christianity as could be. Considering the vast and confused spiritual marketplace that has overrun the world, critical analytical thinking is advised.

who speaks in a tongue speaks not to men but to God; for no one understands him, but he utters mysteries in the Spirit." Now this verse is connected with Romans 8:26–27 by most charismatics and Pentecostals:

> Likewise the Spirit helps us in our weakness. For we do not know what to pray for as we ought, but the Spirit himself intercedes for us with groaning too deep for words. And he who searches hearts knows what is the mind of the Spirit, because the Spirit intercedes for the saints according to the will of God.

Here I am not as certain as I would like to be. It was private prayer language in which I most often engaged and which slowly went away without return to this date. I must admit that I am still convinced that this type of spiritual prayer is genuine. The validity of this form of prayer I observed when casting out demons from people during the 1970s, during the Jesus People Movement. This form of prayer caused dramatic reactions from two different people on two separate occasions, about one year apart. These two raised their hands, covered their ears, and said, "Stop that perfect prayer." However, I do not want to anchor the validity of private and personal praying in unknown tongues on the retorts of demonized individuals.

Whether or not the Spirit intercedes for the Christian in the form of private speaking/praying in tongues I cannot say for sure, but either way, it does not violate Paul's concern that, in the congregation, tongues must be interpreted.

Of Greater Concern

The shaman, while in an ecstatic state, claims to go to heaven or to hell to deal with angels, deities, demons, or the souls of the dead. Pentecostal Christians are also claiming to have met with angels, either in heaven or on the earth. Some describe taking a journey to heaven and conversing with angels. Some even claim to have talks with Jesus in the "throne room." These assertions have been made for several years now. One wonders if this is not simply an example of one-upmanship—"I am more spiritual and closer to God that you"—since pride is a powerful motivator, even in the broad Christian community. Or perhaps it is delusion, or trickery, or lying. Who knows, but it is reminiscent of the shaman's "soul journey." Talking with Jesus in heaven—how could this find acceptance with Bible-oriented Christians?

The rationale runs something like this:

Since we are living in the last days,[5] *God is doing something new. We are off the charts now, being so close to the rapture*[6] *and the years of tribulation. The Bible, while perfectly fine, does not cover the final period and so God is speaking with some specially chosen servants directly. God's chosen anointed will communicate what God is saying to the Church. So, why be limited by the Bible when you can go direct? And the Church, the real and true last days Church, becomes those who listen to and obey the words of the chosen anointed.*[7]

And if someone like me questions such assertions, the rejoinder is: "Well, how do you know God is not doing this?" Or, "Aren't you in jeopardy of committing blasphemy against the Holy Spirit?"

Many will retreat if so questioned. They may even be cowed into accepting and joining in. I personally have been confronted with those exact statements, and I found it difficult to give a credible answer. It is like being asked, "Have you stopped beating your wife?" There seems to be no good, at least no direct reply to the accusations.

---

5 We do expect Jesus to return, but no one knows when this will be. Some try to set dates only to find themselves embarrassed and the Christian community is scandalized as a result. There is nothing in the biblical record that reveals even signs of a run-up to the Second Coming. A careful study of Matthew 24 makes this clear.

6 A study of 1 Thessalonians 4:13–18 shows that the "rapture" and the Second Coming are the very same event and not two separate events.

7 This is a formula for the development of a toxic faith, or to put it another way, this is how cults come to be.

TAKING A STAND

It is not established in the New Testament that there will be a time prior to the Second Coming of Jesus that sends us off the charts, requiring direct communication with angels or deity. There is no passage of Scripture that indicates Christians will do this; nothing even close.

The Revelation of John, the last book in our Bible, details the very end of history. In the last chapters of that apocalyptic book are the accounts of the defeat of Satan, the victory of Christ, His return, the celebration of the Marriage Supper of the Lamb, and the inauguration of the Kingdom of God. What began in Genesis is completed in Revelation. What more is needed? The Holy Spirit has not been taken from the Church or individual Christians. When we gather in Jesus' name, He is still in our midst, and He will be with us until the end of the age (see Matthew 28:20).

Then lastly, there are the words of John himself. He gives readers a warning not to add to or subtract from the revelation given to him by Jesus. Such warnings were not uncommon in that era; they served as a kind of an ancient copyright mechanism. John inserted it for a reason, and it is applicable to those who insist that we have moved beyond the Book:

> I warn everyone who hears the words of the prophecy of this book. If anyone adds to them, God will add to him the plagues described in this book, and if anyone takes away from the words of the book of this prophecy, God will take away his share in the tree of life and in the holy city, which are described in this book. (Revelation 21:18–19)

THE ROLE OF FEELINGS IN THE CHARISMATIC/ PENTECOSTAL EXPERIENCE

Since 1968 I have been involved with those who are charismatic and Pentecostal. While not a terribly emotional or feeling-centered person, still I enjoyed the rock and roll bands of my teenage years. My friends knew me as a rather even-tempered person without major highs and lows, emotionally speaking.

During my years as pastor of a charismatic church, increasingly I found myself the odd-man-out. In our services and other gatherings, the "worship time" was the centerpiece, and it was assumed to be the time when God showed up. Feeling good became identified with God's presence. Quiet times, silent prayer, reflective listening to Bible portions, the repeating of creeds, and reciting of prayers we considered to be lame, even sub-Christian. Over time I began to question these assumptions.

Through my pastoral counseling efforts I found that people would be worried if they did not feel good. Emotions of sadness, depression, uneasiness, and discomfort were to be avoided. I began to hear, "Doesn't God want us to feel good?" "If God is present shouldn't I feel good?" "God wants me to feel bad?" "Doesn't God care about how we feel?" "Aren't praise and worship enhanced when we feel good?" And so on.

These are tough questions, especially for the generations that have grown up to think that everything has to do with feeling good. After all, sad is not the goal of life. But from a biblical perspective, both in terms of precedence and warrant, our feelings are pretty much downplayed if mentioned at all. Yes, there is joy, real and legitimate joy, but upon further study it becomes evident that joy and feelings have little to do with each other. Joy can be present in sadness, even despair.

Sometimes I think that feeling good in worship can be an attempt at assuring oneself of salvation. I learned that healing was that way, too. If you are healed, it must mean you have God's gift of salvation. Right? If you feel good this must be a sure sign of genuine conversion? Right?

Paul, in Romans 8:14, speaks directly to the issue: "The Spirit himself bears witness with our spirit that we are children of God." This is what counts. Here there is a gentle but strong assurance of salvation that is not dependent upon feelings. We may be sad or glad, no matter; we may be struggling mightily or rejoicing with "joy that is inexpressible and filled with glory" (see 1 Peter 1:8), no matter.

Growing up into Christ we learn to distrust our feelings and rely instead on the finished work of Christ, both for our salvation and our sanctification. Walking through the "valley of the shadow of death, we fear no evil because God is with us," David said in Psalm 23. We will endure times of distress, pain, and grief, until gladness appears, and this may not come until we are in the presence of God in heaven. It is the inner witness of the indwelling Holy Spirit that we cherish. Feelings come and go, but Jesus is with us until the end of the age. To that I say, Hallelujah.

CONCLUDING THOUGHTS

Why we cling so tenaciously to that which is contemporary rather than to time-honored points of theology and practice is not completely understood. We tend to embrace what is new and exciting, large and loud. If crowds of people are flocking in, this must be evidence of genuineness. Numbers, influence, popularity, and money are the proof of the pudding.

Charismatic and Pentecostal are adjective/nouns still divisive and growing more so as people pray for and earnestly desire the authentic moving of the Holy Spirit in revival and awakening. There is a kind of desperateness apparent, and along with it a rush to sanctify anything that looks like it is attended by miracles. The desire is a good and true one. But it is here in the hunger and the yearning where mistakes are made and well-intentioned people go off the charts, ignore boundaries, and depend on supposed power gifts and miracles as evidence of a fresh move of God. According to Jesus and Paul, we should expect demonically inspired signs and wonders (see Matthew 24:24 and 2 Thessalonians 2:9–11, among others). Maybe some of us who lived through the Jesus Movement and who had to deal with the dark aftermath of it may have a helpful word to speak here. This is what I am hoping to do in this essay.

September, 2013

Essay Ten

SARAH YOUNG AND *JESUS CALLING*

Sarah Young practices "listening prayer," in which she hears messages directly communicated from Jesus. It is a technique she describes in her bestselling book *Jesus Calling*, which has sold over 9 million copies in 26 languages. This book is the 5th bestseller for the first half of 2013 for all books, not just Christian books. Through it all, the author maintains a low profile, partly due to physical disabilities, and thus she is relatively unknown. She has experienced chronic physical difficulties for many years and writes inspiringly of her loving connection with whom or what she thinks is Jesus; the messages comfort and encourage her.

HOW DID THIS START?

It all began with Sarah wondering if she could receive messages during times of prayer. She hoped God would talk to her personally. And it began to happen. And yes, she believes that Jesus is really and actually speaking with her. She prays then listens, and He answers. This has been her experience for many years.

As she hears she journals what she hears, and after a number of years she published some of what she heard. (She does note that when Jesus says things that are not biblical, she does not record them.) Readers and prayer groups are encouraged and comforted by the messages, and as sales of books demonstrate, she has a growing audience. Many thousands are now taking up the practice of listening prayer.

THE KEY QUESTION

The key question which must be asked is, who is speaking? Is it possible there is a clever demonic counterfeit here?

Over the centuries Christians have thought that God does speak to them. Richard Foster, who champions contemplative prayer or meditative prayer, defends Young's practice. He has modeled his own recommendations for deep meditation and contemplation on what Theresa of Avila, St. John of the Cross, Ignatius Loyola, and many others practiced and experienced centuries ago. What Young does is the same as or quite similar to the exercises of these so-called Christian mystics.

Sarah Young describes her own custom as meditating on Scripture and then waiting quietly to hear a reply from Jesus. When Jesus speaks she writes down what she heard or was placed on her heart. The words or messages are not revelatory in the sense of prophecy or fortune telling, she insists; the content of the messages are fairly ordinary and biblically based. The Bible plays a major role in Sarah's life, and she firmly believes it is the inspired revelation of God. However, and it is a huge however, she wanted more than what the Bible offers. She indeed got more and has come to rely on these communications, the "encouraging directives from the Creator," as she likes to say.

A TROUBLING TWIST

But there is a worrisome twist. When Young journals the words spoken by Jesus they are written in the first person with Jesus as the person speaking. It is not, "Jesus said," rather it is, "Focus on me." Since she purports to write down whatever Jesus says, readers of her book must conclude that her journal is as authoritative as the Bible, almost a fifth Gospel. If this is not so, then *Jesus*

Calling is a false writing, an imitation, albeit very clever, of a revelation from God.

Young's error then is serious and similar to that of the *Course in Miracles*, supposedly communicated by Jesus to Helen Schucman in the 1970s. Schucman's Jesus dictated profoundly spiritual concepts to her, which she wrote down, and one of the most successful new age cults was born. Schucman's Jesus bears little resemblance to the biblical Jesus, unlike Young's Jesus, but could this make the counterfeit even more difficult to detect?

Young's book sales are phenomenal, and again I cannot help but be reminded of Helen Schucman and the *Course in Miracles*. As I study *Jesus Calling* I do see a difference in the two books. Young's book is far more biblically Christian than Schucman's. The difference is clear, and I am tempted to embrace Young's claim to hear the voice of Jesus. But it will not work. There is neither biblical precedent nor warrant for quieting oneself, praying, and then listening for Jesus to speak. This is perhaps the most serious and dangerous counterfeit to be found in the broad spectrum that is Charisma today.

The Jesus supposedly speaking to Sarah Young is very affirming and encouraging, but little else. The messages lack the doctrinal content of the real Jesus found in Scripture. In fact, when one orders one of Sarah's books on Amazon.com one sees that those who bought Sarah's book also like the books of Joyce Meyer and Joel Osteen—purveyors of the health, wealth, and prosperity gospel. Sarah's Jesus is more like a warm fuzzy teddy bear.

WHAT DOES GOD PROMISE?

Let me note that nowhere in Scripture does God promise to speak individually to believers or answer prayer by speaking directly to the one praying. This is the critical point. What I discovered in my decades of ministry is that, if you want to hear audible things from God you will, eventually. But the communication is not from God, however real and spiritual the communication might be.

John 10:27 is quoted by proponents of Young's book as proof

that Jesus speaks directly to His '"sheep." "My sheep hear my voice, and I know them, and they follow me." To "hear" is to know Jesus as the Good Shepherd as distinct from a false shepherd or a wolf; the literal application of "hear" does not work here. It is the Holy Spirit who indwells the believer at conversion who "bears witness with our spirit that we are children of God" (Romans 8:16).

An instruction for believers to listen for the actual voice of Jesus is foreign to the New Testament writings. There is nothing in Scripture about praying then listening for a response. It is surprising that so many do not know this. Churches across the country have "prayer" groups devoted to Young's methods. It illustrates the fascination with feelings and direct experiences rather than seeking to learn what the Word of God actually teaches.

God's Way

We are all hungry to know more of God, and little by little we do grow up into the fullness of the stature of Christ (see Ephesians 4:1-16). Following Jesus is a lifelong process and there are no short cuts. Quick and easy methods of "going direct" to the source can be addictive and difficult to disengage from. Christians, yet sinners and living in a sinful world, are pilgrims on a road that is straight and narrow and often filled with pain and sorrow. God hears our prayers, strengthens and comforts us, but speaks to us through the Scripture. That is enough for us. We do not need more.

October, 2013

Essay Eleven

Charisma: The Fourth Branch of Christianity?

Christianity is traditionally divided into three main branches: Roman Catholic, Eastern Orthodox, and Protestant. Without going deeply into the whys and wherefores, it will be enough to say that this essay recognizes the distinctions. While there are doctrinal differences among these three, their core theologies are surprisingly similar.

This essay suggests that there is now emerging a fourth branch of Christianity, which I am referring to as Charisma. Another way to designate this fourth branch is charismatic/Pentecostalism.

Charisma

The apostle Paul lists the gifts of the Holy Spirit in Romans 12 and 1 Corinthians 12. In the Greek text the word translated "gifts" is transliterated as charismata. From this we get both "charismatic" and "charisma." Most commonly, a charismatic is a person who speaks in tongues and accepts all the gifts of grace.

Some Christians are cessationists, viewing that the writing of the New Testament and the death of the Twelve Apostles ended the need for and viability of the charismatic gifts of the Holy Spirit in the life of the Church. Their belief is that these gifts are no longer operative and therefore are not seen.

In marked distinction, some Christians are continuationists, believing that the charismatic gifts never ceased and are yet operative in the life of the Church today. This belief lies at the heart of the idea that there is emerging, or has already emerged, a fourth branch of Christianity.

Semis

Some Christians, like me, are semi-cessationists or semi-continuationists. To clarify, I think that during times of awakening, when God pours out His Holy Spirit to sweep many into salvation, the charismatic gifts of the Spirit may be in evidence. But during "normal" times, which are most times, the gifts are more rarely observed.

At the church I pastor we pray for people to be healed and follow James 5:14: "Is anyone among you sick? Let him call for the elders of the church, and let them pray over him, anointing him with oil in the name of the Lord." We do this on Sunday evenings and also give an opportunity for deliverance, which is when demons are cast out of those who understand their need for this ministry. No one that I know of speaks in tongues at our services, and we don't have much of a praise band, so we are fairly tame. "Semi" is the right word for me.

Moving in the Flow of the Spirit

There are large and growing numbers of Christians world-wide who claim to be "moving in the flow of the Spirit." They further claim that God's Spirit is being poured out on all those who are open to it. This predominantly occurs in charismatic/Pentecostal churches, but not solely.

During the Jesus People Movement of the late 1960s and early 1970s I was a charismatic. We saw the miracles, we spoke in tongues, we had prophecies, and we had healings by the hundreds. Now, we did not understand that we were right in the middle of a national awakening and that all over the country similar things were happening. We flattered ourselves in thinking we were part of a special elite group of spiritual commandos taking the world for Christ. We had power, spiritual power, and we could not seem to help thinking more of ourselves than we ought to have.

The movement came to an end in 1972 or somewhat later, depending on where you were. But this insight was hindsight, as we did not learn of this until decades later. It was almost panic time when the conversions dramatically slowed and the healings were few and far between. What happened? Who took the power away? What will we do now?

Since we were flexible, we learned how to infuse people with excitement like in the good old days, and we accomplished it mostly through music. No, I am not against praise music. To this day, decades later, I still play the guitar and lead a kind of praise band, but we sing solid Jesus-centered songs and don't get carried away with the beat of the drum and a cranked up amp. We play and sing for short periods with nothing like the now famous 7-11 routine, that is, seven words sung eleven times for at least a half hour.

More, More, More

More is what so many want. Many want to experience more of God, they want to be touched by His power, and they want the power to heal and do miracles. Sitting quietly in the pews listening to doctrinal sermons from uninspired preachers simply will not do. They want moving, shouting, falling, soaking, shaking, burning, and prophesying— charismania. They want more!

And more is what they are getting. It is all over YouTube from IHOP in Kansas City, Morningstar in South Carolina, and the Bethel Church in Redding, California. Young people, who have largely vacated the churches of the three branches, are present and fully engaged in intense activity. It is very compelling.

Why Not Us?

If Charisma is enjoying incredible success, why don't the rest of us get on board? We would, but we sense something is wrong, and it is not merely jealousy or envy or because we are stuck in our ways. Neither is it a rejection of what God is doing by the power of His Holy Spirit.

We sense something wrong in the craving for more. We think it opens the door to deception.

We see disproportionate attention given to the Holy Spirit, or what is thought to be the Holy Spirit, while the Trinity, as a complete entity, is ignored. Father and Son seem to drop out of sight or are only peripherally mentioned. We cannot but notice Jesus' teaching in John chapters 14, 15, and 16 to the effect that the Holy Spirit will glorify Jesus; the Holy Spirit will not glorify the Holy Spirit.

We are dismayed at the notion that the Scripture is no longer authoritative for both practice and belief, for that is the implication in the claim that we are "off the charts" or that we can receive truth directly from angels, Jesus, or even the Father.

We smell a mediumistic odor here, emanating from the mouths of those who sway seekers into avoiding their Bibles in favor of rolling on the floor straining to hear the actual voice of God in their entranced ears. To many of us this is repulsive and even demonic.

"OFF THE CHARTS"

Off the charts—this is the new phrase that opens the door for the prophets and prophetesses and others who claim God, angels, or whatnot, are speaking to them and revealing the future in "these last days."

The rational is that due to the nearness of the end, the coming rapture and tribulation, God is revealing things that are not in the Bible. Questions like, "How do you know He is not?" and "How can you be so certain this is not happening now?" are frequently heard. You can expect these folks to say that the admonition not to add or subtract from the Book of Revelation (see chapter 22:18–19) is merely an ancient form of copyright and is not applicable to these times.

On this particular point, that the admonition not to add or subtract applies only to Revelation and not to the rest of the Bible, an examination of two other passages shows this idea to be faulty. First, Deuteronomy 4:2: "You shall not add to the word that I command you, nor take from it, that you may keep the commandments of the LORD your God that I command you." Second, Deuteronomy 12:32: "Everything that I command you, you shall be careful to do. You shall not add to it or take from it."

Despite the obvious, those who are already trapped into the commitment to believe the "lying prophets" will find it difficult to turn from them and expose them.

A final statement on this issue: Revelation 22:18–19 may be in fact an ancient form of stating, "Don't touch this writing," and legitimately so, as it is a thoroughly biblical warning. In addition, the attempt to justify "new improved truth" and revelations by contemporary prophets ignores the fact that the Book of Revelation brings us right up to the grand finale, right to the Second Coming of Christ, the Day of Judgment, the Marriage Supper of the Lamb, the new heaven and the new earth—there is no more history, only forever in the presence of God. And Revelation perfectly corroborates both what Jesus said in Matthew 24 and Paul in 2 Thessalonians 2.

Sarah Young, Kat Kerr, Patricia King, Lorna Byrne, and Many More

Jesus is talking to people now, like He is on the other end of the phone; Kat Kerr gives instant messages about what she just heard the other day directly from God; Patricia King is in on it as well, receiving messages from the Source. And one of these King predictions is that we are going to be experiencing a whole lot of contact with angels close to God, who will be revealing things. Though in a bit of a different category, the Irish lady Lorna Bryne is constantly, minute by minute, in touch with all sorts of angels and souls. And those who read books by these folks want to have such exhilarating experiences too.

It is all okay, because we are off the charts. The Bible is not needed now; all we need is an angel, a direct call from Jesus, or even a chat with the Almighty in the "throne room" to find direction, comfort, and wisdom.

Give Me that Old Time Religion

Worship for many of us means gathering together with other Christians to pray, sing, study the Word, hear the Word proclaimed, and enjoy fellowship with each other. We love reciting the Lord's Prayer, saying the Apostles' or the Nicene Creed, listening to prayers written by brothers and sisters long gone, and thinking through what our God means to us. We do not think we have to "experience" God, especially since there is nothing in the Scripture that teaches us to do so. It is a life of faith and service, sacrifice and giving, prayer and praise. It is decent, orderly, respectful worship of the Triune God, Father, Son, and Holy Spirit.

Unity, and if Not, Respect

We do not need a gigantic organization that enfolds all the world's Christians. There is no need, and it simply will not happen until, and there is an until, the kingdom of God comes in all its glory. Then there will be unity.

Respect is what we can hope for. Respect for each other, however many branches there may be, respect that comes from the fact we all worship the same God—the Father, the Son, and the Holy Spirit. And in that sense of respect, we can learn from each other out of humility. We can critique, evaluate, repent, confess, ask for forgiveness, and work together, even with those whom we consider a little off track in terms of doctrine.

The enemy who wars against Christ's Church loves to divide and conquer. An elitist attitude divides. The thinking, "I have more of the Spirit than you do" divides. When Jesus is not the center of worship and praise, then there will only be splintering and factioning, not unity.

February, 2014

Essay Twelve

THE ANOINTING. THE ANOINTING. THE ANOINTING.

The Anointing—this is the whole thing, isn't it?"

That is what I heard Paul Cain say some ten years ago at a nearby Pentecostal church.

Reverend Cain is a big name among the so-called Kansas City Prophets, along with a number of others like Bob Jones, Mike Bickel, Rick Joyner, John Paul Jackson, Francis Frangipane, Lou Engle, and James Goll. The Apostolic-Prophetic Movement,[1] sometimes known as the Third Wave, was to be the re-establishment of the Five-Fold ministry of apostle, prophet, evangelist, pastor and teacher as found in Ephesians 4.[2] These leaders see themselves

---

1 C. Peter Wagner is often recognized as an "apostle" in the recreation of the "Five Fold Ministry," and by virtue of his position as a professor at Fuller Theological Seminary in Pasadena, California, and his part in launching the Church Growth seminars at Fuller (of which I was a part), he provided prestige and clout to the fledgling "Third Wave" revival.

2 Rather than five ministries of apostle, prophet, evangelist, pastor, and teacher, many combine pastor and teacher, since the two are joined by the Greek co-coordinating conjunction *kai* meaning "and." More correctly, it is the four fold ministry. And it may be noted that, while these ministries or offices may not always have been formally established,

as part of the reconstitution of the fabled biblical model meant to operate in the "last days." And for such a grand vision a special and super powerful anointing would be required.

RODNEY M. HOWARD-BROWNE

I was wondering then if the anointing Cain talked about was the same that Rodney M. Howard-Browne purportedly brought to America from his home in South Africa. It was Howard-Browne who strongly influenced the "revival" that came to the Toronto Airport Vineyard Church in Canada in the 1990s. It was there that Randy Clark received the anointing from Howard-Browne and spread the "fire" of the revival.

Howard-Browne, in his books *Flowing in the Holy Ghost* (FHG) and *Flowing in the Holy Spirit* (FHS), describes that anointing.[3] It is essential and necessary to define what Howard-Browne means by anointing as presented in the two books mentioned above.

In FHG he says, "the anointing is the presence of God"... "that will come and begin to touch people" (p. 13). "I wait for the unction all the time; I wait for the burning of the Spirit of God within. That burning, that churning, bubbles like a boiling pot inside, because that's what the word 'prophesy' means" (p. 14).

Howard-Browne says, "you must stir yourself up for the gifts to begin to operate" (p. 14). Therefore, after stirring, "it will happen automatically. God will begin to move" (p. 15).

In a section labeled "When the Anointing Falls" he says, "I began to speak supernaturally. I became another person! . . . It's almost like I'm standing outside my body, hearing myself prophesy. . . . People begin to shake and fall out under the power of God in their seats as the word of the Lord comes forth. No one touches them" (p. 31). He goes on: "You can't say, 'I'm going to get up and prophesy now.' However, you can prepare for the anointing to prophesy. You do this by stirring yourself up, by preparing your

---

they have never been absent in the long history of the Church.

3 The two books are virtually identical in content, having only minor variations and additions. To read one is to read the other.

heart, and by waiting on the Spirit of God. Then, when the anointing comes, you flow with it. But you can only prophesy when the anointing comes!'" (p. 31).

Randy Clark

Not everyone got the anointing, not even those who actually touched Howard-Browne. Randy Clark, who had reportedly gotten the anointing, was also able to pass it on to others, or so it was claimed. Clark was in Toronto, too, and people touched him; and some got it, but most didn't.

A contingent from our local ministerial association visited Toronto, and after they returned we gathered in a meeting. There we were, expecting something big. But even for those who got close to the "anointed" people and even touched one of them, nothing happened. Though disappointed, we planned another trip.

I saw Randy Clark personally some years back now in Redding, California, when he visited the Bethel Church pastored by Bill Johnson, whom I guessed had gotten the anointing as well. The anointing was power, and power was what it was all about, the power to heal and do miracles. Many members of Bethel had miracle stories to tell: crowns of gold on teeth; gold dust in their hair; feathers mysteriously floating down from the ceiling; people raised from the dead (none were confirmed); people with stomach and back pain, healed; folks with chronic migraines, healed; youth who smoked pot and were popping pills, healed on the spot. Oddly, the people I was with and who were members of Bethel, both with some serious bodily ailments, were never themselves healed, nor did they know anyone personally who had actually been healed. The miracle stories circulated around town, one here, one there, but somehow the ones healed could not be located. This was no doubt a miracle, too.

Do I sound irreverent or judgmental? Am I being a God mocker and thus in danger of committing blasphemy against the Holy

Spirit?[4] Could I be standing against the flowing of the river of the Spirit now moving in these last days? Am I foolishly, even rebelliously, refusing to ride the wave? Frankly, these kinds of mind-think, conformist charges are enough to satisfy and shut-up most questioners, but not everyone is falling in line or is so lacking in confidence in the saving grace of Jesus that they stop thinking and evaluating.

Cain's Anointing

Paul Cain rambled on for an hour and finally stated he was about to reveal the bigee, the real deal, the ultimate, that one great thing that meant absolutely everything. Wow, the anticipation; it was palpable. Cain moved toward the front of the stage. He stood stone still. He stretched out his left arm, his brown eyes scanning the congregation, while we waited without a sound. And then it came, what we were all waiting for: "The Anointing. The Anointing. The Anointing." He said it was the anointing.

To demonstrate the anointing he stared at a number of the faithful sitting in the front row.[5] One by one he described what would happen to them in the future, essentially telling their fortunes. He said he saw a television set type thing over each one's head and could watch their futures unfold before his very eyes. One would be a great prophet in Africa. Another would be greatly used of God in Asia as a healer. One young lady would found a school for orphans in South America. Without exception each person would do something great and wonderful in the kingdom of God. Cain could see it on the television screen. It was the anointing that made it all happen.

---

4 *The God Mockers* is the title of a book written by Stephen Hill who was the principle evangelist for the Brownsville Revival in Pensacola, Florida during the mid-1990s. All those who rejected the idea that it was a genuine outpouring of the Holy Spirit he so labeled.

5 I had gotten in place early and was a little surprised to see ushers bring in a group of people and seat them in the row directly in front of the platform. The reason for this became clear later on.

Kundalini and Shaktipat

Over the years I've talked with a number of so-called prophets and healers who spoke like Howard-Browne. A burning power rising up in their bodies that gave them power to do miracles was how it worked. During my days in the Jesus People Movement when we did see miracles, I never experienced or heard anything like what Howard-Browne described. However, I had and actually continue to have conversations with those involved in various spiritual practices that do sound like Howard-Browne's anointing. I turned to Wikipedia for the material I suspected I would find:

> Kundalini is described within—eastern religious, or spiritual, tradition as "an indwelling spiritual energy that can be awakened in order to purify the subtle system and ultimately to bestow the state of Yoga, or Divine Union, upon the 'seeker' of truth." "The Yoga Upanishads describe Kundalini as lying 'coiled' at the base of the spine, represented as either a goddess or sleeping serpent waiting to be awakened." In physical terms, one commonly reported Kundalini experience is a feeling like electric current running along the spine.
>
> Kundalini can be awakened by *shaktipat*—spiritual transmission by a Guru or teacher—or by spiritual practices such as yoga or meditation. Sometimes Kundalini reportedly awakens spontaneously as the result of physical or psychological trauma, or even for no apparent reason.
>
> One man said he felt an activity at the base of his spine starting to flow so he relaxed and allowed it to happen. A feeling of surging energy began traveling up his back, at each chakra he felt an orgasmic electric feeling like every nerve trunk on his spine beginning to fire. A second man describes a similar experience but accompanied by a wave of euphoria and happiness softly permeating his being. He described the surging energy as being like electricity

> traveling from the base of his spine to the top of his head. He said the more he analyzed the experience, the less it occurred.
>
> Kundalini can also awaken spontaneously, for no obvious reason; or it can be triggered by intense personal experiences such as accidents, near death experiences, childbirth, emotional trauma, extreme mental stress, and so on. Some sources attribute spontaneous awakenings to the "grace of God," or possibly to spiritual practice that occurred in past lives.
>
> The popularization of Eastern spiritual practices has been associated with psychological problems in the West. Psychiatric literature notes that "since the influx of eastern spiritual practices and the rising popularity of meditation starting in the 1960s, many people have experienced a variety of psychological difficulties, either while engaged in intensive spiritual practice or 'spontaneously'".

I could go on, but I think the above is enough; however, one last observation might be of value. On the fourth page of the Wikipedia article on Kundalini is a section with the heading, "Physical and psychological effects." In brief, I list some of the items which are referred to as "Kundalini syndrome":

> Involuntary jerks, tremors, shaking, itching, tingling, and crawling sensations; energy rushes or feelings of electricity circulating the body; intense heat (heating) or cold; trance-like and altered states of consciousness; disrupted sleep pattern; loss of appetite or overeating; mood swings with periods of depression or mania.

The Quest for Power

Certainly Howard-Browne and any of the Kansas City Prophets and those associated with Rick Joyner of Morningstar in South Carolina, Mike Bickle of IHOP in Kansas City, Bill Johnson at Bethel

Church in Redding, California, or anyone else associated with the Third Wave would not knowingly embrace anything to do with Kundalini or Shaktipat, but there is an obvious association if not direct connection. That association could well be the quest for power.

Power, the one great and overriding drive behind the occult, is the great lure. So much of the tragedy of humanity has been the direct result of a striving to acquire and retain power. The quest for magical powers to heal drives shamanism and religions like Santería. Neo-pagan religions like Wicca also focus on power to heal and perform magic. How thin the line is that separates the occult and pagan from the biblically orthodox.

Anyone who has either read of or experienced firsthand a great moving of the Holy Spirit desires to see it happen again. Most of the time we have the normal Christian experience. Awakenings and revival come and go according to the will of God. But this is not enough for many who need more, more, and more.

Certain people think it is possible to force or precipitate a revival or awakening. It is not too difficult to "work up" a crowd of charismatic/Pentecostals, but almost any group of people immersed in pulsating music, expectations of miracles, and high excitement from a dynamic preacher can interpret their experience as a genuine move of the Holy Spirit. We must never forget that in authentic Christianity Jesus Christ and Him crucified is front and center.

Off the Charts

But then I think: no, wait a minute. These guys up in Redding at Bethel and in Kansas City say we are "off the charts." Their prophets declare that these are the last days and the Bible is not so important anymore. After all, many are conversing with angels now, even big name angels, some speaking directly with Jesus as one would in a phone call;[6] people like Kat Kerr are going direct

6 This is what Sarah Young does in her book, *Jesus Calling*.

to God, bypassing angels all together. Yes, face to face meetings with the Creator of heaven and earth in the "throne room" to get the real scoop for the last of the last days. Apparently, we are right up there at a few seconds before midnight on the great cosmic clock. Wow, I'm a believer!

Going Corporate?

Am I making fun? Yes I am to a degree, in order to highlight the ridiculousness of the whole thing. And one wonders, what comes next? I mean, how can miracles be topped? After hearing from God personally and getting the definitive word about the wrap-up of history from the Big Guy, everything else seems second rate, not to mention a waste of time. A Christian friend living near the Bethel Church in Redding and who has followed the whole enterprise up to the present day said to me last month that there has been a shift into a "corporate" mode to fill a possible void, and by that he meant the selling of product—everything from worship music, dietary supplements, t-shirts and other kinds of clothing, paperback books, and who knows what else will these entrepreneurs come up with? God help us.

Is it possible for the newly and self ordained apostles and prophets to change course? Think of the humiliation, the embarrassment, the decrease in salary, invitations to speak drying up, the rejections, the falling book sales, the payments due on the improvements to the property, the silence of the crowds? What do you do—retire, repent, step down, and confess, with your whole life exposed as a fraud? What do you do after making shipwreck of your faith and that of many thousands of others' faith as well? Here is where the miracles are needed.

Closing Comment

I am one who has made major errors in my life and ministry, and from these I am yet greatly pained and will be until I get home. Indeed, the sufferings of this present time, whether the result of the Fall or my own rebellious folly, are not worth comparing with what God has prepared for us. My repenting will last my whole life, and though I may be embarrassed in certain circles, yet I take confidence that all my sin has been atoned for through the shedding of the precious blood of the Lamb. Thus it is with confidence that I continue following Jesus and rejoicing in the ability to yet be a servant in His kingdom. The audience, after all, is not in the pews but in heaven.

July, 2014

Essay Thirteen

The Testimony of Jesus Is the Spirit of Prophecy

Many self-proclaimed prophets like Mike Bickle and Kris Vallotton insist they are hearing words from God. For instance, "God is going to do something big in our church." "You are going to have a music ministry to the nations." "God is raising you up to be a pastor of prophets." "You will be greatly used of God to speak truth to the nations." "Your healing ministry will go international." "The peoples of the world will be blessed through your prophetic words." "You will father nations and kingdoms." These are stereotypical of the kinds of prophesying one will hear during "ministry time" at churches and conferences with NAR-aligned people.

And it is not acceptable to "touch an anointed" prophet either, thus the "word" from God must go unchallenged.

A Fundamental Error

Revelation 19:10 is used by some to give Biblical legitimacy to the prophetic words coming from the mouths of those holding the office of prophet amongst NAR aligned churches and groups. The assumption is that Jesus, in these last days, is speaking through His prophets.

The last sentence of Revelation 19:10 reads "For the testimony of Jesus is the spirit of prophecy" (ESV). The passage overall is about the marriage supper of the Lamb. John is speaking about what will come to pass at the triumphant return of Jesus. The messenger assures John he has heard "the true words of God." John begins to worship the messenger/angel but hears the messenger say, "I am a fellow servant with you and your brothers who hold to the testimony of Jesus. Worship God."

"The testimony of Jesus." This is the witness that followers of Jesus present to others in fulfillment of the great commission, as found in Matthew 29:19–20. It is a bold proclamation of the timeless Gospel of Grace. It is the broadcasting of the person and work of Jesus Christ.

New Testament prophets present the testimony of Jesus. The prophets are the preachers. Those who testify about who Jesus is and what He did are prophets. The witness is one who testifies and preaches. Nothing new need be added; the Scripture gives us all that is necessary.

The "spirit of prophecy" is the God-ordained, Holy Spirit-blessed, and inspired word of the victory of Jesus on the cross, His resurrection, His ascension, and His continued empowering of His Church. Prophecy is preaching and not giving a word such as, "you will father nations."

The writer of Hebrews is very clear on this point: "Long ago, at many times and in many ways, God spoke to our fathers by the prophets, but in these last days he has spoken to us by his Son, whom he appointed the heir of all things, through whom also he created the world" (Hebrew 1:2).

The fundamental error among NAR and associated groups, churches, and individuals is a misrepresentation of and/or what prophecy is. They use Revelation 19:10 to mean that the NAR-aligned prophets are the fulfillment of the passage. This is simply made up and flies in the face of the clear meaning of the text.

It is readily acknowledged that in the New Testament, particularly in the Book of Acts, prophecies are given, and these mostly from angels by means of a vision (see Acts 9:10–12). These are few and far between. None of the New Testament writers expect believers in Jesus to receive communications from God by any means other than the revealed written word we call the Bible.

My view is that today, as well as throughout Christian history, Satan has mimicked or counterfeited the genuine. If there is no genuine article there can be no counterfeit. The prophecies we find amongst NAR folk is just that, counterfeit, and especially those who identify with the charismatic/Pentecostal branch of Christianity have learned to accept, with caution, those who give prophecy in the name of the Lord. And for a long period of time, I was one of these.

A CHALLENGE

God is doing today just what He said He would do in the Scripture already provided for us. He is not doing something new.

After reading many hundreds of prophecies uttered by NAR self-proclaimed prophets, I am shocked at the ridiculous nature of the better part of them. Some are weird beyond belief. Most can be so variously understood, if they can be understood at all, that one wonders what the point is.

My appeal is for critical thinking. At the same time I recognize how difficult it is, and for some almost impossible, to pull away from what has become the most toxic and dangerous false teaching ever to invade the Christian Church. Nothing really compares except perhaps Arianism in the fourth and fifth centuries.

July, 2015

Essay Fourteen

America and the New Apostolic Reformation

It is evident to most American Christians that there is a decided tilt away from the Christian and biblical moorings which marked previous generations. This is seen is the continuing acceptance of same-sex marriage, little concern about abortion, and a growing acceptance of the drug culture—among other markers of a deteriorating society.

In California, along with a number of other states, marijuana use is legal and some of my neighbors, here in upscale Marin County, grow the weed. I daily read the *San Francisco Chronicle* and Marin's *Independent Journal*— regularly since 1965—and my observation is that we are living in a "stoner" world that makes the hippie scene of the late 1960s look tame. Every single day in the San Francisco Bay Area people are robbed, mugged, raped, and murdered by addicts of one kind or another. We are now living in a dangerous world, and speaking out against it is definitely politically incorrect. Hard to imagine!

Christians, perhaps more readily than others, are aware that as a nation we are going to hell in the proverbial hand basket. What to do? Well, we preach, we pray, we witness, and we lobby as best we can, but the slippery slope just becomes steeper and steeper.

I have noticed that some Christian organizations that are not aligned with the New Apostolic Reformation, and even would not embrace NAR's core theology, nevertheless cooperate to certain degrees in NAR-organized conferences and alliances. (I have in mind here Focus on the Family and Cru.) The question then is: If there are major differences in worldviews, why the entanglement?

My suspicion is that NAR leaders and organizations hold that God is establishing the kingdom of God on earth right now, at least in America. The seven mountains encompass, among others, the family, education, and government. Yes, government, and thus the effort to bring major politicians into the movement. Some of the names mentioned by NAR people are Sarah Palin, Ted Cruz, Rick Perry, even President Trump. Of course politicians need a voter base, and evangelicals are one of the largest. (I understand an NAR-aligned lobby group has nice offices in Washington, D.C.)

A Connection with Islam

The NAR is both political and religious, as is Islam. The goal of Islam is to see Sharia Law extend globally. Islam does not distinguish between politics and religion; for Muslims the two are wed.

Islam does not cherish the separation of church and state. I have read the same in some of the NAR writings. Clearly the goal is to see the Kingdom rule over the globe, especially and foremost in America, and this does not mean the conversion of everyone to Christ. There is talk of a "Christian civil war"[1] and with some writers it appears as though this could include violence.

In Islam it is enough that non-believers submit themselves to Muslim authority. Yes, the other option is death: it is join, submit, or die. And soon, it is peace, peace, peace, which is what is meant by Islam being the religion of peace. Does NAR, or some portion

1 On one side are those aligned with NAR apostles and prophets and on the other are those "opposers" who are not, people such as me.

thereof, have a similar view to Islam?

NAR people believe God is establishing His rule when the offices of apostle and prophet are again in place. And when the mountain of government is dominated through the apostolic and prophetic authority, the Kingdom comes and Jesus descends from heaven.

The above view is termed dominionism. Simply put, the Church dominates, and everything is under its authority. American is pristine once again. Then the world follows. Heaven then is not an eternal fellowship with God in His presence, but is a rule over the world. Heaven may follow, but not before dominion.

The Mission of the Church

We are not called to rule; we are called to witness. We are to make disciples of all nations. We preach Jesus and teach new believers, starting with baptizing them in the name of the Father, and of the Son, and of the Holy Spirit. Plain enough. And the Holy Spirit equips us to do all this (see Matthew 28:18–20 and Acts 1:1–8).

Jesus will return and establish His kingdom exactly when He chooses. Once again, plain and simple. This is biblical Christianity. The NAR agenda is unbiblical and thus is sub-Christian.

Is this an unfair or inaccurate evaluation?

July, 2017

Essay Fifteen

WHY I MUST OPPOSE THE NEW APOSTOLIC REFORMATION

I met and talked a great deal with C. Peter Wagner in the late 1980s at Fuller Theological Seminary in Pasadena, California, while I attended the beginning and advanced Church Growth Seminars. He had read two books of mine, *A Manual of Demonology and the Occult*, published by Zondervan Publishing House in 1973, and *The Deliverance Book*, published by Bible Voice in about 1977.

Either in Charles Kraft's office or Dr. Wagner's, the three of us talked about the ministry of deliverance and the signs and wonders I had experienced during the Jesus People Movement, roughly from1967 to 1972. At those meetings I had no idea I was contributing, in some small fashion, to what would later become known as the New Apostolic Reformation (NAR).

For many years I have followed what was going on in the NAR to some degree, read some of the books flowing out of it, and visited on several occasions the Bethel Church in Redding, California, to hear a number of the leaders speak there, Randy Clark being one of them. I witnessed the gold dust, feathers, and wind of the Holy Spirit (a wind that was actually produced by a large movie-set fan). In addition, an old high school buddy and his wife talked with me about their involvement with the Bethel Church. They were long time members and participated in both Sozo and Soaking Prayer ministries besides going on numerous mission trips to other countries. (They ceased attending Bethel some years back, saying things were "just too crazy.")

After seeing the NAR impact two people in the congregation I pastor (in my 33rd year) at Miller Avenue Baptist Church in Mill Valley, California, events occurred that essentially forced me to speak out against a movement that is far more errant than I first imagined. Though I have written about this general situation before, the scope and magnitude of it now requires a stronger response.

Following are some of the reasons that brought me to this position.

Unconverted people drawn to the NAR may experience false conversion

Recently I learned of people who are not Christians but are more aptly called thrill seekers being attracted to some of the venues where the NAR operates. Mainly they are looking for excitement (huge emphasis on drum and base guitar-heavy music) and maybe a miracle or two. There are also some who suffer some sort of disability or illness that they hope will be healed by the miracle-working apostles and prophets who are "bringing heaven to earth by the power of transformed minds."

Attendees at NAR gatherings are most often presented with a weak Christianity that does not focus on the biblical Gospel. Some claim healing, for a while at least, and some see what they think are miracles and buy into the whole package but without becoming born again followers of Jesus. They hear Christian-like sayings peppered throughout, but most of what is presented is severely lacking in biblical content. It is no exaggeration to say that the NAR is not evangelistic in nature except to promote themselves, though proponents of it would deny such an evaluation.

New or Weak Christians Hoping to Find Assurance

Not only are the falsely converted attracted to signs, wonders, and miracles, but so are those who struggle in their Christian lives and are looking for confirmation that they are on the right path. The NAR seems to answer this need for many. After all, if you witness a miracle, then God must be real, and you are not being misled.

Trouble then arises, because seeing one miracle is not enough. It can become addictive. Faith that rests on signs and wonders is no faith at all. Christian faith is in Jesus alone, both who He is—Emmanuel, meaning God with us—and what He did—taking our sin upon Himself and carrying it away forever, dying in our place, rising from the grave, and freely giving us eternal life. This is biblical faith.

Christians Becoming So Disillusioned They Give Up on Church Completely

This is exactly what has happened to my friends in Redding. Their trust in pastors and church organizations is shattered. It may take years before they and others burned by the shallowness and miracle-oriented gimmicks typical of NAR gatherings will venture out and look for Christian fellowship again.

My sense is that when the NAR implodes, and it will implode, there will be many thousands of Christians who will sink down in despair and experience a loss very similar to someone who loses a loved one to death. This is why I am preparing a recovery program especially designed for those who will be devastated by such a collapse of hope and commitment.

The NAR will implode, because literally hundreds of their major prophets predict things that have not and will not come to pass; because the signs, wonders, and miracles no longer serve as a shot in the arm; because leaders fall away, corporate greed takes over, and there are power struggles; and because when even tame-sounding prophecies fail to materialize, more bizarre prophecies are given out. The NAR says it is the vanguard, indeed the very instrument that God is using to bring the entire globe under the authority of the apostles and prophets and thereby establish the kingdom of God on earth. They claim that when all the facets of human existence—the "seven mountains" of business, government, media, arts and entertainment, education, family, and religion—are Christianized, then Jesus will return.

This scenario is known in theology as post-millennialism and more recently tagged Dominionism, the concept whereby the world is brought under the rule of God by His Church. The fantastic claim is that this is what God is doing now, as revealed to the super-apostles, people like C. Peter Wagner, Bill Johnson, Mick Bickle, Rick Joyner, Chuck Pierce, and a growing list of other apostles, prophets (and a new designation coming into frequent use—generals). The Bible does not teach this clearly, and past attempts to usher in the kingdom of God have proved to be errant, so how is it that so many have climbed on board with the NAR? A powerful delusion maybe?

The non-Christian world views the NAR as a laughing stock

If you type "New Apostolic Reformation" into a Google search you will be shocked at what you find. Wikipedia has many contributors to the discussion. And what is seen in the countless videos of folks like Heidi Baker, Stacy Campbell, Bill Johnson, Rick Joyner, and Kris Vallotton, to name a few, is scandalous and embarrassing to the point that Christian witness is compromised, bias develops against anything Christian, weak Christians are stumbled, and ordinary Christians are hurt and confused.

As time has passed, with the official beginning of the NAR pegged at 2000 or earlier, the movement has become even more ridiculous, and I think this is due to power struggles, money running out, greater scrutiny from news organizations, and reports from those who have left the movement in disgust. And these are only increasing.

IS THE NAR A CULT?

During the 1830s and 1840s America saw the rise of several Bible-based cults. Two of these, the Jehovah's Witnesses and the Mormons, developed their own sacred books, The New World Bible for the Witnesses and The Book of Mormon for the Mormons.

The Jehovah's Witnesses needed a new translation of the Bible in order to insert material that supported their rendition. The NAR folks have done the same, and it is called *The Passion Translation*.

In addition, the NAR is speaking of a "civil war" amongst Christians. Those not aligned with the movement are referred to in disparaging terms, resulting in the classic, cultic, "we-they" mentality. The small evangelical church of which I am pastor would never be visited or attended by someone affiliated or aligned with an NAR church except for the purpose of drawing people away from the congregation.

"Are you hearing about the new things God is doing in these last days? Are you seeing the miracles and the healings like we are? Are you moving in the flow of the Spirit?" These questions are calculated to entice the unwary to attend a church aligned with God-appointed apostles, generals, and prophets, and this strategy has proven to be quite effective.

For six years, from 1988 to 1994, I conducted a cult recovery support group. The recovery focused on how people view themselves in relation to others. I needed it myself, because I recognized I had been part of a group with a cultic mentality: "We" were moving in the Spirit, attuned to the voice of God, operating in the gifts, bringing heaven to earth, and filled with the Spirit, while "they" were dead Christians, merely singing old dull hymns and listening to boring sermons. And "we" were praying for these poor souls that they would wake up and get on board.

That is only a fragment of the cultic mindset, and this view of others who are not rightly submitted to the apostles and prophets who are bringing the kingdom upon the whole world is delusion and deception.

Will Christians be led astray?

The simple answer is, "Yes!" Who among us have not been deceived at some point in our lives? I have been, and I suffered significantly as a result. To some degree I am yet having to deal with my past mistakes, misdeeds, and sinful behavior.

Jesus Himself answered that question in the affirmative. Let us take a look at three verses from Matthew 24:

And Jesus answered them, "See that no one leads you astray. For many will come in my name, saying, 'I am the Christ,' and they will lead many astray" (vv. 4–5).

"And many false prophets will arise and lead many astray" (v. 11).

"For false christs and false prophets will arise and perform great signs and wonders, so as to lead astray, if possible, even the elect. See, I have told you beforehand" (vv. 24–25).

Jesus was speaking about events leading up to the closing of the age. Notice above the phrase, "if possible." This is a conditional clause. Greek has four of these grammatical constructions, numbered one to four. One means, yes, it is so. Two means, no, it is not so. Three means, yes, it is possible. Four means, no, it is not likely. This is the shortest possible presentation of the conditional clauses, but it will serve us here.

The "if possible" of Matthew 24:24 is a first class condition and means that yes, even the elect, those truly born again of the Holy Spirit, may be led astray. Shocking and scary, but there it is.

I have been led astray. Is it possible that others, even those who embrace NAR proclamations and practices will be led astray as well?

An even more troubling possibility

Trances, visions, hearing of audible voices, body parts becoming warm, out-of-body experiences, talking with angels, the Father, the Son, and dead apostles—what indeed is going on here? Signs and wonders, healings, miracles of all sorts—is this all real?

During the Jesus People Movement, 1967 to 1972, I personally saw and experienced real miracles, real healings, and demons cast out. I am no denier of the reality of the charismatic gifts of the Spirit. However, it appears that much of the signs and wonders going on now are false and might open one up to being invaded by demonic spirits. As a matter of fact, my wife and I are now engaged with people from NAR-affiliated congregations who have been possessed by demons and with whom we are now engaged in deliverance ministry. Yes, you read right.

The point or means of invasion is usually while in a trance state, experiencing what is thought to be an out-of-body experience while involved in soaking prayer, periods of being "drunk-in-the-spirit," or even in a state of mind that comes with wild praise and worship.

In the third section of this book the focus is on recovery from the loss experience, since many are now leaving NAR-affiliated groups and congregations. It is common then to question Christianity, even the existence of God. Many become reclusive and withdraw into isolation. The possibility is that some may need to be rid of demonic spirits, and if so, should not be embarrassed about such a thing. It happens, and the point is to live in the freedom we are called to in Christ.

DIVISION IN THE CHURCH

I will admit there is now a kind of civil disturbance going on within some parts of Christianity, which is sad, because most of those aligned with NAR groups and churches are genuine brothers and sisters in Christ. It is for this reason, above all others, that I am writing this essay.

My appeal to NAR advocates is twofold. One, critically analyze what you hear and see. It is not blasphemy of the Holy Spirit to do so, but this is what is often communicated. Please realize that you are part of spiritually oriented intimidation. Two, return to being a simple follower of Jesus—read your Bible, have prayer time, and seek out other believers for fellowship. If you have been critically injured you will recover. Every born again believer has his or her name written in heaven and is completely safe and secure. We continue to look to Jesus, the author and finisher of our faith.

August 2017

Section Three

Recovery and Other Issues

Who has not been tricked and deceived? I cannot raise my hand. This is tragic enough, but then what? The object is to recover and get back in the race again. This is what section three is all about.

The first essay, "Recovering from the Ending of a Relationship with NAR Churches and Groups," is straight forward and rather ordinary. It is based upon my experience with cult recovery and divorce recovery programs. The second essay is far different.

The second essay in section three is "What about Demonic Elements? Here I may lose some readers, but I would hope that despite doctrinal differences, the basic message might be given at least critical attention.

Recovering from the Ending of a Relationship with NAR Churches and Groups

My Recovery from Loss

Now that many are questioning, even leaving NAR-affiliated churches and groups, our attention must turn to recovery from one of the most serious kinds of losses anyone will ever experience.

During the 1970s I was informed that the church I pastored was cult-like though our theology was in keeping with traditional Christianity. I rejected this with all I had, at first. However, my informer happened to be the major professor for my doctoral program. He was also recognized as one of the nation's leading authorities on cults and conversion, so I could not easily ignore him. As I attempted to face up to a very real tragedy, I became confused and isolated from the church I pastored, especially from the other pastors.

This struggle led to my resignation as senior pastor of the church and plunged me into a "dark night of the soul." A divorce followed, and a steady stream of losses descended upon my family and me, some of which I am still coping with decades later. This all began in 1978.

In January of 1986, at the Miller Avenue Baptist Church in Mill

Valley, California (where I still pastor), we began a Divorce Recovery Workshop program developed by Sherry Coppin. I still direct this eight-week workshop, presented four times each year. Many hundreds have attended and it is something my wife and I greatly love to facilitate.

In 1988, based partly on the general format of the divorce recovery workshop material, I developed a twenty-three week course designed to help those who had come out of various religious cults and sects. This workshop continued until 1994. As in the divorce recovery program, here again we dealt with the loss experience. And it became clear that the loss from being either voluntarily or involuntarily separated from such a group was every bit as shocking and devastating as the ending of a personal relationship.

Nature of the Loss

The loss, first of all, is real. Once a person has committed so much to what he or she so strongly believes is the will of God, and commits his identity, reputation, huge blocks of time, large amounts of money, and perhaps much more, and then sees it all collapse—this is overwhelming to say the least. Friends, family, co-workers, neighbors, maybe a husband, a wife, a child—these relationships might be broken or even dissolved. It is absolutely crushing!

What now? Is this Christian thing all just garbage? Is there no God after all? Should I just quit and throw my Bible away? I was cheated, lied to, deceived, and for what? Well, no more church, that's for sure! I don't trust any of those preachers, prophets, and apostles! I am trashing all those books I bought! I am going to find a safe group that helps people or engages in social justice, if I ever reach out again!

This does not even begin to capture the pain. Yet, to recover, the pain must be faced head on. To drown our misery only puts the pain off, and unhappily, may result in something much worse, like suicide. Yes, suicide. Some 90% of those who suffer significant loss have thoughts of suicide. Depression is likely as well. Here we are, living our lives, struggling through, and now this. Such embarrassment, too. Many just want to hide.

Let me mention the worst-case scenario: you may have recruited others into the movement, and they did not fare well. Here is where the guilt comes flooding in. In my case, I brought hundreds in, and I have to admit that I am still bothered by it. Still worse, those I helped dupe will from time to time confront me with my own duped-ness.

You, dear reader, may be a leader in the movement, a follower, a member of an intercessors group, a dancer, a flag waver, on a soaking prayer team, in sozo ministry, a fledgling prophet, or a member of a praise band engaged unwittingly in moving "worshippers" into a trance state—the list is long. It is now time to face up to what happened.

Before moving to the first level of recovery—denial—I want to mention something I have discovered through both research and personal experience. It may take many years before a person is even willing or able to look at his or her loss experience. The number I usually throw out is ten years—ten years after exiting a cultic or toxic group for whatever reason, before one is willing to engage in a recovery process. I am not sure of the accuracy of this, but in the cult recovery groups I facilitated from 1988 to 1994, this was the surprising number—ten years. The quicker then you are able to face up to the hell you went through, the quicker you will recover.

DENIAL

Here is where it all begins. No or little growth toward a normal life is even possible until we admit what happened. We got duped! We were deceived! Yes, that happened, and now there may be depression, anger, murderous and vengeful thoughts, and suicidal thoughts. Fears that we might be crazy and ready for the locked ward would not be surprising.

We face reality and we do not do so alone. We still belong to Jesus; what happened does not change that. Do not give up, because the best is yet to come. And as I say to people in recovery, once we struggle through the recovery process, we are better able to help others recover. In fact, a significant ministry may just be opening up.

Here are some common reactions when dealing with denial:

» Shame for having been duped.

» The question, "Why me?" coming up continually.

» A tendency to minimize the effects of the movement.

» Blaming others for our involvement.

» Idealizing our experiences in the movement.

It is helpful to look at possible factors leading to involvement with the movement:

» Loneliness

» Spiritual confusion

» A traumatic event, a serious illness, the death of a loved one

» Fear of living, of being overwhelmed, of being unable to cope

» Running away from problems

» Bad experiences with a church or a church leader

» Fear of death and hell

» Needing assurance of salvation

It is also helpful to examine the factors that led to leaving the movement:

» Fear of the world and other fears diminished

» Influence of parents, children, friends, and professional counselors

» Bad experiences in movement

» Realizing the unbiblical nature of the movement

» Spiritual events that were frightening

» Excommunication or being somehow rejected by those in the movement

To partially restate several points: It is painful to admit to being duped. It is so difficult to separate from friends, even family, who remain in the movement. Being found alone, a contrarian even, is emotionally overwhelming at times.

We may feel alienated from our Lord. We may feel like we are doomed. We may want to reject Christianity all together. And most do feel this way. I did.

If you can identify with some of what I have been presenting here, you are beginning to deal with denial, the first step in the recovery process. Don't give up; keep facing up to reality. Things will get better.

GUILT AND REJECTION

These two emotions—and that's what they are, emotions—are very powerful. I experienced both of these, almost at once. Yes, my own actions were to blame. I felt terribly guilty, and although I fully understood that all my sin is covered in the blood of Jesus, knew also that God does not even remember my sin, still I knew what happened and this bothered me (and still does to some extent).

Guilt—we may feel guilty for leaving the movement. We wonder if we are doing the right thing. We feel guilty for having been "captured" by the movement. Most toxic groups build into their identity that they are right and those outside are wrong. In Christian oriented movements, those outside are deceived, demonic, opposers of the Holy Spirit, are committing blasphemy of the Holy Spirit, are dead, or are simply bad people. And no one is invulnerable to such awful notions. We feel terrible for pulling others into the movement, especially when we see them being taken advantage of. There are innumerable ways and reasons for guilt to come crashing in.

It helps to admit to ourselves that there are times in our lives when we are vulnerable, particularly when we are young. The NAR is very youth oriented, focused on the music and promises of great and mighty ministries. It is rock 'n' roll in spades. And, whether calculated or simply part of the environment, toxic movements are very sophisticated and powerful, demonstrated by the fact that millions fall prey to such groups.

Rejection—this is what always takes place. Those still mired in the movement are bound to reject the one who wakes up and walks away. It must be so, because admitting that something is amiss must be avoided. The feelings of rejection can be severe, especially if family members and close friends who are yet in the movement begin ignoring and excluding the one leaving. It is very hard to face.

Toxic groups sometimes reject in a formal manner, as part of their doctrine or methodology, those who drift away, with the assumption that the rejection will bring the wayward one back. It goes to the point that cultic groups will order their members to reject those who leave. The group may teach that God loves only those who follow their leaders, since these are God's anointed ones.

» The ex-member may now find he or she is alone in a scary and confusing world.

» Here are some questions that may help in dealing with guilt and rejection:

» What about leaving the movement causes guilt?

» Do you feel humiliated for having been involved with the movement?

» If you do feel guilt and rejection, how have you dealt with it?

» In terms of self-esteem, how is it now?

» If you have experienced rejection, how are you coping with it?

» Have you thought of going back into the movement to overcome or escape from the cascade of bad feelings?

Fear

Arguably the emotion of fear is the strongest of them all. Toxic groups and movements inspire fear in their members. Among the most common fears are fear of the devil, of the world, of being deceived, of opposers, of going to hell, and of being punished by God with illness or poverty, to name a few.

Generalized fear can result in developing phobias to cope with and relieve tension, stress, and anxiety. Since my teen years I have been subject to anxiety, which was the reason I intended to become a psychologist. During the entire 1970s while pastoring a church, I was the lone counselor of the Marin Christian Counseling Center. By far the greatest number of those who came to see me suffered from phobias. Most of my phobias are under control, but if they had blossomed, I might have become worse than neurotic.

Phobic reactions are many and varied. It might be compulsive hand washing or fear of bugs, diseases, and people. Compulsive and obsessive rituals and habits can develop and if left untreated can move into more serious psychological disorders. Religious people may turn toward long hours of chanting prayers, singing songs, reading the Bible, quoting biblical phrases in order to protect against demons, or speaking constantly in "Christianese"—stereotypical Christian language.

Fear may inspire the desire to go back to the movement, especially when insiders are trying to lure the leaver back inside. Being alone can bring on a powerful sense of loneliness, and in that circumstance fear looms larger.

Another fear is that there will be no normal again, that life has forever been damaged and distorted. Fear can result in an abiding sense of sadness, a dissatisfaction with life, and a desire to end it all in suicide.

Dealing directly with fear is a chief way of moving away from it. One way to do this is to list the fears you have beginning with the big ones first then continuing to the lesser ones. Once you have a list, it is helpful to look back over them and evaluate which are appropriate and which are not appropriate. Another way to say this is, examine which are realistic or unrealistic. An example might be: "My life is ruined." This is unrealistic and not appropriate. "My life has changed." This is a realistic and appropriate. "God does not love me." This is unrealistic and not appropriate. I could go on, but you get the picture. Face your fears directly and their sting will diminish.

It is vital to continue in fellowship with other Christians. We know now that there is no perfect church or denomination. In every church fellowship there will be disagreeable people, people who will say weird and insulting things based on misunderstandings or fears of their own. Will you find a church body that believes just like you do? No, of course not; no one ever finds this. Indeed, there is a sense in which every church fellowship is a bit of a minefield. You may be blown up, but not usually in an irreparable way. I have been damaged, and I have seen it happen to people at our Miller Avenue Baptist Church. Would we expect anything else?

With all this said, it is yet vital to rebuild our lives, and being with others is a big part of that. My usual suggestion is, find a church where the Scripture is taught, verse by verse if possible, and where there is an evangelical witness going out calling people to be followers of Jesus. I also suggest looking for a smallish church, one where there is more of a family atmosphere.

ANGER

Anger is an emotion, too, and is by far the longest lasting element to face in recovery. We will be angry with the leaders in the movement, angry with any who were instrumental in getting us involved, and angry at ourselves. Anger at ourselves can be the most devastating of all.

Anger can also be a sign of health. When things go wrong and we have been victimized, there must be anger. It is what we do with the anger and rage that matters.

In the case of divorce, for instance, anger can be both a friend and an enemy. A friend in that anger helps blunt the sense of rejection. It serves an as insulator at first. It may even be justified. Anger is an enemy, if it continues for a long period, leading to depression or an acting out that in turn leads to hospital, court, and jail time.

For divorce or loss of relationship anger can be problematic; if involved with leaving a Christian group or movement, anger can be quite dangerous as well. It is almost a stealth emotion; it comes and goes and can creep up on us suddenly and move us toward criminal behavior. In a moment, an instant, deep-seated anger can boil over and do great damage. Anger must be dealt with head on.

We cannot talk ourselves out of anger, and repressing it can cause serious forms of depression. What then? We give voice to the anger. When I experienced anger as a result of certain events, I took up the punching bag like the one I had when I boxed as a kid. I took it out on a body bag and it helped to dissipate the anger. Anger must be talked out and worked out, not hushed up or covered over.

As Christians we have an advantage when it comes to dealing with anger. That advantage is called forgiveness. One, we can learn to forgive those who harmed us. In the case of NAR involvement, I doubt if any of the players decided to be deceptive and take advantage of others. We remember that the devil prowls around looking for someone to devour, and we know the devil's favorite hunting ground—the church where he finds us Christians.

Two, we forgive ourselves. This is by far the hardest form of forgiving. Most of us forget to forgive ourselves. It is plain from a reading of 1 John 1:8–2:2 that God knows we will sin, so He provides grace, love, and forgiveness in the name of Jesus. At least we Christians usually know when we are sinning, which is actually a blessing, since we can come to Him who delights in forgiving His dear sons and daughters. After all, our sin has been separated from us as far as the east is from the west. We do not take advantage of this great grace, but it is there, ready and waiting.

I urge that you evaluate the anger you have. Are you angry with yourself? If so, admit it, pray about it, confess it to someone else, and ask for forgiveness. Are you angry with a friend, family member, or Christian leader for involving you in the first place? Are you angry with outsiders who said, "I told you so."? We know what to do now—bring it to the Lord in prayer, and as many times and for as long as it takes.

LONELINESS AND LOW SELF-ESTEEM

These two again are emotions, though less tangible than those above. They are words that express how we feel.

Loneliness—especially if family members and close friends are still in the movement and who may very well be estranged from us. Low self-esteem—especially if we had widely let it be known of our devotion to the movement.

Loneliness can be absolutely crushing, even dreadfully painful, depending on the circumstances. Self-esteem is now at a new all-time low, and it may not have been very strong in the first place, which is true for many of us. The loneliness may be the result of humiliation, in that having others know of the goings-on would be unbearable. So one isolates, however miserable that might be.

Those in the NAR movement have enjoyed a really fast paced and interesting world with all kinds of new and exotic ideas. And once away from the excitement, boredom sets in, so much so that one is tempted to get back into it.

Again, as Christians we have an advantage. Though it does not always feel that way, the fact is that we are never alone. We have the abiding presence of the Holy Spirit. And this is not based on our feelings, thankfully. We have fellowship with the God of creation—Father, Son, and Holy Spirit. And this is ours, particularly when we are disciplined in our Bible reading and prayers. I urge each believer to methodically go through the Scripture reading several Old Testament chapters each day, beginning with Genesis, then reading several Psalms, then three chapters in the New Testament, beginning with Matthew's Gospel. Then, pull out your prayer list, which notes the date of the beginning of the prayer request, the request itself noted, then the date of the answer, if there is a clear answer, one way of the other.

I like to say I am religious and not spiritual. This counters the popular saying, "I'm spiritual not religious." I am religious, because I practice my spiritual discipline on a daily basis, since it means so much to me. The early believers, as evidenced in the Book of Acts, were called disciples, meaning they studied Jesus and the written Word. There it is, we are not alone.

Improved self-esteem follows on the heels of the above as we soon learn that we are beloved children of God. Our heavenly Father never gives up on us no matter how stupid we may have been. Each day is a new day; the old is behind us and, behold, the new has come.

Letting Go

I will never be able to completely let go of what happened back in the 1970s, and I do not mean my extensive involvement in the Jesus People Movement from 1967 to 1972. It was a wonderful time, but as so often happens following an outpouring of the Holy Spirit, "wild fire" or what is called the "dark sides" of revival or awakening times ascends from hell. It did come and is still with us, for that is how I see the New Apostolic Reformation.

I and so many, many others have to live with our mistakes, but the sharpness of that lessens with the passing of years. I refuse to deceive myself by saying I am completely healed of all the self-inflicted and other-inflicted deceptions and misdirections in which I was trapped. It happened; it will not go away; and for the most part, it is behind me.

Letting go then means remembering but not dwelling on what happened. It can also mean using your experience to help others.

Letting go means admitting you were involved, and maybe not a little bit, in something that was not of God.

Here is where letting go begins, without forgetting that it will all never completely go away. I am now thirty-seven years away from direct involvement and association, and I consider that I am about 85% recovered, but no more.

As time goes on, we usually think less and less about "those" days, but since we are discussing recovery from a religious cultic experience, the possibility of confusion over doctrine and theology remains. Some of the doctrines I held dear then I retain today, so I must continually sort out and distinguish between that which was solidly biblical and that which was clearly not. The time has not been utterly wasted either. Some good has come out of it, and I am again in fellowship with many who were part of the mess back then.

Our God has a way of turning defeat into victory. He does it all the time.

WHAT ABOUT DEMONIC ELEMENTS?

Throughout this book, I have mentioned the possibility that what NAR-involved people are experiencing in their dreams, visions, and trances, in which they hear the voice and see the appearance of God the Father and Jesus the Son and angels and other divine-like beings, might not be what they perceive it to be. More than a hint, I have made some direct statements about what this really is likely to be.

When we hear and read that some apostles and prophets are being taken to the "throne room" and speaking with the Father, the Son, and various apostles like Paul, that some are seeing angel armies while being escorted around heaven by angels and speaking with them, even touching them—what are we to conclude?

Is all this real? The thousands upon thousands of prophecies given to those who call themselves prophets—are these the true words of God?

Are the "last day's prophets" reporting what God is doing now because we are "off the charts" and only these chosen ones are hearing the voice of God? Is it true and of God? Or, is it something else, something real enough, coming from spiritual entities, but are not Godly at all but are in fact demons from hell?

Let me explain why I am including this potentially controversial essay. Several weeks ago my wife and I were contacted by a woman in Europe who had been involved with an NAR-aligned church ten years previously, but recently became aware she has demons in her. She found us through a book or two I wrote on the subject, the most recent being *Deliver us from Evil: How Jesus Casts Out Demons Today*.

Using Skype we have been in contact with her on several occasions. She is friendly, healthy, intelligent, biblically literate, and obviously a Christian. She was fully engaged in all the regular experiences one would find in a NAR-related church that was fully involved in the practices. Over the course of nearly a month now, we have seen her delivered of a number of unclean spirits. During the 1970s, and to some lesser extent, since 1980, I have had opportunity to conduct this ministry.

It is clear that not all Christians think a born-again follower of Jesus can be indwelt by the Holy Spirit and an unclean spirit at the same time. Of the many hundreds of people I have been able to minister to, however, it is rare to have a non-Christian even want to have demons cast out. That is correct: it is almost always the Christians who both know they have demons in them and want them out. I could abundantly illustrate this with actual accounts of the real thing, but I am hoping my word will be enough. And for those whose theology or doctrine differs from my own, at least we can categorize it as an intra-mural debate among believers and not an extra-mural debate with the outside world.

Here is what I think happens. With a combination of powerful music heavy on the base guitar and drums, with "spiritual" moving and grooving to the beat, the ecstatic dancing, maybe falling out, getting drunk in the spirit, lying under the power perhaps for hours or days, could an evil spirit take advantage? I say an emphatic YES, because this kind of activity was reported to me as the initial opening experience to later demonic attacks by dozens of people seeking help to be rid of these evil entities. For some, it happened during rituals or practices of non-Christian, pagan religions before their becoming Christians, but for others it was and is happening in decidedly Christian venues.

What about our trying to hear the voice of God or waiting to hear a word of prophecy? Those who want to hear an angel, Jesus, or the Father talk to them may hear an impersonation, but it will be an "angel of light" and not the real thing (see 2 Corinthians 11:14). Scripture teaches us to pray and read His Word and nothing more.

I am not trying to sell a book here, but a few years ago I concluded a study of shamanism, neo-pagan religions like Wicca, the West African religion called Santeria (with millions of followers in Brazil alone), and charismania. I concluded that these were connected by means of what is variously called the passive state of mind, the altered state of mind, the shamanistic state of mind, or the ecstasy, the trance, the out-of-body soul travel, and so on. The book is entitled, *The Soul Journey: How Shamanism, Santeria, Wicca, and Charisma Are Connected*. This research and book was necessitated by the fact that I pastor in a town where Wiccans are more common than Christians, where the Institute for Shamanism headquarters is located, where Buddhism has permeated the environment, and where the practice of yoga and other forms of Eastern meditation are ubiquitous.

What I discovered in the research for the *Soul Journey* book is that much of what is characteristic of these shamanistic practices is also present in NAR worship and in the reported experiences of NAR prophets and apostles.

The deception Jesus spoke of in Matthew 24 alone is enough to alert us to the possibility that Christians are vulnerable. Study these verses spoken directly by Jesus. The context is when the disciples wanted to know how to recognize the coming of the end of the age.

> And Jesus answered them, "See that no one leads you astray. For many will come in my name saying, 'I am the Christ, and they will lead many astray'" (vv. 4 and 5).

> And many false prophets will arise and lead many astray (v. 11).

> For false christs and false prophets will arise and perform great signs and wonders, so as to lead astray, if possible, even the elect (v. 24).

If one thinks that only non-Christians will be led astray, let it be noted that the phrase, "if possible," above is a first class condition and means that Christians, the elect and chosen ones, can be led astray, not out of salvation but into deception. All one has to do to be open to deception is be wowed by powerful signs and wonders.

Stating the potential of becoming demonized through some of the spiritual practices of those involved with NAR-aligned groups and churches is one thing, and in fact is an important step. But then what? We are talking about brothers and sisters in Christ who, by no fault of their own, have been deceived and are in harm's way. And who among us is clean?

There is a spiritual battle to come, is here already, and has always been with us, but the battle is already won. Jesus came to destroy the works of the devil, according to 1 John 3:8. He has done so, and His authority over the evil presence extends throughout human history. There will likely come a time when the need for Christians to cast out demons in the name of Jesus will expand. I have found over the years that Christians, by turning from that which is error and confessing such, do see demons flee and even cast demons out themselves.

Indwelling demons are not just an interesting power show. They always cause trouble, from annoying to devastating and debilitating somewhere along the line. Mental and emotional disturbances are common. Strange sensations may be experienced, such as sounds, feelings, pains, and for no apparent reason. Hearing voices, falling into trances, irritation with and desire to avoid normal Christian worship and ministry, difficulty maintaining a normal active life, and more are possible. The devil will tip his hand at some point, in some way, and when this happens, it is time to seek deliverance.

There is deliverance help out there. Consult with a local pastor, although many mainstream denomination pastors and priests do not have extensive experience with this. A web search might yield results in your area, but I caution against enlisting the services of for-profit "ministries." Also, I must put myself out there as a resource. My email address is: kentphilpott@comcast.net. I may or may not be able to help much from a distance, but there is Skype.

May the words of Martin Luther's great hymn, "A Mighty Fortress is our God," ring out loud and long.

A mighty fortress is our God,
A bulwark never failing;
Our helper He amid the flood,
Of mortal ills prevailing;
For still our ancient foe doth seek to work us woe;
His craft and power are great,
And armed with cruel hate, on earth is not his equal.

Did we in our own strength confide,
our striving would be losing;
Were not the right man on our side,
the man of God's own choosing.
Dost ask who that may be? Christ Jesus, it is He—
Lord Sabaoth His name,
From age to age the same, and He must win the battle.

And though this world, with devils filled,
should threaten to undo us,
We will not fear, for God hath willed His truth
to triumph through us.
The prince of darkness grim, we tremble not for him—
His rage we can endure,
For lo, his doom is sure: One little word shall fell him.

That word above all earthly powers,
no thanks to them, abideth;
The Spirit and the gifts are ours,
through Him who with us sideth.
Let goods and kindred go, this mortal life also—
the body they may kill;
God's truth abideth still: His kingdom is forever.

May God bless you with His indwelling presence and give you the peace that passes understanding. May you be filled and satisfied with His Word, both written in the Holy Bible and living in His Son Jesus Christ, our Lord and Savior.

Characteristics of a Toxic Faith

Over the years I have collected lists of practices, ways of thinking, and mindsets that experts who specialize in cultic groups, whether they be religious, political, educational/psychotherapeutic, or economic have developed. These are the four areas where the cultic or toxic mentality are usually found.

Following is a short list of traits I think apply to the NAR. It is essential that Christians understand these dynamics so that we can remain both emotionally and spiritually healthy.

1. Inability or reluctance to question doctrines of the group
2. Black and white thinking with no shades of grey
3. Judgmental attitudes toward those who think differently
4. A shame-based view whereby a person thinks he is unworthy
5. Magical thinking whereby people think God is obligated to take care of them
6. Unreasonable financial demands made upon followers
7. Conflict with education, science, and medicine
8. A view that outsiders—those who do not directly affiliate with or hold to the group's doctrines—are part of the "evil" system
9. A gradual detachment from the world
10. The breakdown of relationships with those outside the group

11. Claims to be receiving special revelation
12. Practices entailing entering into trancelike states
13. Requiring that negative or critical opinions be avoided
14. Minimization of tough questions in general
15. Requiring that the group's image must always be upheld
16. Teaching: God loves a person based on good behavior and right belief
17. Teaching: true believers will have peace when things go wrong—no grieving allowed
18. Teaching: God will heal based on one's true faith
19. Teaching: All the group's spiritual leaders can be trusted
20. Teaching: Wealth is a sign of God's blessing
21. Teaching: A faithful follower can become God-like
22. Teaching: God hates non-believers and wants to punish them
23. Teaching: All things that happen to members of the group are good and are from God
24. Teaching: If someone has problems, sin is at the bottom of it
25. Teaching: A person must always submit to spiritual authority
26. Teaching: The more money given to God's causes the more God will give back
27. Teaching: God uses only spiritual giants
28. Compulsive religious activity
29. Obsession with right thinking
30. Growing intolerance of others not in the group
31. Addiction to a religious high
32. Going outside the group for counseling or seeking a second opinion is severely frowned upon
33. Growing dependence on leaders for direction in one's life
34. Fear that leaving the group might mean loss of salvation
35. Fear that leaving the group might expose one to the demonic
36. Thinking that only my group is hearing the voice of God

The list could be much longer but the above covers most of it. Developing a toxic and dangerous mindset is a slow process, one that few would recognize in themselves.

Appendix

MAJOR PLAYERS, ORGANIZATIONS, AND NETWORKS OF THE NAR

The are two parts to the appendix: one is a list of the major players in the New Apostolic Reformation, the other is a list of the major organizations and networks associated with the New Apostolic Reformation. Both lists could be considerably longer; I note only those that are regularly mentioned in NAR associated writings, videos, or evaluations by persons and organizations not associated with the NAR.

Not all the persons listed in Part A are necessarily directly connected with the NAR but are mentioned by various writers as somehow connected or peripherally associated.

Not all organizations and other entities listed in Part B are necessarily directly part of the NAR. There is no overall homogeneous and hierarchical organization that is the NAR; rather various groups are in some way involved or aligned. Some groups may be "claimed" by various NAR personages but are involved only tangentially.

Part A
Major Players Associated With Or Aligned With The New Apostolic Reformation

Che Ahn, Senior Pastor of Harvest Rock, Pasadena, California; Apostle, Harvest Apostolic Center

Gary R. Allen, former Executive Editor of Enrichment Journal, General Council of the Assemblies of God

Elizabeth Alves, President of Increase International

John and Carol Arnott, founding leaders of Catch the Fire, Toronto, Ontario, Canada

Heidi Baker PhD, co-founder and Director of Iris Global

Roland Baker, PhD, Director and founder of Iris Ministries

John S. Baylor, Jr., M.Div., Fuller Theological Seminary

Todd Bentley, Evangelist/Revivalist, founder of Fresh Fire Ministries

Tony and Cynthia Brazelton, founders and pastors, Victory Christian Ministries International

Michael L. Brown, PhD, host of The Line of Fire Radio Broadcast, and president of Fire School of Ministry

Paul Cain, one of the early Kansas City Prophets

Stacey and Wesley Campbell, co-founders of New Life Church and of Canadian Prophetic Council and Be A Hero

Paul Carden, Executive Director, The Center for Apologetics Research

Mark Castro, Omega Center International, Mark Casto Ministries, Cleveland, Tennessee

Mahesh Chavda, Chavda Ministries International, Charlotte, North Caroling, Senior Pastor, All Nations Church

Mark Chironna, PhD, Mark Chironna Ministries, Church on the Living Edge, Orlando, Florida

Yonggi Cho, founder of the Yoido Full Gospel Church (Assemblies of God), the world's largest church, in South Korea

Mike Clarensau, Senior Director of Healthy Church Network, General Council of the Assemblies of God
Dr. Randy Clark, overseer, Apostolic Network of Global Awakening
Kim Clement, Kim Clement Center, Tulsa, Oklahoma
Gerald Coates, leader of Pioneer International, London, England
Graham Cooke, Brilliant Book House
Dennis Cramer, President, Dennis Cramer Ministries
John Dawson, International President Emeritus, Youth With a Mission
Jack Deere, former professor at Dallas Theological Seminary, now moved into the charismatic movement
Peter Drucker, leader in the "Church-State" movement
Colin Dye, Senior Pastor, Kensington Temple, London, England
Dick Eastman, International President, Every House for Christ
Harold R. Eberle, founder of Worldcast Ministries
Lou Engle, The Call
Ellyn Davis, co-author of *The Physics of Heaven*
Dr. Don Finto, founder of Caleb Company
Becky Fischer, founder of Kids in Ministry International and founded Kids on Fire School of Ministry
Francis Frangipagne, founder of In Christ's Image Training and the Advancing Church Ministries Association
Judy Franklin, co-author of *The Physics of Heaven*, Staff Minister, Bethel Church in Redding, California
Woodie Fultz, Pastor of Valley Worship Center, Dayton, Ohio
James W. Goll, PhD, founder of Encounters Network, Prayer Storm and GET eSchool
Jay Grimstead, founder of Coalition on Revival or COR
Tim Hale, Pastor of Harbor Christian fellowship, Lebanon, Ohio
Bishop Bill Hamon, Christian International Ministries
Apostle Jane Hamon, Vision Church at Christian International Ministries
Jim Hodges, founder and President of the Federation of Minters and Churches International, Duncanville, Texas
Jack Hayford, Chancellor of The King's University; founding pastor

of The Church On The Way, Van Nuys, California
Jane Hennesy, Pastor of Trinity Church, Cedar Hill, Texas
Leif Hetland, Global Mission Awareness
Marilyn Hickey, Marilyn Hickey Ministries
Brian and Bobbie Houston of Hillsong Church
Jane Hansen Hoyt, President/CEO of Aglow International
Ray Hughes, author of *Sound of Heaven: Symphony of Earth*, founder of Selah Ministries
Cindy Jacobs, author of *The Voice of God*, co-founder of Generals International
Harry R. Jackson, Jr., Senior Pastor of Hope Christian Church, Bishop of International Communion of Evangelical Churches
Beni Johnson, wife of Bill Johnson of Bethel Church in Redding, California
Bill Johnson, Senior Leader of Bethel Church in Redding, California
Bob Jones, one of the early Kansas City Prophets
Rick Joyner, founder of Morningstar Ministries, Fort Mill, South Carolina
John Kelly
R. T. Kendall, author of *Total Forgiveness*
Patricia King, founder of XP Ministries and Patricia King Ministries
Joni Lamb, co-founder of Daystar Television Network
David Lane, American Renewal Project
Jennifer LeClaire, Senior Editor, *Charisma* magazine, Director of Awakening House of Prayer
Banning Liebascher, founder and Director of Jesus Culture
Phil Mason, New Earth Tribe, Byron Bay, Australia; author of *Quantum Glory: The Science of Heaven Invading Earth*
Dr. Art Mathias, President, Wellspring Ministries
Dan McColllum, contributor of "God Vibrations" article in *The Physics of Heaven*
Doctors Bob and Audrey Meisner, TV Hosts, MyNewDay, New Day Ministries, Canada
Dick Mills, International Conference Speaker
Sudhakar Mondithoka, Director of Hyderbad Institute of Theology

and Apologetics, India

Dr. Patrick Murray, Senior Pastor, The Living Word Church, Vandalia, Ohio

Gary Oates, International Conference Speaker

Rod Parsley, Senior Pastor of World Harvest Church in Columbus, Ohio, founder of Valor Christian College, The Center for Moral Clarity, and Breakthrough (a media ministry), Bridge of Hope missions organization, Harvest Preparatory School, World Harvest Ministerial Alliance, The Women's Clinic of Columbus, and ifarv.tv.

Karl I. Payne. Pastor of Leadership Development and Discipleship Training, Antioch Bible Church, Redmond, Washington, Chaplain, Seattle Seahawks

Dennis Peacocke, involved with COT in Santa Rosa, California

Mark W. Pfeifer, Senior Pastor, Open Door Church, Chillicothe, Ohio

Cal Pierce, Director, Healing Rooms Ministries, Spokane, Washington

Dr. Chuck D. Pierce, President, Global Spheres Inc., and Glory of Zion International

Phil Pringle, C3 Church, City Harvest Church

Mario Ramos-Reyes, Director of the Institute for the Study of Culture, Ethics, and Development; Visiting Professor at the School of Law and Philosophy, Catholic University of Paraguay

Larry Randolph, International Conference speaker

Rev. Dr. Samuel Rodriguez, President, National Hispanic Christian Leadership Conference

Sid Roth, host of It's Supernatural!

Dmitry Rozer, Senior Editor, *The Center for Apologetics Research*

Cheryl Sacks, CEO, BridgeBuilders International Leadership Network

John Loren Sanford, founder of Elijah House

Brian Stebick, Regional Director, CSB Ministries, Bachelors of Biblical Studies Baptist Bible College

Robert Sterns, founder and Executive Director, Eagles' Wings

Ministries

Dutch Sheets, Author, Apostle, Dutch Sheets Ministries, Colorado Springs, Colorado

Tim Sheets, Author, Apostle, Pastor of Oasis Church, Middletown, Ohio

Steve Shultz, Founder, The Elijah List

Vinson Synan, Dean Emeritus, Regent University School of Divinity

Dr. Hope Taylor, Ministry Director of International Leadership Embassy, in Washington, D.C.

Jack R. Taylor, President, Dimensions Ministries, Melbourne, Florida

Varghese Thomas, Hindustan Bible Institute and College, India

Rev. Jen Tringale, Jen Tringale Ministries, Fort Worth, Texas

Kris Vallotton, Senior Associate Leader of Bethel Church in Redding, California, co-founder and Senior Overseer of Bethel School of Supernatural Ministry

Dr. Mary Frances Varallo, President, Mary Frances Varallo Ministries, Nashville, Tennessee

Lance Wallnau, President of the Lance Learning Group

Jonathan Welton, author of *Normal Christianity*, Destiny Image Publishers, 2011.

Barbara Wentroble, President, International Breakthrough Ministries

Steve Witt, Senior Leader, Bethel Church, Cleveland, Ohio

Randall Worley, Headwaters Ministries

Barbara J. Yoder, Lead Apostle, Shekinah Regional Apostolic Center

Part B

Major Organizations and Networks Associated With Or Aligned With The New Apostolic Reformation

The Call
Bethel Church in Redding, California
Campus Crusade for Christ (This organization founded by Bill Bright can be found listed with groups that are somehow connected with the NAR.)[1]
Charisma House
Charisma Magazine
Christian International Ministries Network, Santa Rosa Beach, Florida
Daystar TV Network
COR, Coalition on Revival
The Elijah List
Focus on the Family (James Dobson and his ministry, Focus on the Family, will be found listed with groups that are somehow connected with the NAR.)
Fresh Fire Ministries
Global Awakening Ministries
GOD TV
Healing Rooms Ministry, Spokane, Washington
Hillsong
Identity Network
IHOP (International House of Prayer) in Kansas City, Missouri
International Coalition of Apostolic Leaders[2]

---

1 NAR-sponsored conferences often have speakers, both from the Christian community and secular organizations, even politicians who have nothing or little to do with the NAR, but for varying purposes will attend and have fellowship with the very influential organizers.

2 The International Coalition of Apostolic Leaders is the world's largest network for the apostles and prophets of the New Apostolic

International Coalition of Prophets
Iris Global, the ministry of Rolland and Heidi Baker
Joel's Army
Leadership Network
Manifest Sons of God
Ministry to the Nations
Morningstar Ministries, founded by Rick Joyner, Fort Mill, South Carolina
New Life Church
Partners in Harvest
Praying the Bible International
Trinity Broadcasting Network, TBN
Women's Aglow International
Youth With A Mission

Reformation. It has hundreds of members from many of the world's nations.

Other Books by Kent Philpott

ISLAMIC STUDIES

IF ALLAH WILLS

MEMOIRS OF A JESUS FREAK

CHRISTIAN BASICS:
LESSONS, DEBATES, AND CONVERSATIONS

THE SOUL JOURNEY:
HOW SHAMANISM, WICCA, SANTERÍA, AND CHARISMA ARE CONNECTED

IF THE DEVIL WROTE A BIBLE

AWAKENINGS IN AMERICA AND THE JESUS PEOPLE MOVEMENT

HOW JESUS CASTS OUT DEMONS TODAY

A MATTER OF LIFE AND DEATH:
UNDERSTANDING TRUE AND FALSE CONVERSION

ARE YOU BEING DUPED?

WHY I AM A CHRISTIAN - VOLUME 2

FOR PASTORS OF SMALL CHURCHES

HOW TO CARE FOR YOUR PASTOR

Available at www.evpbooks.com

CPSIA information can be obtained
at www.ICGtesting.com
Printed in the USA
BVHW061042240321
603332BV00002B/194